CHOICES WOMEN MAKE

Choices Women Make

Agency in Domestic Violence, Assisted Reproduction, and Sex Work

Carisa R. Showden

University of Minnesota Press
MINNEAPOLIS • LONDON

11/7/11
Lan
$25—

Published by the University of Minnesota Press
111 Third Avenue South, Suite 290
Minneapolis, MN 55401-2520
http://www.upress.umn.edu

Library of Congress Cataloging-in-Publication Data

Showden, Carisa Renae.
    Choices women make : agency in domestic violence, assisted reproduction, and sex work / Carisa R. Showden.
        p. cm.
    Includes bibliographical references and index.
    ISBN 978-0-8166-5595-3 (hc : alk. paper)
    ISBN 978-0-8166-5596-0 (pb : alk. paper)
        1. Women—Identity. 2. Autonomy (Psychology). 3. Feminist theory.
    4. Domestic violence. 5. Reproductive technology. 6. Prostitution.
    I. Title.
    HQ1206.S497 2011
    305.4201—dc22

                                              2010032602

Printed in the United States of America on acid-free paper

The University of Minnesota is an equal-opportunity educator and employer.

18 17 16 15 14 13 12 11   10 9 8 7 6 5 4 3 2 1

CONTENTS

ACKNOWLEDGMENTS

On the path from initial inkling of an idea of how to think about the problem of postfeminism, to a finished book on agency and choice, I have acquired many debts. For intellectual, material, and/or emotional sustenance at either discrete points or throughout the ten years it took to move this project from start to finish, I am indebted to Jean Babyak, Frankie Babyak, Susan Bickford, Barbara Blinick, Merike Blofield, Steve Bos, Alice Carlston, Charles Carlston, Pam Conover, Bill Crowther, Shirin Deylami, Ian Down, Maxine Eichner, Ruth Hartland, John Hartland, Rebecca Hirsch, Sarah Honer, Dustin Howes, David Lefkowitz, Steve Leonard, Mike Lienesch, Greg McAvoy, Elizabeth Markovits, John McGowan, Rachael Murphey-Brown, Denise Powers, Larry Showden, Mary Showden, Holloway Sparks, Erin Taylor, Jamie Taylor, Jonathan Weiler, Hadji, Edgar, and even Alessandro.

Pieter Martin shepherded this project from prospectus to book with skill, kindness, and great humor. All academics should be lucky enough to have such a caring, capable editor.

Kathryn Abrams and Susan Hekman both read later versions of the manuscript in its entirety, offering me invaluable feedback and helping push past points of paralysis in my thinking and writing. Their generosity is inspiring.

A special thank-you to the Santa Clara University Women's and Gender Studies program, especially Linda Garber, Jessica Gagnon, Sharmila Lodhia, Sherryl Booth, Juliana Chang, Laura Ellingson, Eileen Razzari Elrod, and Janet Flammang. Without their support over the crucial six months spent finishing this book, it would still be but a set of computer files sitting on my hard drive.

For all of that and everything else: Erin G. Carlston.

Anything the reader might find useful or illuminating in this book bears the stamp of the people just mentioned. The rest is on me.

Introduction

The theme of this book is women's agency—how it is developed, how it is deployed, and how it can be increased. Having "agency" involves both deliberating on choices and having choices on which to deliberate. It is thus a product of both autonomy (the individual capacity to act) and freedom (the conditions that facilitate action). A full understanding of agency therefore requires consideration of both the subject who acts and the conditions within which she operates, particularly the conditions that produce her self-understanding. This book lays out a conception of agency as both a process and a capacity that is shaped by subjects' temporal and relational circumstances. It begins with the theoretical underpinnings of what makes an agent and how she interprets the conditions of her agency. It then examines the development and deployment of agency in particular contexts in order to see how agency plays out in the messy living of imperfect lives. All of this work is done from the perspective of feminist commitment to honoring women's ways of knowing and living in the world, and to improving the conditions within which that knowledge is cultivated and living takes place.

When feminist theorists try to tease out the sources of and possibilities for agency, we often become entangled in the terms of the modernism/postmodernism contest over the nature of subjectivity, which pits the self-constituting Cartesian, transcendental subject against the socially constituted, contextually bound subject. Even though most feminist theory of the subject relies on social constructionism to some degree, that theory often reflects a need to retain a modernist core, the ideal of an essential self beyond construction. There is an inherent, seemingly irresolvable tension in feminist work on agency arising from the fear that without at least a semiessentialist notion of the subject, the agency that is fundamental to feminist struggles is lost. The vestiges of modernist conceptions of agency mean that at some point, even a constructed subject needs to be able to liberate herself. Yet any gesture toward essentialism is also viewed with skepticism because of the need to account for differences among women and the political nature of gender identity. So the problem of agency that arises from the tension over the nature of subjectification is that one is either a victim, a dupe of power unable to see her way clear of her situation, or a heroic individual, an agent who liberates herself, either individually or in conjunction with others.[1]

In this work, I contend instead that agency exists in the space between these two essentialized and impossible-to-realize categories; that agency is manifest in the mediation between structural determinism and self-determining autonomy. In locating agency in the interstices of discursive production and material determinism, I am not offering a way out of this hero–dupe impasse so much as I am suggesting a way to work within this tension.[2] I do this not to save the possibility or impulse for liberation, which would require adopting a particularly modernist view of autonomy, but to balance a sedimented and constructed self with the potential for discursive and material challenge that animates politics, allowing for change that comes from both individuals and groups while also constituting them. In considering material constraints on agency, as well as the discursive possibilities for production and protest, I hope to highlight the way that being simultaneously subject and object of politics makes agency possible but means all choices are limited and often suboptimal. Economic, political, and social structures of exclusion and domination are all too real, yet our relationships to them are differentiated enough that subjectivity is not just an effect of power but a lived relationship to and within it.

In the chapters that follow, I draw together feminist political and legal theory, as well as phenomenological and poststructuralist theory, to offer a more nuanced account of the status of women as political and social beings than any of these theories alone provides. The novelty of my approach is not in the individual components of agency I draw on but in my insistence that agency cannot be understood without relying on all of them. The interaction of these aspects of politics, psychology, and social life creates the conditions of—the possibilities for—agency.

Agency is a form of resistance in that it opens up or reorders one's life circumstances in some positive way for the individual who is acting, and contributes to a broader understanding of the conditions that both limit action and construct what kind of action makes sense in different circumstances. Thus the constitutive aspects of agency emphasized throughout this book are, first, the critically reflective component composed of one's internal dispositions and individual intentions (autonomy) and, second, the external impediments to, and resources available for, achieving one's goals (freedom, and its limitations). Projecting one's will into the world in a way that attempts to alter the structures of one's life can be an effort to increase choices. Such projections of the will change the development of internal capacities for autonomy and the external relations shaping one's creative capabilities. Because choice evaluation is part of exercising agency, agency cannot be a capacity that relies only on internal dispositions. Good choices (and not just any choices) need to be available for this capacity to develop, and the presence of choices depends on the interrelationships between people and their environments. One can evaluate choices that are all suboptimal in their service to the achievement of life plans, making subtle distinctions between worse and less bad options. To take this evaluative capacity and use it for increasing freedom requires political and social interventions in most cases.

This book offers a description of agency that takes seriously the critiques launched against both the modernist and the poststructuralist subject while showing how action is possible, though constrained in different ways for different people. The chapters that follow show how and when resistance to hegemonic pressures is feasible and why it erupts in different configurations in different places. Although many theorists discuss some of the related elements of agency that I present here, few people bring them all together so that we can see the distinctions among autonomy, liberty, and agency, as well as the relationship between individual and collective manifestations of agency.

This project contends that each of us is an individualized nexus of various discursive forms of juridical and social power that "exceed us," to borrow Judith Butler's language. If agency lies in the taking up of these forms of power to construct a livable life for ourselves, then both the capitulation to and the resignification of these discourses is important; the way that someone combines her resignation with her resistance is critical to her identity and her sense of agency, as well as how she can make sense of agency more generally. Given where and how agency currently exists and the subjectification processes that enable it, this book links the development and exercise of agency to political and social institutions, drawing the connections between the interior individual aspects of agency and the exterior social and juridical workings of power that affect agency. The point of doing this is to analyze where agency is present; to consider how and why it looks different for different women; and to consider what kinds of interventions feminists should strive for. Underlying the entire discussion is an understanding that agency is an intersubjective achievement and not simply potentially evident in the individual acts people commit. Developing the conditions that encourage agency within the individual—the psychological and the sociological elements that make agency both possible and robust—is a collective endeavor—a political project, broadly conceived.

If agency is the project of figuring out how to insert one's will in the world in the service of creating a life that respects the norms, values, and needs of others without subjugating one's creativity to those norms, then, in the cases examined here, women's agency and the potential for feminist agency are clearly evident, yet also complicated and constrained. Part of what is at stake in the lives and choices examined in chapters 2 through 4 is the insistence by women that they are indeed agents, that they are taking up and reworking the forms of power that shape their self-understandings, their ideal of the good life, and their sense of both the possible and the righteous, even when their choices conflict with what others might consider the correct choice in these difficult circumstances.

I argue that one key to expanding women's choices, without dictating one objectively correct way of making decisions, is to name the source and power of different constraining norms and practices and to see where, how, and why women are resisting or adopting the roles and opportunities presented to them—for example, when they are confronted with an abusive partner, or with the opportunity to buy or sell the means of creating a baby. Once one has a better sense of how women are affected by and respond to these relations of power, then it becomes possible to argue for public policies and legal solutions, as well as cultural and economic interventions that allow for differences in the needs of various groups of women, and that increase the space within which more women make choices about their lives. One cannot simply say that anything a person does is evidence of agency. The primary criterion for whether one is an agent must be whether one's actions foreclose other possibilities, not whether they make some observers squeamish or are not what we would do in the same circumstances.

In the pages that follow, I illustrate how agency as the interplay between autonomy and freedom is given form through the effects of identity (as both a personal and political construct); the force of material and discursive institutions (juridical and economic structures, embodiment, and cultural discourses) and their combined role in the development of individual habits; the ambiguity of social life and the products of the workings of what Foucault called "capillary" forms of power; and iteration of and resistance to social and political power in its hegemonic and insurgent forms. My concerns here are to demonstrate the ways in which discursive and material structures work in concert to give bodies meaning in collective interactions. I examine from phenomenological, legal, and poststructuralist perspectives the ways that social meanings are constructed and the sites where resistance can be developed and embraced. By considering the habits that women develop, the reasonable, practical evaluations that often ensue from living in bodies marked in particular ways by contemporary political and economic cultures in the United States, and the types of projective capacities feminists might like to encourage, I build an account of agency focused on the sources of, and outlets for, women's self-conscious resistance to sexist gender norms.

All of these aspects of agency are interrelated, but I consider them in discrete sections of the work in order to examine fully the multiple variables affecting how individuals and groups of people come to see certain acts as agentic ones and come to understand what kinds of choices are possible and desirable in different situations. In chapter 1, I explore how the origins of the subject and her many possibilities are found in the interplay of structure, ambiguity, and resistance, and I demonstrate throughout this book how these features work together to create persons who are always partially determined by influences that exceed their potential domination and understanding of these influences, but who are never fully dupes of power either, without critical consciousness of any sort. Illuminating the personal and contextual factors that need to be analyzed in order to understand what makes agency possible for different individuals and groups enables me to explain why agency does and does not erupt in particular ways across time and circumstance. To think about what is required to facilitate agency, I spend the final part of chapter 1 arguing for a view of politics as trivalent, and thus for political interventions that focus on recognition, redistribution, and governmental policies. The conditions for agency are produced through the interaction of culture, economics, and politics, so all three need to be targeted and creatively reworked.

The value of defining agency as the outcome of both individual and contextual factors developed over time and across circumstances becomes apparent when examining three distinct social and public policy issues: domestic violence, assisted reproduction, and participation in commodi-fied sex, specifically prostitution and pornography. The rhetoric, laws, and public policy initiatives surrounding these areas operate in very different ways to reinforce existing norms about heterosexuality, family relations, and distinct binary gender categories. Instead of reading domestic violence and sex work as cases in which women are simply victims with limited agency, and assisted reproduction as a case where, in contrast, they have clear autonomy and choice, I offer an intersectional analysis that is instructive for understanding the political and discursive construction of women and their options.[3] Taken together, these chapters show how the binary conceptions of women as "victims" or "heroes" do not pertain. Instead, this project illustrates the ways in which agency actually develops, in all its messy, complicated, and compromised inglorious drudgery.

Sometimes one can act—and act in a way that makes one's life livable and endurable on a day-to-day basis—but such actions are not necessarily expressions of agency if there is no effort to disrupt or interrupt or corrupt the material weight of determinism through a creative, generative challenge.[4] Equally important, however, are the moments of generative challenge that are too easily characterized as co-optation, capitulation, or false consciousness because they fail to conform to the actions that are commonly deemed feminist or resistant. I highlight particularly the second challenge to conventional thinking about agency in the cases I examine. For example, through empirical studies of the dynamics of domestic violence and different forms of sex work, we can see the agency in some instances of staying in an abusive relationship or in certain practices of prostitution. I also look at these examples to point to specific juridical, economic, and cultural interventions that might improve the life conditions for women and make their development of agency easier and potentially more effective beyond their own particular circumstances.

Observers can thus appreciate a number of different choices women make as difficult yet importantly right for them, while they also argue for an alteration in social and political practices that could make the deployment of agency less fraught and stunted.

In chapter 2, I consider not only the ways in which women are oppressed by intimate partner violence and the roots of this victimization in discourses about and laws enforcing traditional gender norms, but also the ways in which women already enact resistant agency in situations of domestic violence, both when they stay with and when they leave abusive partners. Exploring the contradictory demands on battered women and the reasons they make the decisions they do demonstrates that to understand and judge agency, one has to examine not just the actions that individuals take but also the opportunities that are open to them and the multiple identity categories they simultaneously inhabit and navigate. This examination reveals the many grounds that women have for staying in situations of domestic violence, as well as the agency-enhancing power that can accompany the claiming of a victimized identity like "battered woman."

Although violence is an obvious way of enforcing power inequalities, many of the most effective mechanisms rely on nonviolent, continuous, subtle, and productive forces in everyday life. These subtle, penetrating, capillary forces of power can work at the level of desire and self-understanding to produce self-surveying subjects who support (at least to some degree) their given roles in the status quo of social relations. In chapter 3, I look at the intersection of new reproductive technologies with ideal mother norms to examine how pronatalist female gender ideals are both reproduced and contested through the particular ways in which these technologies are adopted.

Dominant norms guiding social life are regenerated through self- and other surveillance, daily practices of the individual body (gesture, habit, and desire), and a sense of the necessity of certain actions and roles to fulfill one's gender and racial identity imperatives. The freedom to reproduce outside of heterosexual marriage and over a longer period of one's lifespan has become another form of gender discipline through a corollary rise in the pressures for women—or at least certain groups of women—to become mothers. An opportunity increasingly becomes an imperative. At the same time, conditions of reproductive freedom for some groups of women are undeniably more open. Thus technologies that reinforce "compulsory" motherhood both support dominant models of family life and provide the means to challenge the implicit race and class configuration of normative sex roles.

In chapter 4, I turn to sex work. Radical feminists have argued widely that sex work is violence, that there is no way to understand sex workers except as victims, with no agency. Sex radical feminists have argued the flip side: sex work is a heroic overcoming of gender norms, a high-water mark of autonomy and agency. Most sex workers, however, place themselves into a third category (sex as work), and through this position attempt to undermine (or resignify) what counts as erotic and what counts as labor. I argue that only this third position allows activists and sex workers to engage fully with the trivalent nature of politics and to ground a trivalent approach to reshaping the contexts in which sex workers find themselves. These contexts—and these questions of labor, agency, and violence—are further complicated by the different concerns raised both across various forms that sex work can take and between groups of prostitutes. I consider in the sex work chapter the greater possibilities for agency presented by prostitution as opposed to pornography, in addition to the different meanings of prostitution for economically advantaged and disadvantaged women.

Chapter 5 shows how our contextual, local understandings of agency translate into the possibility for broader, systemic change. The beginnings of political protest are found in the micropractices of everyday life, but turning them into political change requires the collective action of people committed to similar ends. Coalition building brings together autonomy and freedom by encouraging critical reflection, increasing exposure to alternative ways of approaching situations, and providing the discourses that help women understand and articulate their goals and desires. Successful coalitions encourage the discursive and intersubjective development of agency and effect change in the social and political arrangements that leads to identities that are maligned and discriminated against. These systemic changes ultimately feed back to the individual level by reshaping horizons and expanding the sense of the possible.

Agency, then, like writing is always "in process." As I conducted the research for each of the cases I discuss here, I often arrived at conclusions at odds with my own instincts going into this project. And my conclusions are not, of course, settled, as I continue to think through the complex issues that domestic violence, reproduction, and prostitution raise. I hope that, like me, readers will find the issues discussed in the following pages challenging and this book both an opportunity and an invitation to reflect on their own ideas and beliefs.

CHAPTER 1

Conceiving Agency

Autonomy, Freedom, and the Creation of the Embodied Subject

Agency is often used interchangeably with *autonomy* and *freedom,* so that debates about the meaning and possibility of autonomy or freedom get shifted to agency as well. Although I agree that these are deeply interconnected ideas, I argue here that agency is in fact distinct from and broader than autonomy or freedom considered alone. Autonomy is self-governance, even if governing through a relational sense of self. Agency is autonomy plus options; thus, agency includes not only the personal but also the political.[1]

Rather than bifurcating self and society, an adequate theory of agency foregrounds the way in which the subject is developed by powers that transcend it. These powers that exceed the person are, as philosopher Axel Honneth writes, the "constitutive conditions for the individualization of subjects" (1998, 198). A theory of agency then helps to make sense of the socially determined subject's ability to act in the world because it emphasizes the social embeddedness of the individual choice maker and the way in which she is understood through salient, politically produced group identities, while also collecting within it the individually specific modes of taking up these external forces (see Bevir 1999, 67). Thus, I center this discussion on agency, as opposed to freedom or autonomy, because agency encompasses both doing and being, suturing together critical aspects of both freedom and autonomy that we might miss if we looked at either alone.

Agency, like freedom, is deployed in specific contexts and is manifest to varying degrees in specific choices and actions. But, like autonomy, agency is dispositional and needs to be considered over the span of a person's life, because the development of agency is a lifelong process.[2] Agency is buttressed by an ability to choose from an array of viable options to improve the quality of one's life by allowing one to fulfill a range of needs and desires and to influence the contexts in which those desires take shape. Additionally, the conditions producing preferences must be as fully open as possible. It is important to examine not only what a person wants but how and why she comes to want those things. Self-interest does not have to entail atomism or crass liberal individualism; rather, it here points toward active reflection on the conditions of our lives and care for making them better. Women all have the potential for agency; the point of politics is to create a world that maximizes women's ability to exercise the full range of this potential to make both possible and desirable a life plan that is open to new experiences and possibilities, rather than closed to the exploration of various ways of being in the world.

The notion of feminist agency additionally contains a self-reflective, critical consciousness about the productive workings of power.[3] Under conditions of constraint or oppression, agency may manifest itself in resistance to hegemonic power structures. Feminist discussions of agency often assume that agency "resist[s] those structures, practices, or images that contribute to gender-based oppression" (Abrams 1995, 306n11). Thus feminist agency as resistance has a critical, political element of reflective, systemic analysis. Critically conscious feminist agents recognize the way in which their options, identities, and ethical sensibilities develop intersubjectively, and through the interplay of juridical and nonjuridical laws, norms, and customs (i.e., hegemonic power structures).

In this chapter, I situate agency as both a capacity that one has and a process of development at the intersection of freedom and autonomy.

I do this to see how external forces shape internal development and how, in turn, personal development leads one to order and focus on certain overlapping aspects of one's external situation differently at various times and places. After looking at how agency encompasses elements of freedom and autonomy, I turn to the modes of expression of agency: embodied identities. I explain how the body and identities structure one's understanding of one's agency and the political possibilities these offer. I highlight these aspects of agency because they are essential to my effort in the following chapters to balance the undeniable evidence that women are systematically subordinated in various ways—which clearly compromises their ability to choose and act freely—with the need for public policy makers, social commentators, scholars, public service providers, and other interlocutors to see and respect the ways in which women exercise dignity and make choices in the face of subordination. The processes of becoming particular kinds of embodied subjects mean that women's agency has been diminished to various degrees and takes on different forms in different situations, but they do not make agency impossible.

THE AUTONOMY IN AGENCY

Although I focus in this work almost exclusively on agency in the service of increasing one's options for a more open life, it is of course also true that one can express agency in mundane situations or in efforts to thwart progressive action. But feminist theory should serve feminist ends, and the normative commitments of feminism are best served by looking at both the method of decision making and the content of decisions to assess if they open up women's life options. For instance, in my discussions of domestic violence, sex work, and assisted reproduction, I am interested in examining why the same decision can carry different meanings depending on the particular configuration of discursive imperatives and institutional constraints an agent faces.

Theories of autonomy come in a number of guises: procedural, strong substantive, and weak substantive.[4] For the purposes of the contextually embedded and differentiated conception of agency I am relying on here, procedural accounts of autonomy are too "thin" because they fail to account for the socialization that can stunt the ability or desire to act without regard to the judgments of others or the perceived imperatives of social roles.[5] Conversely, strong substantive theories are too "thick," assuming that people are only autonomous when their preferences, desires, and endorsed values have specific contents; these requirements are, in my view, too onerous.[6]

I argue instead for a weakly substantive approach, which allows us to make some normative judgments about the content of people's choices without falling into the problems associated with notions of positive freedom or theories of false consciousness. In the weak substantive model of autonomy, autonomous desires, preferences, and values are constrained but not content specific. If the only options available to a person are "bad" ones, choosing under such conditions does not negate the autonomy of the actor. If one has the capacity to reflect critically on one's situation but few means by which to change it, one has some autonomy and limited agency but not an open horizon for fulfilling life goals. My empirical chapters aim to show that a range of preferences, desires, and endorsed values are compatible with agency, taking into account the role of socialization and material opportunity.

Particularly useful in a weakly substantive autonomy theory is the role of normative competence. In some theories, normative competence denotes only the familiarity with what is required of the actor and prescribes particular actions. But I am persuaded by the work of Paul Benson, who defines normative competence as "an array of abilities to be aware of applicable normative standards, to appreciate those standards, and to bring them competently to bear in one's evaluations of open courses of action" (1990, 54).[7] This notion of normative competence is useful to my project because it allows for the translation of one's practical judgments into appropriate actions that conform to certain social expectations, but it now also includes the ability of those actions to reveal something about the significance of our relationships with others and our self-understanding as developed in relationship, in addition to the availability of external resources and alternative models of action that can foster such intersubjectively developed identity and purpose (Benson 1990, 54–55; Emirbayer and Mische 1998). In other words, normative competence means more than simply reiterating conventional wisdom about right and wrong; it also requires that one can evaluate the actions possible in the course of decision making and, if appropriate, take actions that are *not* sanctioned by hegemonic powers, where the social and political situation leaves room for this possibility.

The normative domains within which one needs to be competent include insurgent and resistant discursive constructions, in addition to hegemonic ones. Norms generated by subaltern communities or alternative models of approaching a situation might give one a sense of authority to speak (a sense of self-worth, in Benson's terms) that one might not have if only hegemonic normative codes are considered.[8] The beauty of this weakly substantive account of normative competence is that it both suggests that insurgent norms can be brought to bear on practical decision making and provides a way to account for greater and lesser degrees of freedom as these affect the autonomy of the agent. It does not require one always to act in a particular way to demonstrate agency (or autonomy), but it saves agency from being anything an actor does.

In adopting normative competence as part of my definition of agency, I am interpolating into Benson's theory a Foucauldian understanding of norms and our ethical relationship to them. The norms about which we need to become competent to exercise agency are not, in Judith Butler's words, "the same as a rule, and [they are] not the same as a law. A norm operates within social practices as the implicit standard of *normalization.* . . . Norms may or may not be explicit, and when they operate as the normalizing principle in social practice, they usually remain implicit, difficult to read, discernible most clearly and dramatically in the effects that they produce" (2004a, 41). The sense of normative competence that I am relying on here is as a Foucauldian *ethical* relationship to normalizing structures. Foucault defines ethics as "the conscious practice of freedom" (1994 [1984], 284).[9] An ethic "constitutes a practice through which an individual can negotiate his relationship to [moral] requirements and restrictions" (Bevir 1999, 75). I am arguing that the ethical practice that agents need to adopt is one of normative competence; that they exercise agency when they develop an ethical—rather than an unthinking—relationship to morality or social norms. This ethical relationship entails self-reflection on a life plan that interrogates and takes up uniquely the political possibilities of one's situation and helps make possible a wider array of actions (see Abrams 1999, 823–34). However, such reflection and interpretation are distinct from the ultimate result of one's action. One can live an ethically competent life moving toward one's goals even if those goals cannot always be achieved in the optimally desired way. Agency can be—and frequently is—partial.

If we consider the application of Foucault's definitions to gender, for example, we see that although norms have tremendous power to produce the social meaning of identity categories such as gender, we are not "competent" at enacting norms only when we engage in normative femininity or masculinity. Put slightly differently, gender is not only its normative expression, but also its normative misexpression. The latter is still an enactment of gender, one that resignifies what the gender norms mean. Gender constrains, but it also produces; it enables us to become more than the system of norms about which we have to become competent in order to rework or resignify them (see Butler 2004a, 42). The work of normative competence is to interrogate the norms that recognize subjectivities in certain ways but exclude other models of being and understanding. This is the link between subjectivity and agency, where agency is the work to contest and change discursive power relations—normative understandings and processes of normalization—in order to make more forms of subjective power relations possible.[10]

Of course this ethical relationship to norms is not simply a matter of individual reflection; it is also shaped by social practice and can be enhanced through dialogue with sympathetic interlocutors. To care for oneself, to work on oneself, to embrace the possibilities for agency "implies complex relationships with others insofar as this ethos of freedom is also a way of caring for others. . . . Ethos also implies a relationship with others, insofar as the care of the self enables one to occupy his rightful position in the city, the community, or interpersonal relationships" (Foucault 1994 [1984], 287). Whereas autonomy in the liberal sense is fundamentally a property of individuals, agency is deeply intersubjective; the conditions that make agency possible are social ones, and the development of one's strategies of resistance are engaged by being with others not stepping back from them.

An ethos engaged intersubjectively links normative competence to action. Different kinds of actions can be protests against normative construction. And inequality means that the content of the action one takes will look very different depending on where one is inserted in the world. Inequality also means that the kind of resistance one wants to enact and can enact will be different for different groups of even similarly situated people. Furthermore, the same action can be undertaken to launch different kinds of ethical protest, as we shall see in the case of sex work, where sex radical prostitutes and sex-as-work prostitutes claim prostitution as resistance, but on very different grounds and as very different kinds of ethical care of the self.

The concept of normative competence is significant to this project in several ways. In part, agency resides in the ability to articulate the content and source of the norms for judging right and wrong and governing our sense of what choices we wish to make in a particular situation.[11] Directly related to this is the ability to evaluate the value of those norms to one's life plan, seeing how they influence its content and affect one's ability to pursue goals or not. Normative competence can lead to greater critical consciousness about one's ability to project one's will into the world and to participate in the authoring of the social horizon in which we are embedded. Finally, normative competence brings us to a way of coping with liberal—and specifically procedural—autonomy theory's insistence that we can be autonomous only when the source of our needs and desires and the means through which we have acquired them are fully transparent to us. In contrast, I argue that given the intersubjective constitution of individual subjectivity and the various and subtle ways that hegemonically valued ideals are sedimented in the micropractices of daily life, some motives that constitute the individual's drive are harder for her to pin down than others. Thus the ideals of "need transparency" and biographical consistency across time and context should be replaced with a conception of needs as shifting and contextual (see Honneth 1998, 204–6).

Agency is evidenced, then, in the ability to reflect on the demands of particular environments and determine a course of action from the needs presented by each environment, yet in accord with more general principles. For example, most people would argue that a life lived without violence is better than a life lived with it, as a violence-free life frees one psychically and physically to pursue a broader range of goals. But within that general principle, there are many context-specific considerations for how best to achieve that goal. Normative competence is thus weakly substantive in that there are some choices that open up freedom more than others, but those choices cannot be determined by abstract universal principles.

So autonomy is important to understanding agency because of the role normative competence plays in both resistance and identity development. The weakly substantive understanding of autonomy also points us to considering the substance of a decision and not just the process of making it. Yet weakly substantive understandings of autonomy and agency leave room to see how the same action can be more or less agentic depending on who is acting, and how actions that might not on first glance seem ethical or agentic are in fact so.

THE FREEDOM IN AGENCY

I turn briefly to locate my argument about agency in the context of freedom, again to show its relation to and distinction from this concept.

When I talk about freedom, I mean to invoke only the structural conditions of life options facing individuals and socially mediated groups; I am not developing a theory that directly tackles questions of collective political struggles to transform society in the way that scholars such as Linda Zerilli and Lisa Disch have done. Rather, I turn to the relationship between agency and freedom to consider more carefully the situational context specificity of agency. This situational context specificity means that social determinism is real, but finding agency within determinism—seeing how people are both determined and determining—is my effort to explain how women are more than simply dupes of power, though they are shaped by the material reality of their situations. Some situations are more properly understood as fields of domination—defined by Foucault as ossified, static, and consolidated forms of power to which resistance is much more difficult—and others as situations of governmentality, fields of power within which individuals exercise self-development in negotiation with conflicting norms and power relations (Foucault 1994 [1984], 283, 300).

The structural conditions I discuss are both material (economic, legal, political) and discursive (the norms and discourses produced by these material systems and through which people understand and experience them). Material structures and ideological discourses working together create the conditions for freedom to emerge or, alternatively, to be stifled. That the material and discursive conditions in which we are embedded set the possibilities for agency means that, as Judith Butler has argued, "agency is always and only a political prerogative" (1992, 13). Agency only exists within the structural conditions of one's life. These conditions produce the subject who acts.[12]

To take advantage of the possibilities for freedom requires both the ability to choose and options to choose from; enabling conditions must be present in our material and discursive situation. In situations of oppression, this demands a radical material restructuring so that the external barriers to freedom are lowered and the concomitant changes to the internal barriers can also be realized, but it is important to stress that increasing choices is not just about making more things or paths available, or increasing money or goods. Rather, as Nancy Hirschmann has argued, making more and better options available so that agency can flourish "entails engaging the social construction of desire" (2003, 202). That is, understanding agency as a political prerogative means working to understand, and where appropriate to change, the very things we desire—or, more aptly, changing the material and discursive relations that bring into play particular sorts of desiring subjects.

This kind of change happens slowly and through social, collective action. The terms on which resistance occurs are socially constituted and already "out there," although part of what is at stake in resisting those terms is challenging the social conditions that produce them. Conceiving of the production of the conditions for freedom as an aspect of agency brings together the material and the discursive aspects of freedom—challenging the conditions of possibility for how we can live and be in the world.[13] In holding autonomy and freedom together in this view of agency, we can begin thinking about using practices of freedom to create what works, creating what we can be rather than what we should be or should want. Challenges to the discursive understandings of what makes life possible for us are efforts at materialization as well; freedom is an aspect of agency in the efforts to rework the possible ways of being in the world, and these possible ways of being in the world regenerate the ethical norms and material structures within which we operate.

This materialization occurs in part because, following from Foucault, all power, whether hegemonic or insurgent, is productive of persons, of subjectivities; we do not have a "true" interior that is thwarted by the evils of exterior, false powers. We are who we are because of, not in spite of, the workings of dominant power structures. So materialization links the conditions of freedom and autonomy because ideology creates "the very social phenomena that it claims to describe," comprising behaviors, ideals, and relationships between people (Hirschmann 2003, 80, 78–85). To speak of the social construction of the desiring subject is to speak of the ways that, for example, femininity as an ideological construct, the role of motherhood, and ideological normative dictates about what makes a good mother are intertwined within individual women and similarly situated groups of women to create one's gender identity. This gender identity forms well before what can be called the age of reason and helps to direct what becomes one's sense of autonomy and capacity for normative competence (see Meyers 2002, 7–8, 36–37).

The subject is subjected to power and becomes recognizable (an agent) because she is in relation with others—this is what power is—and our positions within these relations make us recognizable as subjects. These relations, being recognized and recognizable, are the subject's conditions of possibility. She is possible because she is recognized, and her efforts to challenge the ways in which she is recognized—so that she can become a different kind of subject—are generated within the fields of power relations creating her. Put simply, there are a variety of norms about how we are supposed to live that are contradictory, or at least not perfectly mappable onto each other, and because there is contradiction and multiplicity, we have opportunities to reshape the social world. As we shall see in later chapters, sex workers, nonmother women, and domestic violence victims who stay with their abusers but contest the abuse are also trying to be possible in their own ways within existing discursive constructions of women and sexuality.

The multiplicity of normative discursive power relations, then, marks one's situation—the conditions of freedom—as ambiguous.[14] Discursive understandings, normative regulations, and material structures are mutually constitutive of each other, and all are productive of the subject of agency and the subject of politics. Because of the multiple, overlapping structures within which we are embedded, there is ambiguity, a lack of determinate meaning, in every situation, despite the presence of extant and worthwhile value structures. To understand who someone is—her sense of herself and her capacities for normative competence—we must locate her within the imbricated regimes of discourse and materiality, normative regulation and the structural, situated institutions of the social world. The discursive is how we make sense of a material world that is inescapable. Further, we need to rely on the material for limits on our projects and not just potential openings for new modes of being. Each situation thus is marked by the confluence of multiplicity with stability. People have agency through the ambiguity of situations, but it is an agency constrained by the collective meanings and understandings generated within existing relations. It is up to humans to reveal, create, and discover new possible meanings in the field of existing ones in the overlapping sedimenting and projective (forward looking) dimensions of living in one's situation.

Degrees of freedom must be assessed in the concrete situation of choosing or acting. This means, in part, that agency is not a capacity that we have equally across situations. This situated agency also means that we are not free to ignore others, although we can choose to some degree how we position ourselves in relation to others' judgments of us (Merleau-Ponty 1962, 435). We can disregard their disapproval if we are peers or if the threat of violence does not attend to that disapproval. We might be quite tied to and limited by others' judgments of us if the others can threaten or harm us in some serious way. Other people are thus central to our own capacity for agency because agency is engaged in community; we are situated "with others in various institutions such as a language, family, race, class, or nation, each with its own history" (Compton 1982, 585). We have delimited roles in each of these institutions that we have to take up and engage as part of our situated (partial) agency. We are not free to shrug off or ignore these roles and the expectations that others have for us, nor do we have to conform unthinkingly to them. Once we are critically conscious of the source and meaning of these roles and expectations, we are in a position to negotiate our place in and responses to these roles and expectations. Such being-with others permits both collective projects and alienation and conflict (586). Thus agency is always both socially determined and socially enacted. The aspect of agency that incorporates freedom exists because of our social situation, which means that freedom requires other people. One's situation is never, strictly speaking, one's own; one must always engage other people's readings of what one is and what one's actions mean (Kruks 1990, 145).

IDENTITY AT THE INTERACTION BETWEEN
FREEDOM AND AUTONOMY

Identities are both individual and social constructs that serve as mechanisms through which agency is developed. Identities are not fixed or unitary phenomena. Rather, I invoke a phenomenological understanding of identities as complex facets of subjectivity that are rooted in concrete experience and change over time. So an identity is neither a deep psychological trait nor a (mere) self-ascription but an emergent relation to and within the institutions created through praxis. In this view, identity is not only the product of situation but also of the things to which we pay attention and the way we take up elements within our situation.

Identities are central to agency because agency is both an ontological and an epistemological issue, a question both of who I am (and how I come to understand who I am) and of what I am capable of doing. Identities are the founts of our agency; the process of becoming a subject is bound up with the production of agency. The subject, produced by power, is the engine of agency, but the agency that is mobilized to protest the current ways in which power works is not synonymous with subjectivity. Agency is found in the interstices between identity categories, both public and personal, and between domination and governmentality, where autonomy and freedom meet. Agency is thus better thought of as a dynamic expression of pieces of the subject rather than being conflated with subjectivity. If we understand the subject to be complex, with some identities more relevant in some contexts than others, then when those pieces that are better configured and situated for engaging resistance are brought to the foreground in different situations, agency in the dynamic, critical sense I am developing here is more likely to be evinced.

Because agency is what enables us to engage in politics, identity is intimately and undeniably linked to politics. Subjects do not have "an identity." They have many identities, and these comprise both a personal sense of self and the political categories into which we are slotted. Political identities follow from political and social organization and exist in an interactive relationship with one's personal identities.[15] Who we are is animated and dynamic because we are made possible through intersecting, sometimes even paradoxical, situations.[16] Thus our identities are not seamless wholes uniformly grounding our autonomous attacks on the external forces oppressing us. Rather, the identities to which we are attached are the product of our paradoxical situation within conflicting social structures. These structures provide the mechanisms of the social construction of the desiring subject and place the possibility for agency firmly within one's social situation. We become attached to our social location and take it up as our identity, which is our means of furthering our own projects; we become attached to our selves—we adopt our identity—through the social norms that make sense of the relations of power in which we are embedded (see Butler 2004b, 190).

Agency is made possible because of the instability of institutional norms and rules and the ethical relationship developed toward those norms and rules (Butler 1990, 143). This is why agency is a political prerogative and not simply a personal attribute, existing as it does at the intersection of (internal) personal identities and (external) political ones. So, for example, if we change the signifying practices, we change the rules of gender performance; thus, we change the way we "do" gender, one hopes, by exploding the life possibilities that are assumed to attach to variously gendered bodies. We thus also change the desires we have as gendered subjects. That is, in producing who we are, discursive relations produce what we want, because desire stems from situation. This is why engaging in Foucauldian practices of freedom (resistance) is so important to understanding how agency is developed and deployed. It is developed through the sense of the possible created by social construction. It is deployed through reworking norms against themselves, through launching particularized actions that work in particular contexts.

Although this political engagement alters the norms and the situation within which we make sense of ourselves, it does not, of course, thereby entirely disrupt our personal identity. Personal relations, identities, and commitments work as a ballast to anchor one's sense of self as it negotiates the evolving terrain of social and political life. We can think of our identities that attach to our subjectivities not so much as rigid, essential structures, but as "general forms capable of accommodating sets of variables" in the way that Maurice Merleau-Ponty tried to conceive of our open—but not indeterminately so—situation in the world (Smith 1971, 46). As we resignify or attach differently to the norms constituting our identities, our sense of self can then entertain some new variables, but this is likely to close off some of the old meanings that were possible as well.

As subjects, we need some sense of stability to preserve our sanity. Multiplicity is the condition of agency, but multiple identities and discourses cannot all be entertained; we are limited by the weight of past and present commitments and external resources, and we self-limit because we need some coherence to be understandable to ourselves and others. We also self-limit through the ongoing development of normative competence, our ethical relationship to these multiple forms of power. These stable personal identities are pliable but not endlessly reinventable. One can have a stable sense of self that is still able to respond to changes in the world by evaluating and then incorporating or rejecting—or some middle ground between those actions—normative contests. Some of us are more open to change than others, given our particular personal and political commitments at a particular time.

There are patterns to identity that come from the social influences that construct who we can be and how we can be in the world, but we filter socialization through various personal experiences to create difference. The political aspect of identity is important for understanding the basis on which we come together in public when a political issue has an identity valence to it, for understanding how identity is a publicly formed aspect of the self, and for understanding the constraints on defining ourselves, on our autonomy. These public identities are an example of the norms about which we must become competent as we work to challenge the identities where they are constraining and/or marked by marginalization or stigma. These identities can be broad ones like "woman," but they can also be narrower, like "battered women" or "prostitute." Claiming them as political marks them as ripe for contestation. The personal aspect of identity helps to explain why some members of the identity group are better able to muster the resources to resist the identities and the various ways in which it occurs to them, or seems possible to them, to engage in normative struggle.

To specify the sources of openness or resistance to change, we need to look at how we perform our identities within the constraints of power. The accumulated effects of this performance are the sedimented weight of our own history that give consistency and coherence to our identity. We become who we are, and that becoming has a facticity— a flux as well, for certain, but a substance that cannot be jettisoned or radically reworked by fiat. As Merleau-Ponty says, "an attitude towards the world, when it has received frequent confirmation, acquires a favored status for us" (1962, 441). Explaining this constraint on free action, Merleau-Ponty gives the compelling example of a lifelong inferiority complex. Although it is not impossible that I may just up and drop it someday, it is highly unlikely that I will be able or willing to do so. Past actions, habit, and custom all constrain our ability to act and our sense of the possible. Our agency "does not destroy our situation, but gears itself to it: as long as we are alive, our situation is open, which implies both that it calls up specially favoured modes of resolution, and also that it is powerless to bring one into being by itself" (442). Thus the past helps locate the future, and sets up the "probabilities" of future actions.[17] The notion of probability makes much sense in thinking about not only what we can do in a given situation but also what we actually do. As Sonia Kruks explains, "If women, or other oppressed groups, have 'geared' their freedom to an oppressive situation—one that effectively denies them the possibility of action that opens onto the future—then resistance, while not precluded, is improbable" (2001, 45). So seeing and insisting on the imperatives of women's situation, and the sedimented identity of the agent that develops from it, help to contextualize agency, help to illuminate where and why some aspects of identity might be emphasized and why some women resist while others conform.[18]

Following from this history or sedimented habit, while we can conceive of a number of options for how to act, or do something unexpected and new in a particular moment, there are good reasons why we are not likely to. For example, the consequences might be unknown and therefore frightening, or a rational-emotive calculus of known consequences might mean that the penalties for novelty would be too high for us to handle emotionally or intellectually. This subject of politics with a history and situation and freedom-in-constraint is an ethical subject. She has to contend with her own and others' habits and expectations, but she also has new horizons opening up through her self-reflective engagement with others and as a result of the competing imperatives from different institutions and discursive constraints. Agency to act otherwise (other than expected) is an especially high bar for people in the most oppressive nexus of power relations. External resources need to be amassed for sufficient internal resources to be mustered and sustained.

One way we can think about the balance between stability and indeterminacy is to keep firmly in mind the function of time in the development of agency. Subjectification is an ongoing process of production or creation, while agency is both a capacity and a process. As a capacity, it may well be latent, and it may be used for furthering or hindering life works; its strength ebbs and flows. As a process, it is a nonlinear, temporally and situationally specific mode of being, developing, and reflecting on the stipulations of the present, the weight of the past, and the possibilities for the future. Agency as a process and capacity in time can perhaps best be understood by considering Merleau-Ponty's idea that living in time means "taking on deliberately what I am fortuitously" (1962, 456). By this, he means that we must both grapple with the present conditions of our life and use them to go beyond the constraints of the present. Only by becoming critically conscious of the structures of our time and the habits we have developed can we work to develop projects that open up future possibilities in new ways, which is part of what it means to be a being with agency.

The time of agency is not only one's own history but also the history (and future) of the conditions of one's intelligibility; the conditions of one's subjectivity are embedded in social time in addition to one's personal past, present, and future. This sociality is a source of the instability of the norms through which one makes sense of oneself (Butler 2004a, 15). The agency that is predicated on our social construction is then also temporally situated. Because identity is generated not just within forces of power but across time, the coherence of an identity is achieved in part through its deployment and habitual lived-within-ness over a period of years (see McNay 2000, 17–18).

Thus, in evaluating agency, we cannot consider only the current time slice of someone's relation to structures and discourse. We must also account for the historical development of agency, the process through which an agent acquired her motives, goals, and resources. My work follows from the definition set forth by Mustafa Emirbayer and Ann Mische of agency as "a temporally embedded process of social engagement, informed by the past (in its 'iterational' or habitual aspect) but also oriented toward the future (as a 'projective' capacity to imagine alternative possibilities) and the present (as a 'practical-evaluative' capacity to contextualize past habits and future projects within the contingencies of the moment)" (1998, 962). These elements of agency are temporal in the sense of one's orientation to one's life and situation; they are not sequential, but they are likely to occur simultaneously and to be activated in various orders in particular situations.

Why think about agency as a temporal process or capacity that ebbs and flows through time? Because, I would answer, this highlights how an agent's present evaluations of her situation not only rely on past commitments and evaluations but are also geared toward a future that one is trying to open up. This temporalization makes sense of creativity or generativity of agency as a realizing of one's projects now and into the future but guided (constrained) by the events of the past and the need for subjective coherence. Temporalizing agency helps us to cope with the argument that reiterative agency is unable to account for what motivates subversion, and why some resist when others do not. As political theorist Lois McNay writes, thinking about "the maintenance of a coherent sense of personal identity helps explain the discontinuous nature of change in gender relations in terms of the investments individuals may have in certain self-conceptions that render them resistant to transformation" (2000, 19).

The projective dimension of agency—opening up of one's future horizons by the actions that one takes now—can only be understood in the context of the fluctuating nature of self through both time and situation. Someone may have more or less agency in specific times and places, depending on which aspects of her identity are made most salient at a given decision-making moment. This means that agency can open and close, ebb and flow, not simply grow or increase through time. Understanding agency through time is a means of accounting for both the sedimentation of discursive power in producing relatively stable identities and the generation or creation of alternative modes of being within fields of power (see McNay 2000, 31). As the embodied subject's capacities and locations shift through time and situation, so do the possibilities for agency as both normative competence and projective resignification. To be an agent in this temporal process of subjectification is to build a coherent identity that provides the basis from which to challenge that which is incoherent and unworkable within oneself, those parts of oneself that contest the hegemonic norms one has to navigate. In building this coherent self, one actively configures an identity that is both individual and recognizable to others—one that is determined through social life yet is also constructed as one lives one's life, as one acts as an agent.

One reason that resistance is difficult to motivate is precisely this need for coherence through time. This does not mean that one never changes, but it does mean that some elements of one's identity will become more sedimented and central and more resistant to challenge. For instance, "certain forms of gendered behavior endure long after the historical circumstances in which they emerge have faded" (McNay 2000, 79), a phenomenon that makes less sense on a purely poststructuralist account of subjectification that sees identity formation as an open field of language games of resignification, or even materially enacted appropriations. Sedimented identity constructs may be a source of strength and agency, or they may be a source of oppression, depending on one's ethical relationship to them and the material situation within which one is working. Certainly it can be an act of agency to hold on to what one needs to continue to have a sense of oneself *as oneself*.

The iterational dimension of agency—schematizing social experience, relying on habit—is important for seeing how day-to-day life shapes the orientation one has toward the world and the likeliest places to start evaluating and changing it. Because "actors develop relatively stable patterns of interaction in active response to historical situations" (Emirbayer and Mische 1998, 982), the historical situation of agency accounts for habits, coherence, and another reason that actors do not always resist when they act, even during those moments when they may have the structural opportunities to do so. To turn structural opportunities for opening up future possibilities into action that actually does so will require the input of others to help reframe habitual understandings, to ask questions about the necessity of adaptive preferences that persist despite a change in social relations and locate oneself in this sense of the possible.[19] Engaging in political work, or at least open communication, with others can enable individuals to mediate between the normative exigencies of lived situations and the potentials for other models of life that they can see in others and imagine for themselves. (We will see this most clearly in the responses to intimate partner violence by women who adopt the most hegemonic gender and relationship identities.)

Given the need to be competent in an array of possibilities for action if one wants to act with resistant agency, it is not difficult to see how practical evaluation and the projective dimension of agency traverse each other. Projection involves the invention of new possibilities for thought

and action. Such "creative reconstruction" is "neither radically volun-
tarist nor narrowly instrumentalist" (Emirbayer and Mische 1998, 984).
The process occurs with culturally embedded actors who are negotiating social life and trying to construct changing images of where they
want their lives to go and how they might get there. Although we do
find ourselves thrown into cultures and histories not of our choosing,
the conflicts among the various cultural meanings and institutional em-
beddings provide us some way to create a project of our own out of the
pieces we are given.

The temporal flux of identity is a matter not only of autonomy but
also of freedom, where structures shape the possibilities for agency but do
not determine them. Not only do actors relate to situations differently
through time but structures themselves are not static; one's discursive-
material situation is itself changing, evolving because of human interactions with institutional domains. We relate to structures differently
depending on the specific mix of the routine, purpose, and judgment
motivating particular actions and the particular practice, institution, or
relationship in which the action occurs. Agency and structure are thus
doubly constituted:

> temporal–relational contexts support particular agentic orientations,
> which in turn constitute different structuring relationships of actors
> toward their environments. It is the constitution of such orientations
> within particular structural contexts that gives form to effort and allows
> actors to assume greater or lesser degrees of transformative leverage in
> relation to the structuring contexts of action. (Emirbayer and Mische
> 1998, 1004)

Because we are multiply situated in two related ways, we can do more
than simply reiterate the norms and structural imperatives of our given
situations. We are multiply situated in time in that the present moment
is often a way of refocusing the past and the future. We are multiply situated in relationships to others and to cultural and political institutions

by inhabiting a variety of roles, often at once.[20] Only once we look at this double constitution of agency and structure in particular contexts can we see how we get beyond (mere) reiteration, beyond being a dupe of power. Further, if agency as a capacity and a process exists differentially within one person across time and space, looking at the different types and degrees of the agency of persons within specific situations gives us analytical insights into the development of agency and then, perhaps, the ways in which it can be deployed more generally. As both a capacity and a process, agency is vested in the individual, but it is made possible in particular ways through the social and political contexts in which the individual is embedded.

With its insistence on the dual tendencies in human behavior toward innovation and creativity on the one hand and habituation on the other, the phenomenological lens on human action that I have brought to bear in this section allows us to see the experience of structures and our habituations to them as mediated by creative praxis, situated agency. This approach points us toward general identity structures of gender and sexuality, for example, while reminding us that these structures, like individuals, are constructed intersubjectively and interinstitutionally. With an emphasis on the praxis of agency, we can attend to why simply being a woman is not sufficient to give rise to particular acts of agency. What one does in the world and the ways in which one encounters institutions and focuses attention on existing structures accounts for the agency that results: marrying the promise of action from the discursively constituted "I" to a way to locate why some resist when others do not, or resist differently than others with whom they share some, but not all, social fields. Praxis generates a new horizon: the new generality of background that we share with others. In this new horizon, "we are always called upon to determine once again the sense of our situation and to contribute to the history that carries us forward" (Evans and Lawlor 2000, 3).[21] Agency exists within the constraints of the structures encountered, but agency as praxis also creates what Jean-Paul Sartre calls new "exigencies," which then structure and constrain future praxis.

Of particular relevance in the decision-making contexts examined in the next three chapters is the material weight of embodiment in women's praxis. Agency in any situation as both a capacity and a process is fundamentally grounded by the kind of body one has for two reasons. First, because the sex, race, or abilities of one's specific body create a form of knowledge about the world, gendered (and raced and sexed) individual consciousness is inflected by the body's experiences and capacities. Second, the body has socially imposed meanings and is part of how people are categorized in the world. These are obviously related in that one makes sense of one's specific body through the general material and discursive situation of embodiment. We learn how to be women (or particular kinds of women) in the world before we have knowledge that we need to do certain things to be women or to contest womanhood. This embodiment can serve as both a source of contestation of proscribed ways of being in the political world as well as a blinder to the types of behaviors that might be hindering the fuller development of our agency.[22] This is why a combination of a critically reflective consciousness of the effects of power with an understanding of one's phenomenological embodiment is required to see both the possibilities for and the practical limits on agency in a given situation.

Embodiment serves as the background against which the possibilities for life choices emanate because of the way cultural meanings attach to bodies.[23] Bodies carry with them the habit of cultural meanings and the use or functions associated with particular body types. We can and do come with presuppositions, and in our efforts to change cultural meanings, bodies can be misread or misunderstood in the political, economic, and social lexicon of the day. This can change the sense of agency someone one has or the opportunities offered up to her. Thus the generality of embodiment is "part of the explanation for the ubiquity of woman's oppression" (Kruks 2001, 40) and part of the patterned responses both resistance and habitual iteration take.

Although biology is not destiny, it is nonetheless a relatively stable and common (shared) social construction. Embodiment provides the general framework for our interaction with the world around us, shaping our experiences and our sense of the real and the possible. The body gives rise to identities both personal and political, actively organizing our knowledge of the world by mediating how we take in and use all of the sense data we are presented with, and carrying with it the ambiguity of meaning that comes from living among conflicting and competing discourses (see Kruks 1990, 116; McNay 2000, 33; Alcoff 2000a, 251–53, 261). This generality is formative but not essentializing because general forms still take varying specific shapes.

Understanding the power of crosscutting discourses to engage consciousness while producing docile bodies helps to make sense of "the 'interconstituency' of consciousness and body" (Elizabeth Grosz, cited in Kruks 2001, 53). Here, phenomenology adds to a theory of agency the notion that ethically competent freedom is made possible in part by what my body can do, what it wants to do, and how it is received in the world. "Consciousness is in the first place not a matter of 'I think that' but of 'I can'" (Merleau-Ponty 1962, 137). Because consciousness is bound to embodiment in this way, the body becomes our vehicle for our abilities in the world. This sense of "I can" is attributable not only to levels of physical ability but also to levels of physical advantage, advantage here being constructed by one's situation—the discursive-material nexus in which one is embedded.

In a racially and gender stratified society, for example, one's abilities—the "I can"—are political as much as they are physiological.[24] One's sense of freedom, ability, and possibility can vary by the constraints placed on bodies because of sex markings and the social and political meanings attached to biological being (see Bordo 1997, 181–85). The generalities of embodiment are constraining but not rigid; they are at least somewhat multivalent and malleable. Thus embodiment is both fount of and limit on agency, and there are different ways to take up the identities that spring from our bodies. Given the weight of the past and the way in which one takes up the world in order to resignify it, with occasional opportunities for reflection, evaluation, and perhaps a change of course, there is an agency in the subject, although it is constructed by the tools of the "out there" (the discursive forces of the social and political world). Here is a margin of agency, of self-direction, in the constraints of embodied gender construction.

THE POLITICAL POSSIBILITIES OF AGENCY

Looking at the multiply situated process of subject creation helps to emphasize the complex ways in which identities develop and are taken up in the deployment of agency. If the process of embodied subjectification creates the possibilities for our agency, then identities mark not only our oppression but also our means of resisting that oppression.[25] Even where identities are constructed to limit political possibilities, we can contest those limits while embracing the positive aspects that an identity category brings to our sense of self. The political possibilities that come from understanding agency as I have described it are thus a form of identity politics—admittedly a fraught concept, but one I adopt for specific purposes. Without rehearsing the debates about the usefulness or validity of identity politics in detail, I explain below the relationship between personal subjectivities, public identity categories, and the agency and politics that follow from these external and internal phenomena.[26]

Identity politics enables us to use marginalized categories to assert a place for ourselves within larger structures, a place that needs to be recognized and less stigmatized by articulating simultaneously both the existing harms against, and the real value of, certain social locations. Changing the public contours of identity fundamentally alters the terms on which individual subjectivities are produced, which can open up the ways in which the capacity for agency develops. So some gender identity-based politics is about figuring out what it means to be a woman, and other identity-based politics is about affirming the worth of womanhood. Ultimately, however, the point of identity politics is not to make claims about the validity of identities or the significance of any particular configuration of identities to one's sense of self, but to contest the "circumstances that make identities seem so salient" (Minow 1997, 23). It is a protest against particular configurations of power that produce social inequalities and marginalize people subsumed under narrow normative regulations.

Because identities are created by political means, political contests over meaning require us to engage with identity and subjectifying regulations. Identity—both public and private—is an effect of the confluence of discursive and material relations of power, and the disruptions of those effects provide a potential for seeing and mobilizing resistance. The multiply situated subject finds the various norms of identity one source of her relationship to the political world. Identity cannot be refused as a personal or a political matter, although the precise meanings and boundaries of identities can be protested through argumentation and embodied action. While resignification of discursive norms alone is not a politics, it is one moment of agency, and resignification of gender norms must include moments of positive engagement in addition to critique.[27] Because they serve as forms of self and mutual understanding, identities must be rebuilt (even if only contingently) through collective public action.

We cannot help but act from our identities; thus the question for feminist agents is not whether to engage in identity politics, but how to do so. Although identity politics can be tactical, it is more than that. Identities are indexical and yield the possibility for self-understanding and political action aimed at contesting one's social location (Alcoff 2000b, 337). Identities are partially constitutive of agents' self-understanding and possibility as agents. That identities are formed through multiple intersecting vectors is what gives them their creative potential. One's situation in identity categories is projective, iterative, *and* practical-evaluative. The point of developing an ethical relationship to governing norms is to act, to do something, because agency includes this projective element: action toward a future project.

Further, identities are the terms that we have on, and through, which to launch these projects, to contest social relations producing exclusions and stigmas, and to challenge those social, material, and political conditions. What we are claiming when we claim our identities in public is not some essential truth about ourselves but a ground from which to act. An identity is, as Linda Alcoff makes clear, "a location in social space, a hermeneutic horizon that is both grounded in a location and an opening or site from which we attempt to know the world" (2000b, 335). As the source of our conditions of possibility, identities are the publicly recognizable place from which to start a political argument, not the place where we have to finish it. Because identities are the source of recognition in public, they are real. We are treated in concrete and systematically identifiable ways because of the identity categories that we fall into or that we are assumed to be members of because of our embodied situation, regardless of whether we want those identities to be the most salient aspects of our beings.

When we talk about identity politics, we need to understand that this kind of political activism is both necessary and partial. We are not doing everything with identity—or everything that needs to be done politically to improve the conditions producing our agency—when we engage in identity-based political activism. As both Linda Alcoff and Susan Hekman argue, there are two ways of understanding identity that need not to be conflated yet often are because they are so closely aligned. There is the public identity category—our "thrown" identity, what we are seen as. This public identity flattens out differences between us and others in that category, and it flattens the complexity of our own sense of self. This public identity is, in essence, part of our general situation from which political action is launched. Political action is, as Hekman makes clear, an "interface between public and personal identity. When, for example, I enter the public arena espousing the identity 'woman,' I am acknowledging that I am subsumed under this public category. My political action entails that I *identify* with this category, but I do not and cannot bring all the aspects of my personal identity into that act of political identification" (2004, 7; see Alcoff 2000b, 335–36). One does not, in fact, bring all of the political possibility of one's identity and one's agency into that identification, and the way in which one identifies with "woman" will vary depending on the issue that provokes the identification process.

Then there is private identity, our own sense of self (Alcoff 2000b, 336). This is one's subjectivity created through but exceeding public categorizations. We cannot make political identity categories carry the weight of saying everything that is salient about us. The identities of identity politics are public, not private, which means that they are only ever meant to be partial markers of significant facts about oneself, not the whole story; the use of identity categories is a way of emphasizing common (general) social situation in order to contest the very ways in which the state has grouped its citizens—and the way it treats its citizens on the basis of these categories and the disciplining power of social norms; thus the use of identity categories in politics becomes a way of undermining the very essential nature attributed to them. What I am defending here is an identity politics that relies on an understanding of the power of identity to create temporary political solidarity, as opposed to an assumption that political identity is synonymous with either ontological unity or the totality of one's personal identity.

Obviously there is significant overlap between public and private, external and internal. This is why I have argued that we have to understand both subjectivity and social location in order to see how politics works and also how agency is made possible. What is political in personal identity is the fact that one's identity and sense of self cannot be extracted from—cannot be autonomous of—social location. Thus, politics is always to some degree about identity, about producing certain kinds of subjects, producing conditions that cannot help but create public, as well as individual, subjects and subjectivities. So as social locations are produced by and through power and inequality, and as inequality structures what counts as difference, in order to change subjectivity and produce different forms of desire and subjectivity, we need to change social relations. Social relations can only be challenged through collective action. Hence, agency can be personal, in interpreting what social location means to the individual, but it is also political, in working to open up spaces and meanings of social identity categories so that we can relate to each other differently.

I find it helpful to think about this in the context of Foucault's argument in "Friendship as a Way of Life," where he says the question we confront in marginalized identities is not one of creating an "I" but one of creating certain kinds of relationships; we have to work at becoming, for example, women or homosexuals "and not be obstinate in recognizing that we are" (1994 [1981], 135–36) women or homosexuals. The identity politics debate has been fixated on an iterative concept of identity; Foucault pushes us to remember the projective aspect of identity, the agency that can be activated through identity politics. The process of creating and living identity is an example of the process of agency. We *become* through social practices based on an ethical relationship to governing norms. Rather than thinking about liberating an identity through identity politics, we need to think about (re)creating that identity from the building blocks that we have been provided. We are trying to develop new social relations in order to resist, reorder, and recreate the norms by which we are governed in our social life and thus in our private lives. We are acting as an "I," but in the service of further developing who that "I" is and how she exists in the world, how she is understood through her relationships with others, and, therefore, in her sense of herself as a being in the world.

Claiming a place in the world is an aspect of the politics of recognition. To be seen as existing within the terms of recognizability is to be understood to exist (as human) in some fundamental way. But those terms of existence are also part of what keep us from fully developing as agents, from realizing our lives—from *becoming* as part of newly constituted relationships—in important ways. Thus the struggle for recognition is not only the struggle to be recognized within existing structures and norms but also the struggle for others to recognize the norms and rights that insurgent communities, subordinated groups, and oppressed individuals are trying to create in the interstices of already existing material structures and discursive norms.[28] Recognition has this double meaning that needs to be remembered when conceiving the relationship between identity to agency. To have agency is to develop a critical relationship to the terms of recognition that dominate rights discourse, legal categories, and economic and cultural relationships. Without some distance from the norms, a critical relationship is not possible, but at the same time, too much distance leaves one beyond recognition, with no way of living as one needs to.

This reclamation of identity politics leads to a politics that demands recognition but that also engages juridical and economic relations of power and not simply cultural affirmation. If we demand only to be recognized, then we reify identities: "See me as I am!" we say. To demand to be allowed to become more than my current situation allows is to shout "See me as I (and we) could be!" Identity politics should simultaneously function as a demand for recognition and a demand to change the conditions that make recognition and becoming so difficult. To be able to be recognized in a way that opens up horizons of possible actions and choices requires a reconfiguration of state and economic power relations that interweave to create the conditions—the situations—through which we develop. Because the subjectifying conditions for women are cultural, economic, and juridical, there can be no meaningful recognition of identities without redistribution of material goods. As Nancy Fraser writes, "cultural differences can be freely elaborated and democratically mediated only on the basis of social equality" (1997b, 186).[29] Material redistributions do not merely make life easier by doling out more widely some forms of power; they set the stage for the radical contest of identities. Part of the harm of socioeconomic and political powerlessness is in the way it both produces and reinforces stigma.[30] Redistributive schemes change the sites and vectors of the construction of the desiring subject and the opportunities for proliferating individual and social meaning. Each of the next three chapters will highlight how both engaging the state and keeping redistribution of goods central to politics increases agency by further pluralizing options for identities and life goals, in part by helping to destigmatize certain actions and identities. Recognition is not enough because recognition alone cannot cope with the material restructuring and political inclusion required to open up conditions of freedom and engage the social construction of desire.

In addition to cultural and economic interventions, then, opening up the conditions of agency also requires engagement with the state.[31] When we focus on the state, we are focusing on changing the law in particular. Legal reform has been seen as requiring activists to fix identity categories yet again in order to mark out just who is covered in any particular case. But I am persuaded by arguments about the indeterminacy of the law, and I argue that the law—like the body—is a generality within which specificity must be negotiated. For example, Jodi Dean (1996) argues that the ideals embodied by the law can serve as influential models of the types of institutions we would like to promote as well as the relations we want to encourage to develop in civil society. Dean specifically discusses the role of the law in transmitting a nonessentialist solidarity among groups and individuals, arguing that the law bridges poststructuralist conceptions of difference and the universalism of politicolegal subjects (1996, 9). Building on her point, I argue that legal solidarity is nonessentialist because it is vested in the abstract framework of legal principles within which democratic contestation about concrete meanings of identity categories can take place. Abstract laws require interpretation to be applied in concrete cases; participating in this interpretation is one way of opening up the meaning of legal categories.[32] Such an understanding of the role of the law underlies my legal prescriptions in the following chapters.

Obviously, lawmaking and legal interpretation are highly norm-regulating exercises. Further, although the generality of the law has the potential and the capacity to hold within it the situationally specific considerations that I argue are critical to seeing and understanding agency, it often does not recognize or protect different needs among similarly situated subjects or those who experience similar situations in very different ways. The goal in targeting the state is to end the practice of "legislating for all lives what is livable only for some, and similarly, to refrain from proscribing for all lives what is unlivable for some" (Butler 2004a, 8). By looking at the dangers of the universalizing tendency in the law, I hope to show how legal attention to context specificity can improve the conditions within which agency develops. State power too often looks like ossified forms of domination; collective action to produce a legal regime of governmentality is essential to opening up more women's capacity for agency.[33] We can begin to disrupt legal domination by looking at how the law creates a bridge between our particularity and collectivity through the fostering of relationships among people that create common notions of what identities mean (Dean 1996, 9).

Despite both the usefulness and necessity of the law in enabling or constructing political agency, it can only ever be a partial answer to the problem of fixed identities and the limiting effects this has on agency (see also Minow 1997, 83). The law itself is a construct of the time and place in which we live, expressing our history and our sense of hope for the future. It reflects the social world, our culture and economic structures, as it exerts its effects in shaping persons and presenting sites of contestation over the meanings of identities and the norms of social life. Given its role in constructing and resisting identity, it is important. But because it is only one repository of power and source of agonism, the law cannot be our only focus in considering the construction of agency or in seeking the changes we want—hence my emphasis on a trivalent process of recognition, redistribution, and political inclusion to open up the possibilities for women's agency.

Conclusion

The conditions for agency are set by the interplay of the discursive and material considerations I have outlined; agency emerges from and is shaped by the confluence of these general states in the specific meeting up within the embodied consciousness of an individual and in the discursive space that marks overlapping group memberships. As individual lives and group dynamics give lie to the overweening regulatory ideals of political and cultural norms, the possibilities for agency are created. The deployment of agency is made possible through the particular interplay of external conditions and individual assessment of conditions measured against personal desires, motives, goals, and needs, as well as a sense of efficacy. Because desires, motives, and needs are socially crafted—although taken up uniquely, if in broadly general, understandable terms—each of them can be affected through political and legal collective action. Particularity of existence makes agency possible, even though realizing that agency may at times be impossible or overwhelmingly difficult, given the weight of the crosscutting axes of dominating power within an individual's situation.

Taken together, the various pieces that collectively constitute the processes of and possibilities for agency give us a broader perspective on the availability of different options for engaging self, others, and the state at some times in our lives and not at others. Part of this political vision comes from seeing how subjects are both constructed and self-constructing. To have a coherent life project that can be pointed to as "me"—an actor in social life who is (at least potentially) recognizable across time and space as the same person—we need the sense of a projective horizon with the occasional discursive rupture. To account for why an actor launches resistance in the face of some forms of power relations but not others, in some domains (e.g., cultural) but not others (e.g., political), we need to focus on the interlocking effects of different sites and sources of power and on how individuals and groups (and individuals as members of groups) relate to them.

Even as a poststructuralist view of subjectivity gives us the tools to think about multiple sites of power working in ways that produce subjects rather than simply oppressing them, it fails to give an account of a particularly political psychology that can connect to the roles that deep regularities and broad historical forces have in shaping our sense of how and where we can act in the world through our somewhat ordered relations to institutions and social discourses.[34] A phenomenological understanding of identity is useful in explaining how the development of agency relies on others, on the temporal, lived body and the generality of structures ordering our lives. Although phenomenology is useful for understanding the presence of the collective in the formation of agency, it tells us less about the collective deployment or activation of agency. My efforts to recuperate identity politics, and in chapter 5, coalition politics, are a step toward remedying this absence.

Thus phenomenology complements poststructuralism through its assertions of how we can "confirm or repudiate but not annul" (Merleau-Ponty 1962, 447) our social position through our interaction with given norms, structures, and imperatives for how to be in the world. Our sense of this type of insertion into the world comes both from the knowledge we achieve through our lived body (the conception of bodily experience as central to epistemology) and the sense of the ongoing project through praxis which is part of developing an expressive (creative and generative) and not just performative (iterative) self. Although praxis shares some similarities with Judith Butler's theory of performativity, and Butler's theory is important for the way in which it raises the specter of resistance, existential phenomenology offers a critical expansion of Butler's theory. It adds the determining aspect of life to the constructed nature of beings in the world. Once we are in the world, the human will to express, project, create, and reflect can help to account for how we get from performance as reiteration to performance as resistance.

Still only partially answered is the question of the norms for judgment that are needed at the level of political activism but not provided by poststructuralism. Action should be geared toward opening one's situation, such that choices become less constrained, as a matter of recognition, redistribution, and political inclusion. The performance of resistance should respect the self-professed needs of members of the group, a norm that fully contains the understanding that preferences and needs shaped by oppression or exploitation can be challenged. One goal of political action is to open up opportunities to evaluate needs and desires, allowing people the opportunity to reconsider political needs as we more equally distribute the division of labor, the organization of decision-making power, and the construction of cultural meanings that enhance the self-respect and self-expression of all members of society. These are abstract, guiding norms. To see how they guide judgments and actions in particular cases, I turn in the next chapters to specific examples where women's personal and political agency are related in complicated ways, and then to the political ideal of coalition politics. As we shall see, agency (or its absence) is neither a foregone conclusion nor encapsulated in an easily predetermined action in cases of domestic violence, use of assisted reproduction technologies, or sex work. Further, agency is not a discrete capacity that can be easily measured, nor can its presence or absence be determined without investigating the specific and imbricating contexts within which decisions are made.

CHAPTER 2

Should I Stay or Should I Go?

Intimate Partner Violence and the Agency in "Victim"

In this chapter and the next two, I use the theory developed in the previous chapter to examine the multifaceted nature of agency and choice in women's lives by considering how agency develops and is deployed. In looking at agency in particular contexts, I consider together the development of internal capacities for autonomy and the external relations shaping the creative capabilities of particular persons so as to see the varied ways in which political and social inequalities shape how one believes oneself able to engage the world. The political and social constructions of desire (autonomy) and possibility (freedom) are the political prerogatives of agency discussed in chapter 1. In these three chapters, I hope to illuminate the processes of subjectification that give rise to gendered agency, which is always intersected by and understood as simultaneously raced and classed agency.

Why examine domestic violence as a site of agency? On the one hand, it seems to be a pretty clear-cut case of compromised agency. Bodily integrity is one of the primary principles of and requirements for agency, and bodily integrity is lacking in most cases of intimate partner violence.[1] On the other hand, domestic violence is one of the primary areas of political contestation over the nature of women's agency, particularly in terms of placing "victimization" in direct opposition to agency. Whether the issue is battered women who kill their partners, funding for domestic violence shelters, making domestic violence a civil rights crime, mandatory arrest at all domestic dispute police calls, or any of the many other public policy and legal issues that arise in this case, the debate nearly always centers on whether women are victims of a patriarchal culture and legal system or whether they are autonomous adults who have made bad choices (and who are, anyway, nearly as violent as men). Because the law deals with intimate partner violence too uniformly, because society demands easy answers to this complex problem, and because women's acts of agency and resistance in violent relationships are either overlooked or held against them, this case is a perfect example of where a more nuanced theory of agency is sorely needed.

I will discuss four critical analytical points about the possibilities for and exercise of agency in situations of domestic violence. The first is that not all women who stay with their abusers are dupes or lacking in agency. There are a variety of actions women take, whether they stay with or leave a partner, that could count as agentic. The second point follows directly from the first: to assess agency, one must see victims of violence as they are situated in social and culturally specific contexts. Staying with an abusive partner might well be mere iteration of gender norm expectations in one context but, in another context, it could be an attempt to struggle with, resist, or otherwise assert one's will toward opening up future horizons of action and self-development. One can only understand the individual's sense of purpose, desire, and opportunities by considering her in her environment. At the same time, while there are different ways that women and men react to situations of domestic violence, there are patterns that emerge that are based on socioenvironmental factors.[2] From this insight emerges my third point: that agency and victimization are coincident rather than mutually discrete categories.[3]

My final analytical point is that investment in and adherence to hegemonic gender norms and the heteronuclear family comprise the primary facet of normative competence that confounds resistant agency because it directly affects who stays and why. For women of color and poor women, this effect is even more pronounced than with relatively affluent white women.[4] What this means is that a one-size-fits-all approach to dealing with domestic violence will never succeed. Most theorists, social service providers, and policy analysts would agree—and the discussion here underscores—that racism, sexism, homophobia, and poverty all facilitate violence. Thus, all of those concerned about intimate partner violence must work to eradicate these factors to meet the goal of making domestic violence less frequent.

I am taking a phenomenological approach to seeing and understanding the myriad ways discourse and structure intersect in individual cases of domestic violence, in order to make broader claims that go beyond the individual narrative while still trying to account for significant differences among women. Phenomenology as method focuses our attention on the circumstances and terms within which some ways of being in the world are more possible and probable than others, and on how these terms and conditions come to be actualized in lived experience. In the case of domestic violence, a phenomenological approach means investigating the particular experiences, norms, and interventions that combine to create one's habitus, mundane micropractices of daily life, and larger sense of place in the world, and then considering how this habitus permits one to act and assert a will to change the concrete structures of one's life. As Jacqueline Martinez explains, "By examining the relationships between what is possible and what becomes actually present, phenomenology attempts to articulate the essential existential structures of what is present in the immediate lived experience of the person" (2000, x). These are the habitual dispositions and most relevant discursive schemas that allow one to assess the possibilities for transforming (or not) one's world in a way that is consistent with agency directed toward self-interested action. Agency is also social and includes one's sense of responsibilities to other individuals and groups as well as to oneself. So even though, for example, leaving an abuser theoretically might be possible in many cases, once we consider the power of intersecting norms, obligations, and institutional constraints over the span of a person's life experiences, we may find powerful reasons why the presumably objectively "right choice" of leaving a batterer is not actualized in particular cases, offering another example of the always partial and constrained nature of agency.

In my assessment of the varied responses to domestic violence of differently situated women, it becomes clear that agency is often found in suboptimal choices and, relatedly, that what are considered optimal choices vary by context. The point here is not to say that because one can be an agent in suboptimal conditions, then there is no political work left to do. Rather, the point is to see why these suboptimal choices often were the best exercise of agency in a particular case so that interested parties can point to the discursive, institutional, and interpersonal forces constraining such choices, with the purpose of changing them for the better wherever possible. What "choice" means in situations of domestic violence is complex. It is more than just a matter of staying or leaving, and making optimal choices requires outside social and political assistance, not just psychological changes. In the final section of this chapter, I briefly consider political and legal responses that could and do follow from understanding agency in this highly contextual way.

An Overview of Intimate Partner Violence

Although numbers often obscure as much as illuminate, they can set up the basic contours of a problem.[5] The National Violence Against Women Survey (NVAWS), conducted jointly by the National Institute of Justice and the Centers for Disease Control and Prevention, found that

> 25 percent of surveyed women, compared with 8 percent of surveyed men, said they were raped and/or physically assaulted by a current or former spouse, cohabiting partner, or date in their lifetime; 1.5 percent of surveyed women and 0.9 percent of surveyed men said they were raped and/or physically assaulted by such a perpetrator in the previous 12 months. . . . [Furthermore,] violence against women is primarily partner violence: 76 percent of the women who were raped and/or physically

assaulted since age 18 were assaulted by a current or former husband, cohabiting partner, or date, compared with 18 percent of the men. (Tjaden and Thoennes 1998, 2)

The NVAWS also found that women living with female intimate partners experience less intimate partner violence than women living with male partners (11.4 percent versus 25.5 percent). Men who live with male partners experience higher levels of abuse than men living with female partners (15.4 percent versus 7.9 percent) (Tjaden and Thoennes 2000, 30–31). Results from the National Crime Victimization Survey (NCVS) conducted by the United States Department of Justice indicate a similar asymmetry in perpetration of domestic violence: "Intimate partner violence made up 22% of violent crime against women between 1993 and 1998. By contrast, during this period intimate partners committed 3% of the violence against men" (Rennison and Welchans 2000, 1).[6] And although rates of intimate partner violence have been dropping, according to the most recent NCVS, the gender disparity remains: 475, 900 nonfatal intimate partner assaults against women and 151, 500 against men. "The number of intimate partner homicide victims has declined since 1993, with greater declines seen for male victims. During 1993, the number of females murdered by intimates was 1,571, compared to 1,159 during 2004—a 26 percent decline. The number of males murdered by partners during 1993 was 698, compared to 385—a 45 percent decline" (National Crime Prevention Council 2009).

The numbers above lump all women together, but women are not equally affected by intimate partner violence. Race and class matter, but the significance of these effects depends on the intersection of sociodemographic variables studied, and the precise measure of the differences varies by study. NCVS studies seem to show that African American and Native American women experience higher rates of physical and sexual assault, but the NVAWS found that these differences diminished significantly when the analysis controls for sociodemographic variables.[7] In the United states, youth, poverty, and lack of education are all correlated with higher levels of domestic violence, and African Americans, Asian Americans, Hispanic Americans, and Native Americans are "disproportionately more likely to be young, impoverished, and less educated" than European Americans (West 2005, 161). Native American women have the highest rates of victimization; one reason for this is likely the high rates of poverty among Native communities, ranging from 20 to 47 percent, "compared with 12 percent of the total of the U.S. population" (Hamby 2005, 187). Carolyn M. West found that African American couples had the next highest rates of male-to-female partner violence at 23 percent, "followed by Hispanic couples (17 percent), and White couples (11 percent)" (2005, 163). Within Hispanic groups, "Central American (7 percent) and Cuban American women (7 percent) were least likely to be abused, followed by Mexican American women (14 percent). Puerto Rican women (23 percent) reported the highest rates of partner abuse" (162–65). Again, to be clear, what these numbers indicate is the effect of poverty, education, and age. That is, because communities of color are poorer and less educated overall relative to European American communities, they have higher rates of violence. Within socioeconomic groups, however, race is not a significant predictor of violence. Race is a significant predictor of how police, courts, and community members respond to domestic violence, which means that resistance strategies will vary by race because of the structural differences these groups face.

The NCVS results support the link between poverty and rates of intimate partner violence.[8] Although domestic violence occurs in all socioeconomic classes, in homes with an annual income of less than $7,500, 20.3 women per 1,000 report being victims of domestic violence, a rate seven times higher than that of domestic violence against women with the highest annual incomes (3.3 per 1,000).[9] The qualitative surveys I discuss below help explain some of this difference as a matter of investment in gender norms and its relationship to the question of who reports violence and seeks help from public officials, but this is only a partial explanation.

Given these numbers, I focus in this chapter on domestic violence as a problem of male violence against women. Although lesbian battering and incidents of women who are coercively (as opposed to self-defensively) violent toward their male partners confound simple gendered readings of intimate partner violence, these cases are not the norm. Additionally, there are significant methodological flaws in the surveys that find intimate partner violence to be a problem of mutual violence, a point that is beyond the scope of this project but that helps lend credence to my decision to focus on male violence against women.[10]

The asymmetries in perpetration of violence underscore that gender is a significant factor in understanding the dynamics of domestic violence, but also that how different groups of women relate to and experience violence varies depending on other social positions that they occupy. So while focusing on the trait that many victims share—gender—is useful for figuring out part of the story of intimate partner violence, if we focus only on the similarities, we will fail to see the ways and reasons why women negotiate this violence differently, and we will fail to grasp the fuller range and types of interventions that are necessary for different groups of women. Thus, although gender is an important variable that must be considered, and one that plays a prominent role in my own analysis of domestic violence, it alone does not explain the full range of experiences or point us to the most useful social and political solutions for all women. Before we can consider how other social organizing tropes, identity categories, and normative requirements affect the experience of domestic violence, however, we must start by seeing what gender *does* explain about intimate partner violence.

Domestic Violence as Gender Crime: The Feminist Model of Battering

Feminist analyses of domestic violence that have arisen from the battered women's movement of the 1970s locate the cause of most domestic violence in sexism and women's lack of power relative to men in society, the law, and the economy.[11] Most feminist theories blame much battering on this power imbalance while rejecting the focus of psychological theories on, for instance, a batterer's personal lack of impulse control. Systemic models explaining domestic violence link gender norms to patriarchy, explaining how these norms play out in the law, the labor market, and social expectations about appropriate behaviors for women and men. Battering as a problem of unequal power and (men's exercise of) control is understood as existing within and arising from a framework of gender subordination, which includes gender role socialization and social and economic discrimination in education, the workplace, and the home. While recognizing that much has changed since colonial times, feminists do note the ways that current ideas about familial relations and gender roles have a very specific history that still affects social expectations and legal treatment of spouses.

Specifically, feminist theorists and legal scholars point to the legal and social legacy of coverture,[12] the commonly accepted views about men's duties to keep their wives in line with rights of chastisement, the scope of which varied by state,[13] and women's responsibilities for maintaining the tranquility of the home, moderating men's baser instincts, and providing their children with a father who lived at home. The ideology of family privacy also served, and to some degree continues to serve, to protect batterers.[14] As I will explain more fully below, the continuing strength of these ideals of male dominance and female submission varies by the intersection of race, class, and cultural backgrounds that individuals and groups inhabit, and they are supported in part by the legal and social responses to battering.

Further, historically, there was the understanding that legal marriage was a bargain of sorts: women received male support and protection in a number of ways and, in return, they were to provide sexual, household, and reproductive services. Women were to get material comfort from the arrangement as well as sexual safety and "legitimacy." "The attractiveness of the 'bargain' was ensured through an interconnected web of social norms, practices, and ideologies. For instance, public-sphere labor opportunities for women were circumscribed to such an extent that dependency on a male wage was, for some women although certainly not all, virtually inescapable" (Eaton 1994, 209). That is, the ideology of the family wage, as well as normative ideals about the appropriateness of women in the workforce, and which jobs were suitable for women, kept many women, particularly white women, economically dependent on men.

Many structural explanations for domestic violence also point to gender norms that equate masculinity with dominance and femininity with submission as another pernicious influence on the prevalence and acceptance of domestic violence against women. Studies of Native American cultures lend credence to this explanation of violence against women. Sherry Hamby has found that gender-based violence was lower in Native American societies where gender roles were more evenly weighted. For example, despite the high rates of domestic violence among Native groups today, the Iroquois, Fox, and Papago historically had very low levels of domestic violence, while partner violence was much more common in the Arapaho tribe at least as far back as the 1800s. As Hamby explains, "Societies that lacked family violence were generally characterized by shared decision making, wives' control of some family resources, equally easy divorce access for husbands and wives, no premarital sex double standard, monogamous marriage, marital cohabitation, peaceful conflict resolution within and outside the home, and immediate social responses to domestic violence" (2005, 180). As Western notions of gender relations have come to dominate tribal life and the colonial impoverishment of Native populations has settled in, domestic violence has become more prevalent among all Native groups. Further supporting the gender norm theory, Shamita Das Dasgupta and Shashi Jain (2007) have found that when cultural imperatives compete, patriarchy often overrides teachings of gender equality in religious communities, so that even the avidly nonviolent Jains, for example, have problems with intimate partner violence, and adherents express their belief in men's right to chastise their wives despite an explicit religious teaching of gender equality.[15]

Contemporary feminist theorists account for why men batter by pointing to the lingering effects of patriarchy and the sexism it has engendered in many areas of life.[16] A formal right to batter one's wife was phased out in the states via the courts and legislatures through the mid-1800s to early 1900s. (The first state supreme court rulings recognizing "marital rape" as a criminal offense were not handed down until 1981 in Massachusetts and New Jersey.) But prevailing ideas about heterosexual gender roles and the seriousness, or lack thereof, of intimate partner violence—beliefs that had been supported in part by weak legal responses to battering—continued to hold sway among many people in the criminal justice, health care, social service, and legal communities as well as in the population at large. Many feminists such as Phyllis Goldfarb, Isabel Marcus, and Elizabeth Schneider have argued that the criminal and legal justice systems' reluctance to respond to domestic violence as a serious harm "represents the de facto version of de jure coverture. Whereas physical violence once reinforced coverture . . . so does family violence play an even more crucial role in maintaining the subordination and social control of women now that the formal incidents of marital inequality have been dismantled" (Goldfarb 1996, 600–601).

In the 1970s and 1980s, feminist activists from the battered women's movement used this model of the systemic roots of domestic violence to launch demands for fundamental political and social reforms. Shelters were opened, sex roles contested, economic initiatives won, and lawsuits launched against police departments that failed to treat domestic violence victims seriously.[17] But as the movement achieved some successes, large parts of it were co-opted by the larger institutional structures that were supposed to be challenged and altered. The call for fundamental transformations of social and political life were superseded in many battered women's organizations by a focus on therapeutic responses that are far more receptive to models of crisis intervention and expanded services to individuals than they are to facilitating or abiding fundamental structural change. Within many organizations, battered women are clients—persons to be helped—rather than sisters in a larger feminist struggle.[18] These groups tend to focus on explaining intimate partner violence in terms of individualistic, biologistic sex-role theories that account for problems almost entirely on the interpersonal level.[19] As Karen Kendrick found in her study of battered women's shelters in Southern California, while women gave lack of housing as the primary reason they returned to an abusive spouse, housing is something the shelters specifically will not help with because shelter staff assume "that battered women are suffering from psychological problems and that, through personal transformation, they will be able to leave their partners and meet their family's economic needs" (1998, 167). Even when sexism is viewed as the source of the problem, battered women's services funding needs and the desire for social respectability require a focus on nonpolitical, legal, and social service provision (152; see also Pence 2001).

The legal system, guided by fundamental tenets of liberal individualism, has also driven this mode of analysis, making it difficult for feminist lawmakers and legal advocates to get courts, prosecutors, and legislators to see the structural, extenuating factors shaping women's responses to violent relationships.[20] Instead, domestic violence has been treated like other kinds of assault, and individual beatings are viewed as discrete events falling within traditional liberal understandings of harm. Among other things, this view causes courts and policy makers to miss many significant types of battering behaviors such as emotional abuse and psychological intimidation, the very types of abuse that many women say are the most devastating aspects of intimate partner violence (Goodmark 2004, 29–30). Additionally, these individualistic, therapeutic analyses are problematic because they focus almost exclusively on the victim (why doesn't she leave?) rather than the perpetrator (why does he hit her?). Domestic violence thus becomes a problem of the woman's failure to respond as a rational man would to a stranger assault, rather than a man's manipulation of gender norms and social expectations to exert control over a woman's freedom and autonomy. As Elizabeth M. Schneider explains, "The culture of female subordination that supports and maintains abuse has undergone little change. At the same time, there is a serious backlash to these reform efforts, and many of the reforms that have been accomplished are in jeopardy" (2000, 27).

The criminal justice approach has displaced systemic analyses and community-based responses with individualized analyses and solutions. Where in the 1970s the primary focus was on ending the abuse, which could include ending the relationship but did not have to, the focus has since shifted to ending abusive relationships, not challenging gender norms and the ideology of abuse.[21] This professionalizing has been promoted through the passage of the Violence Against Women Act as part of the crime bill and with its focus on grants for police trainings and community groups with an "established" or "documented" history of success.[22] All of this is not to say that there is no room for the criminal justice system in responding to domestic violence, or that I want to return to a time when the police, courts, and prosecutors failed to take domestic violence seriously as a problem. As I will explain below, the mere option of criminal justice interventions is an exceptionally important resistance tool that women use when contesting intimate partner violence, even if they stay with their partners. But the criminal justice model focused on extricating individual women from individual relationships so dominates thinking about intimate partner violence that most of women's resistance strategies are now read as pathological or masochistic, as opposed to ways of coping with competing norms, identities, and structural conditions within which the abuse is always wrong but the relationship (without the abuse) might be desired. Thus the law fails to see the agency of the women in domestic violence situations—as well as the factors preventing the further development of their freedom and autonomy. And because of its partial capitulation to the funding imperatives of the federal government, the battered women's movement has had a mixed response to being the social interlocutors who can help battered women escape violence and fundamentally challenge the patriarchal norms structuring intimate relationships. Until these norms are successfully challenged, battering will continue to plague intimate relations, welfare and immigration policies will continue to work against women's agency interests, and the law will fail to hold men accountable for the specific forms of coercion and terror that constitute domestic violence.

To see intimate partner violence as a unique phenomenon—different from stranger assault and deeply structured by patriarchal values—one has to understand the motives and actions of the batterers and not just consider the actions of the victim-survivors. Battering is a form of coercive control that engages the processes of subjectification in trying to manipulate the actions, feelings, identity, and sense of self-efficacy of the battered woman. As she is battered, the phenomenological facts of her life are changed. The use of isolation, physical assault, verbal abuse, and often sexual sadism challenges women's subjective sense of self and forces her to adapt to the environment into which she has been drawn. Asserting resistance is always a matter of engaging the institutions and the other people who comprise the habitus of her life, and in battering relationships, it is no different.

Evan Stark and Martha Mahoney have been at the forefront of pushing this legal and political reclassification of intimate partner violence from discrete assaults to a pattern of coercive control. This model respects the complexity of battered women's situation by demonstrating that the identity of "battered woman" is created by the entrapment they experience rather than existing as a central function of the individual woman's essential identity; that is, it allows her to claim her victimization without demanding that this serve as the sum total of who she is or who she presents to the courts, police, and social service agencies (Stark 1995, 1025). Further, the coercive control model explains why women stay in abusive relationships without resorting to individual psychological theories. The actions one takes to contest the violence are presented as agentic and help to explain the distinct nature of domestic battery as opposed to other forms of violence (Stark 1995, 1023). "In marked contrast to the [psychologically based battered woman syndrome] defense, women's attempts at autonomy are the starting point from which the coercive control theory reframes battering relationships in terms of pro-gressive entrapment." While the abuser's past violent acts are important in assessing the presence of entrapment,

> the assumption behind the coercive control defense is that these assaults were possible only because a woman's efforts to escape and/or resist the violence were compromised by isolation, intimidation, and control, as well as by the failure of helpers to respond appropriately. Thus, an assess-ment of entrapment involves an examination of the dynamic of coercive control over time, including control over money and food, social rela-tionships (primarily friends, family, children and workmates), sexuality (where, when, how, how often, etc.), work, access to helpers, communi-cation and transportation, minute facets of everyday life (such as access to the remote TV changer), and it includes attempts by the woman to leave as well as the response these elicited. (Stark 1995, 1024)

All of these mechanisms are as much a part of the intimate partner vio-lence as the use of fists or other objects to physically assault the part-ner.[23] If we only look at battering as discrete episodes of physical assault, we facilitate the position that leaving the relationship is the only ap-propriate form of self-assertion. "But battering reflects a quest for con-trol that goes beyond separate incidents of physical violence and that does not stop when the woman attempts to leave. A focus on control reveals the danger that violence will continue as part of the attempt to reassert power over the woman" (Mahoney 1994, 75). The coercive con-trol model starts from women's lived experience of violence and what they have learned about how best to be agents for themselves in this context.

Where domestic abuse is understood as coercive control, it becomes easier to see how violence that is infrequent or nonsevere can still signifi-cantly alter one's sense of herself.[24] This relationship of coercive control can be more or less severe. Women often report that the psychological abuse is more difficult for them than the physical abuse, but the courts do not see or respond to psychological abuse as abuse. Phenomenological experience of violence means that pain and self-protection drive behaviors, but physical pain is not always the most acute aspect of abuse; psychological pain at the failure to be taken seriously—not to have one's existential self recognized and valued—is often the most brutal aspect of an abusive relationship. One cannot become oneself fully and in a relationship when that relationship fails to provide a habitus of understanding. Creative self-development still happens, but the creativity is aimed at negotiating space for existential recognition and physical integrity; that is, the basic components of agency, not the fully flourishing life plan that one might otherwise develop and enact, are all that can be expected until there is some structural change.

With this understanding of intimate partner violence, we can see why the individual assault model and attempts to use the criminal justice system and liberal jurisprudence alone to cope with it are flawed. Resistance strategies are formed in a context of coercion, not discrete assaults, so any assessment of whether or not women who stay in—or stay for some time in—abusive relationships has to account for the ongoing and multifaceted nature of abuse, which occurs in a relationship that is a central aspect of one's sense of self. Agency and resistance also develop and thus have to be seen in the context of "relationship time," which is not precisely the same as the linear time model used by the courts or outside observers. Relationship time is measured by the distance between insults or from insults to physical assaults. One's agency develops in part by learning to read these distances and react to and predict them; responses need to be measured in the time of violence and the effects of or responses to violence. Thus the practical-evaluative aspect of agency (contextualizing the past and future in the contingencies of the moment) develops through individually experienced entrapment in conjunction with—as we shall see below—the iterative and projective adoption of gender and relationship norms. Said slightly differently, one's ethical normative competence develops through the time and situation of coercive control.

One example of the way that coercive control works comes from Neil Websdale's study of domestic violence in poor black communities in Nashville, in which we read "Elaine's" story:

> The jobs I had, every job I had while I was with him for eleven years, had to be to his standards, the clothes I wore . . . he had to go to the shopping mall with me and make sure that my skirts wasn't too short . . . my pants wasn't too tight, um, when we went out to eat I had to sit with my face like this in the plate and eat. I couldn't look at nobody. Somebody recognize me and he says, "Who that?!". . . . You know and stuff like that, and then, you know, a lot of times I blame myself for stayin' with him as long as I did because I figured if I hadn't stayed with him as long as I did, he wouldn't been able to continue to abuse me. But, when you in love with somebody you take stuff like that. . . . This man stabbed me in the leg with a butcher knife, he beat me up . . . and then would try to have sex with me. After he done beat me, he talk about how I look beautiful with my face all swelled. I got knots on the top of my forehead, but I look beautiful to him with all these knots and stuff. He like just to see me like that because he knew that nobody else would want me. But he beat me up one time too many. (2005, 144)

Similarly, Ann Goetting's study *Getting Out* details sixteen stories of coercive control in relationships of women from a range of racial and socioeconomic backgrounds. One of those women is "Rebecca," a Northern Arapaho, Lakota, and Mexican American social worker who explains her marriage as follows:

> I was very isolated. I never got off the pueblo, maybe once a week. He didn't want me to go back to work, we had no contact with my parents by then because I had no telephone. If we went to get groceries, he was there and he wrote all the checks and drove the car. It was a joint account, but he kept the checkbook and balanced it. The Saturday afternoon that we went to get groceries, it was a big deal. It was 28 miles one way to

Santa Fe to do groceries, we might got out to eat. Once we got back to the pueblo it would start all over again. He would go into rages. There was always something wrong with the kids or the food or something. I couldn't do it all, it was too spread out. I felt like a blob trying to cover all the bases. (1999, 100)

Through these examples we can see that intimate partner violence is patterned and, as a pattern, it creates the phenomenological experience of being in relationship, which shapes how one sees herself in the world. In the context of coercive control, women develop habits of being and being together as a way of trying to assert control in a situation where control is precisely what one's intimate partner is trying to wrest from her. Seeing domestic violence in this coercive control model reveals how intimate partner violence works to produce certain kinds of subjects and ways of acting in the world. These behaviors and subjective senses of oneself and what one needs to do might look maladaptive or masochistic to outsiders who cannot see the pattern of behavior, but they can be read as highly agentic—engaging the structures of autonomy and freedom available in a given situation—when seen within this context.

Coercive control is the means through which the "generality" of the social position of gender spans different situations of intimate partner violence. But sexism cannot be examined in a vacuum; it is deeply imbricated with racism and heterosexism. Although abusers use gender power and gendered norms to exert control, they also use relationships of race, class, and ethnicity to control their partners. To see how and why women respond to abusive situations in the ways that they do, it is important to understand these constitutive forces producing their battering context. Thus, a good account of both what women's choice structures look like and the interventions necessary at the political and cultural levels includes analyses of racial, sexual, and economic pressures as well as the forceful power of gender and heteronuclear family norms on different groups of women. In short, what is required is an inter-sectional approach to understanding how violence works, and how and why women respond in the ways that they do.[25] In the remainder of this chapter, I consider these intersections and how they affect women's agency—an agency that includes the possibility of acting for oneself under conditions of oppression.

GENDER, DOMESTIC VIOLENCE, AND INTERSECTIONALITY: UNDERSTANDING WOMEN'S AGENCY BEYOND THE LENS OF SEXISM

In examining how women respond to domestic violence, it becomes clear that agency develops through the process of incorporating intertwined gender, race, class, and sexuality norms into one's identity. As one's subjectivity takes shape, the processes directing the development of one's sense of desire and possibilities are mired in the ineluctable mix of norms to which one is trying to become competent. A woman's understanding of these identity structures and her role in embodying them comes through her interaction with family, friends, community members, and bureaucratic and legal others. To see the complex play of gender, race, class, and sexuality in the decision-making nexus of intimate partner violence, I draw on some exemplary studies of different groups of women and the ways they have resisted the violence against them. These studies do not exhaust the range of iterations of racialized gender class identity, but they provide an illustrative range of ways identity-constitutive norms and rules interact to produce the desires, political possibilities, and future horizons constituting women's agency and resistance modes.

In her 1996 book *Compelled to Crime: The Gender Entrapment of Battered Black Women,* Beth E. Richie presents her fascinating study of incarcerated African American women, comparing battered black women to both nonbattered black women and battered white women also held in the Rikers Island Correctional Facility. The results of her interviews with these women led her to develop a theory of "gender entrapment" to explain the dialectic between being victims and being survivors in their day-to-day lives as poor African American women subject to brutal violence at the hands of male lovers.[26] Richie argues that violence against women in intimate relationships, and the same women's participation in illegal activities, is linked to culturally constructed gender identity development. When she uses the phrase "gender entrapment," she means entrapment very much in the legal sense of being coerced into doing something illegal that one would not (necessarily) do otherwise (Richie 1996, 4).[27] Her theory of gender entrapment is a specification of the feminist model of battering as gender crime, and I borrow from her theory of gender entrapment here because it helps me to explain how gender norms as intersected by race, class, ethnicity, and immigration status construct the conditions of possibility and the specific subjective desires women experience. The studies of battered women I look at here show how gender entrapment works across and within racial groups, and how resistance strategies—the manifestation of agency through time and within contesting and constraining norms—begin to emerge. Gender entrapment in the context of domestic violence (coercive control) very much victimizes women, who nonetheless develop means of resisting under these webs of constraints. Community and racial norms can further victimize women, but they can be starting points of intervention as well, where freedom and thus autonomy—socially constructed desire—are reworked to open up women's life options.

In comparing the battered women to the nonbattered women, Richie found that the factor distinguishing the two groups "was the degree to which they *aspired* to the ideological norm" of the middle-class, stay-at-home mom in a heterosexual nuclear family (1996, 135). For the battered black women in particular, this aspiration, combined with an awareness of cultural and racial expectations, opportunities, and stereotypes, led them to put up with more abuse than the other women and attempt to salvage the relationship rather than jettison it.[28] For the battered black women Richie interviewed, "the establishment and maintenance of a nuclear family was seen as not only desirable, but as a way to provide the protective support that they perceived African American families would need against problems in the future" (139). These women were more critically conscious about and deeply affected by racism than they were by the idea of battering as a specifically gendered violation.[29] Thus, one reason they stayed in these relationships was because of a strong felt need to fight racial stereotypes of the failing black family and aggressive black men. The battered black women in her study were more likely to stay in the relationship than the battered white women, although for both groups, the stronger the attachment to normative womanhood and the nuclear family, the more likely they were to stay (Richie 1996, 143). While they stayed, however, the black women did attempt to stop the violence, often by turning to crime. For some, criminal activity was an attempt to share something with the partner in the hopes that it would bring them closer together. The white women Richie interviewed, who were economically poorer than the black women, used crime as a means of getting out of the relationship (Richie 1996, 131). (I will return to this point in the next section.)

The black women Richie interviewed were more likely to leave a partner who became abusive if they instead exhibited a more critical gender consciousness about external limits on opportunities and expectations due to sex, which existed alongside a strong, but differently articulated, race consciousness. For them, loyalty to race and racial identity was less focused on particular families and men and more on the African American people in general. Their identities were less saturated with hegemonic gender ideals and were less relationship bound (Richie 1996, 62–68). These women were also quite aware and critical of racism, but "the absence of men was accepted with indifference. As such, the African American women who were not battered were less concerned about men's lack of social options and less invested in taking care of them in the domestic sphere than were the battered African American women" (Richie 1996, 44). Both groups of women demonstrate the weakly substantive autonomy requirement I posited as part of agency in chapter 1. Both racial and gender hegemonic norms were evaluated in light of important life goals, and action was taken to rework gender expectations in light of changes desired within racial norms, or vice versa. The ambiguity of different women's situations and meaning-making potential means that some will emphasize racialized gender identity and exercise projective agency to challenge the meanings of black womanhood while others emphasize gendered racial identity to do the same. What we see here is that the interplay of personal and political situation gives rise to different practical-evaluative ethical stances.

These women prioritized their very real commitments to race, gender, and self differently, in significant part because of the influences of relative economic privilege and standing in their families of origin. The battered black women Richie interviewed grew up in homes where they were somewhat economically better off than the other women in the study and were considered "favorite daughters" with greater liberties and a greater sense of possibility for the future. Richie notes that the gender entrapment of these women took root early in life with the family modeling of hegemonic gender roles and expectations (1996, 31–56). Although they were the favorite daughters, this privilege was contingent on them doing the emotional work for others in their families and accommodating their needs (33–36). Strong feminine gender conditioning combined with relative economic privilege seemed to leave these women particularly vulnerable later in life. "For most of the African American battered women, neither growing up with emotional support and relative material privilege nor their optimism could mitigate the negative effects of the social world, which is organized hierarchically by race/ethnicity and gender" (136). That is, while the black women in her study who were abused actually came from relatively more privilege than the nonbattered women, this privilege was overwhelmed by the racism they encountered in academic, employment, and social settings.[30] They had higher expectations of success than the women who were not favorite daughters or who were poorer growing up. When they encountered racism in academic and employment settings and began having difficulty achieving as they expected to, they became more critically aware of the direct impact of racism on their opportunities, and they also felt a greater sense of failure. The desire to fight racist stereotypes of the disintegrating black family, the desire not to fail in this area of life as well, and the greater investment in normative gender and the nuclear family combined to cause them to stay (or at least stay longer) in abusive relationships. Here there is both a critical consciousness of racial norms and a reshaping of that consciousness that begins to form a sort of racial entrapment. The racial entrapment develops because of the favorite daughter ("good girl") responsibility to privilege certain racial duties over personal ones as a form of caretaking. So communal racial duties become personal duties discursively reconstructed over time and more deeply interpolated into one's gender identity. These women are in a racial/gender double bind.

Racial and gender appeals to these women were often explicitly articulated by family members and associates as well. The way in which social and personal discourses, opportunities, and expectations combined led to a sense of self and commitment to others that contributed to their willingness to stay with their partners. Given their varying commitments to the heterosexual nuclear family, as well as differing relationships to race and gender privilege, and the impact this had on their response to violence in the home, the women in Richie's study demonstrate that individual psychologies account for only part of the decision to stay or leave. The normative forces of both gender and race expectations intersect to produce different senses of what women believed to be both desirable and plausible responses to the violence they lived with.

These patterns of gender investment—specifically, gendered family norms—intersecting with specific racial imperatives occur across groups of women, producing individuals with positionalities and possibilities for enacting agency that track along different vectors of normative expectations. For example, South Asian immigrant women bring with them strong patriarchal gender expectations from their countries of origin, if not their families of origin, and this commitment to maintaining the patriarchal family—and the penalties for failing to do so—means that these women are often unwilling to leave their abusers unless and until the abuse is too severe to permit them to live with their husbands or they can get culturally competent assistance to cope with family and community pressures as well as legal immigration issues.[31] One's gender identity is developed very much in the context of family roles, and thus agency develops through the negotiation of community needs and one's strong sense of place in the family hierarchy. The identity from which many South Asian immigrants to the United States express their agency prioritizes community within gender and can produce a sense that the marriage must be made to work although the violence needs to end. For example, South Asian cultures stress the ideas of "family before self," the requirement that one marry, and a strong divorce stigma, all of which socialize young women strongly into living patriarchal gender identity as central to one's ethnic identity (Venkataramani-Kothari 2007, 14–16; Ayyub 2007, 32–33). This is not to say that South Asian women do not leave abusive spouses, but that the way one negotiates leaving will differ for South Asian immigrants than middle-class white women who are coming from a discursively constructed sense of self in relationship prioritizing independence, autonomy, and "love-match" marriages.

Ruksana Ayyub has found that most South Asian women are aware of women's subordinate status and of the abuse of women in their culture. When they have grown up not seeing it in their own home, they "invariably feel indebted to their families' generosity for" not subjecting them to violence and oppression. "They felt protected from the unfairness of society, not by their own strengths, but by that of their parents and family. Therefore, the self that emerges is dependent upon authority figures for its rights and grants" (2007, 35). Because the processes of subjectification are ones that emphasize the familial and the role of others rather than the self, resistance strategies to any violence faced will likely involve others, so a legalistic, individualized emphasis on leaving a batterer is unlikely to resonate with these women in a way that helps them gather the resources they do have to challenge their situations.

Both Shamita Das Dasgupta and Anitha Venkataramani-Kothari emphasize that because of strictly differentiated gender-role socialization and the emphasis on women's familial duties, "most battered South Asian

women feel that marriage denies them sexual control and their husbands are entitled to unlimited access to their bodies" (Venkataramani-
Kothari 2007, 17). Not only do battered South Asian women have very
little sexual autonomy but also, in line with the coercive control model,
this is coupled with a lack of financial independence. Even if women
work outside of the home, the men almost always control the finances
(Venkataramani-Kothari 2007, 16).[32] There is also strong pressure to
keep the marriage intact for the sake of community cohesion and to
protect the social status and ability of siblings to be eligible to marry.
"Furthermore, many battered immigrant women are afraid that separation or divorce might risk their own children's educational opportunities and future happiness, the very reasons they may have migrated
to the United States in the first place" (Das Dasgupta 2005, 64; see
also Erez, Adelman, and Gregory 2009, 47). Leaving one's spouse can
threaten the status of important others in her family and community
and mark a failure of self because one's identity is often defined by two
primary roles: wife and mother. Regardless of the behavior of her husband, a divorced woman is viewed as "damaged goods. . . . To compli-
cate matters, those women who endure a bad marriage in order to keep
their families together are glorified within the culture" (Venkataramani-
Kothari 2007, 16). To fight such strong cultural messages that have
shaped one's sense of self and desire throughout her years of identity
formation requires much time and a variety of social and economic
resources from a range of concerned others. Even mustering those resources can exacerbate the abuse; the more women fail to comply with
expected gender norms, the more the abuse escalates in many cases,
bearing out the gender entrapment thesis (Erez, Adelman, and Gregory
2009, 45–46; Menjívar and Salcido 2002, 906–8).[33]

In the context of the United States, both East and South Asian battered women find that they are battling their communities' "model
minority" stereotype. Many religious and ethnic leaders pit Asian groups
against Latinos and African Americans, holding Asians up as hard-
working, peaceful, and law-abiding, in contrast to the supposed deviance

of other minorities. Thus, battered women from these groups are discouraged from going to the police or other outside services and publicizing any problems within the community that might tarnish the ethnic group's image (see Venkataramani-Kothari 2007, 14–15; Ayyub 2007, 24). As Richie found with the race consciousness of African American women, Margaret Abraham writes of the South Asian women she studied: "The need to belong to one's ethnic community may sometimes take precedence over gender-based abuse within the marriage" (2000, 133). Thus, that battering is a coercive gender assault does not mean that individual or community responses to it can or will be focused only on intervening in gender norms. Both subjectification and situation are too multiple for a singly focused analysis or set of solutions.

Similarly, the interpolation of community and individual needs arises in Native American communities, but here in ways shaped in part by the genocidal history of relations between colonial whites and Native populations. Currently, many Native tribes are quite small, so tribal survival is a pressing issue. As Sherry Hamby found, "Divorce—a recommendation of many domestic violence advocates—may be viewed quite differently by American Indians who will not have the same options for intraracial remarriage that most other women have" (2005, 189). Rather than a prejudice against outsiders, the preference for intraethnic marriage is seen as a cultural survival issue. Here again, it makes sense that women would prefer to end the abuse without ending the relationship where agency and autonomous desires are constructed by one's group identities. Tribal survival is not more important than the woman's safety, but an agentic woman could see tribal survival and ending the abuse as equally important values. Here we have a stark example of how the temporal element of agency reaches well beyond the individual life and absorbs the history—and future—of the entire group. These community pressures play out in similar ways with both U.S.-born and immigrant Orthodox Jewish and Latino communities, as well.[34] The specific ways in which and reasons for racialized gender identity developing as it does vary, but the analytical point remains the same: gender identity is a primary constitutive force driving women's sense of autonomy and freedom, and gender identity is inextricably inflected by norms about how to be a "good" member of one's racial and ethnic communities.

Aside from a socially constructed but very real desire to promote one's community interests and to honor one's identity as Indian or black or Jewish, immigrant women face additional structural constraints on their options for negotiating a violent relationship—constraints U.S.-born citizens do not have to face and that many service providers fail to understand or know how to navigate. In protesting the abuse she faces, an immigrant woman's sense of autonomy and freedom are produced by gender entrapment but also immigration law entrapment. "For many, living with an abusive man who holds the key to her permanent residency in the United States is a better alternative than being forced to return home to a life of scorn and stigma for herself and her natal family" (Venkataramani-Kothari 2007, 17). Dependence on one's spouse for legal status is "debilitating because if withdrawn, it makes immigrant survivors not only extremely vulnerable to deportation, but also ineligible to work, get a driving permit, or otherwise acquire an independent status" (Grewal 2007, 168). A precarious legal situation—arriving to the United States as a sponsored spouse, for example—can undermine one's subjective sense of agency, one's sense of self as able or willing to resist community gender imperatives, because it removes the structural conditions of freedom necessary to gird agency. Thus, legal, familial, and cultural barriers to ending violence all impinge on immigrant women's agency.[35]

Further exacerbating the gender/race entrapment constraining women's agency is that some women are coming from nations in which domestic abuse is not viewed as a serious or public problem. According to one woman in Edna Erez, Madelaine Adelman, and Carol Gregory's multiethnic immigrant study, "Women in Latin America and Mexico are supposed to suffer a lot with their husbands" (2009, 48). Another reported, "A man can do anything; he is the head of the family, and a woman should always sacrifice to make things work. The expectations for men and women are different. Our culture does not welcome outside intervention. We don't involve outsiders in family issues. We do not consider domestic violence as a crime; police do not get involved. We don't go to shelters. Legal system does not get involved" (49).[36] I am not trying to exoticize or "other" immigrant communities as a "them" that is somehow different from "us." Many native-born community groups have strongly racialized gender identities produced through a history of racism and classism in the United States that co-imbricates one's sense of gender identity with community survival imperatives (whether understood as surviving literal genocidal history, as with Native American populations or more figurative, though still potent, genocide like the incarceration of young black men at rates out of proportion to their relative criminality and lethality). Gender identities and community norms do manifest themselves in particular ways within immigrant communities, however, as removal from one's natal country and often one's natal family changes one's relationship to community identity and can make it more salient while also isolating women from some of their sources of resistance to violence. As Erez, Adelman, and Gregory found, "The escalation of abuse was particularly difficult for immigrant women who had left their natal families behind: 'I don't have family here, so he tells me that I don't have another choice but to stay with him.' Another woman argued that 'if he were in Syria, he would take into consideration my parents and would not act abusively as in U.S.'" (2009, 44). Social isolation is a tool of coercive control that is almost built into the immigrant experience for many women, making them particularly vulnerable to abuse and cutting off some of their resources for protesting the abuse and their spouse's sense of entitlement. And while isolation can be a problem, so can living within an immigrant community where orthodox views of gender roles prevail. Even if a woman is able to leave her abusive spouse, she may not receive support from her community. For an immigrant, this can be a particularly daunting challenge because they may be the only people she knows in the United States (Menjívar and Salcido 2002, 904–5).

Immigrants are almost uniquely perfectly situated for an abuser to take advantage of the propensity to abuse. Understanding that intimate partner violence is a means of coercive control and that the primary mechanisms of control are isolation and monitoring, the situation of many immigrants—especially those recently arrived to a new country—is ripe for intimate partner violence to develop or escalate. Where women do not speak the primary language of the new country, where they have been uprooted from their natal families and home communities, and where any job skills they may have brought with them are likely to be devalued because of language barriers—along with a lack of awareness of the legal situation in the United States—conditions are ripe for exploitation if control is what their partners seek (see Menjívar and Salcido 2002; Erez, Adelman, and Gregory 2009, 36).

All of these factors produce resistance strategies that look different from what the liberal criminal justice system–based approach often expects of women if it is to take them seriously as abused women and not masochists or participants in some form of mutual violence. It is also important to be clear that I am not implying that some cultures are simply more violent than others and culture thus somehow excuses or explains domestic violence. Rates of domestic violence are quite high among U.S.-born couples; thus, the "cultural defense" argument—that for U.S.-born citizens domestic violence is an individual, psychological problem while it is a cultural problem for nonnative groups—is specious. My point is to highlight different subjectifying discourses that contribute to particular manifestations of agency and desire, where abuse is always recognized as wrong, but the means by which one deals with it can and will vary.

To that end, I want to examine in more detail the interimbricating force of race and class in domestic violence among U.S.-born women. Although ethnographic researchers and critical race social and legal theorists generally agree that race and class have a noticeable effect on responses to intimate partner violence, a recent study by educational and social policy researcher Lois Weis appears to contradict the specific details of some of these studies. Researchers including Beth Richie, Kimberlé Crenshaw, Neil Websdale, and Margaret Abraham have argued that abused women of color are less likely than white women to seek outside help—particularly from the criminal justice system—given the history of abuse that plagues police departments' relationships to communities of color, but Weis reached precisely the opposite conclusion, claiming that "white women are reluctant to name domestic violence as a 'problem' in the community, although it obviously is, . . . and are unwilling to name the white male 'self' in any consistent way as a perpetrator of violence in their own homes." African American women, though, "speak openly and directly about the violence in their homes . . . [and] hold African-American men responsible for the violence in their homes" (2001, 156). Weis found that what little critique of domestic violence white women had to offer was individualistic rather than focused on gender and domestic relations more generally. In contrast, the African American women in her study were outspoken critics of normative gender relations. She also reports that "they call police (who are generally unresponsive), seek orders of protection (with little avail), flee to shelters" (160). Weis's report that white women are less likely than black women to use criminal justice and shelter resources directly contradicts Richie's finding that white women are *more* likely to do these things. Weis's finding is odd given all of the other work that exists demonstrating African American women's reticence to bring in outsiders, given their legitimate concerns about being called "race traitors" and the reticence to expose black men to police brutality.

There are a couple of ways to begin to make sense of these findings: first by considering the interactive effect of investment in gender norms with a sense of racial solidarity, and second by examining the role played by economic class, and differential benefits gained from the gender and race structure, in affecting who does or does not call in police or other outsiders and why. First, given that the white women in Weis's study offered only individualistic explanations for domestic violence, it is not surprising that they are seeking individualistic solutions. Women who have less critical (less normatively insurgent) gender consciousness are less likely to leave or work with others to mitigate or end the abuse. This part of Weis's study is consistent with both Richie's and Grewal's findings, for example. The black women in Richie's study who were battered (and among them, those who were more severely battered and who stayed longer) were typically those most invested in the normative ideal of the heteronuclear family. For the South Asian women in Grewal's study, the more invested they were in "patriarchally rooted sociocultural understandings" of the husbands as "lords" over wives, the less likely they were to seek outside help (2007, 169). Thus, while the racial analysis seems an anomaly in Weis's work, the gender analysis is more consistent with other research.

Further, the production of gender identity cannot be separated from one's racial or ethnic identity. So the gender norms and gender consciousness as racial constructs produce women who evaluate abuse and its roots in patriarchy or individual men's psychology differently. The responses to violence are gendered in all cases, with gender understood as a racial construct. So although Weis concludes that "white women spend a good deal of time propping up the image of the nuclear family and hiding the abuse, while poor and working-class African-American women are openly suspect of the institution and spend more time in self-healing through participation in group discussion" (2001, 161), it seems more accurate to say that it is the investment in the nuclear, heterosexual family (and the gender roles that attend to that) combined with the racially specific construction of gender that shapes one's configurations of agentic possibility within abusive situations. Further, gender identity is not only crosscut by racial and ethnic community norms, but also by class positioning. Class may not determine consciousness, but it is certainly a central force producing racialized gender consciousness.

This seems especially true as the poorer white women were seen as "hard living women," living outside the confines of heterosexual respectability and heteronormative femininity that is implicitly coded as white. When abused, the hard living white women are more likely to avail themselves of services and to talk to others about the abuse than are the women Weis refers to as "settled lives" women. The hard living women are in some sense a morality tale for the settled women about what might happen to them if they fail to live up to the gendered family norms they are supposed to fit into. In a later study, Weis and her co-investigators observed that "given that the women's role was to sustain family life, with stories of abuse came embarrassment and, ironically, evidence of *her* failure. Silence cloaked abused in the hope that its biting reality would soften and eventually fade away. . . . Living in violence may be better than living on the streets or losing custody of one's children. If she speaks, the 'settled' woman could pay the price of becoming 'hard living'" (Weis et al., 2005, 245).

Here economics and gender norms collide, holding women in between binding ideals: hearth and home are to be achieved by good white women, not homelessness or living too close to the edge. Sometimes the desire to hang onto and repair an abusive marriage arises from norms about class respectability and the impetus to hang onto any slight class privilege one may have, where, in a twinning effect of these norms, class status is reflected in part by adherence to hegemonic heteronuclear family status. Desire for the heteronormative family at all costs is socially produced by the material conditions producing middle class gender norms. The settled lives women's resistance is often overrun by an (excessive, hegemonic) normative competence that drowns out all other options as too threatening to one's identity. If one's gender identity is that of a good girl who lives a respectable life, falling from working class to poverty can damage one's sense of self and one's ability to operate within a radically changing discursive and material framework.

Although class, as both material and discursive element of situation, is clearly important in structuring women's sense of the possible, it is difficult to generalize about what effect economic status has on leaving, seeking outside help, or attempting private, individual solutions. One common argument is that if women had more economic resources available to them, they would be less likely to end up in or stay in abusive relationships because they could (literally) afford to do otherwise. But while much has been made of the role that economics plays in shaping domestic violence, it is an insufficient explanation. The desire for power and control spans economic classes. And though it is true that the overwhelming majority of women who leave their abusers are financially self-supporting, with independent economic resources, so are more than half of the women who stay with partners who have been abusive (Jones 2000, 170). This difficulty in generalizing about the role of class is important to note because it suggests that although economic opportunities are vital for the credible threat of exit and a woman's realistic options for being able to support herself (and her children) if she does leave, the role of economic resources and opportunities in shaping actual responses is muted by the force of and investment in gender and racial discourses.[37] Once desire has been produced and racialized gender habits of thought and action developed, external structures of freedom can override identity imperatives, but economic resources alone are not enough.

Thus, women might want to stay in their relationships for a variety of reasons, as Neil Websdale noted in his study of women in poor black neighborhoods in Tennessee: "Fear of retribution, love of their abusers, shame, embarrassment, wanting to keep the family together, relying on his paycheck, and hope that things might change" (2005, 145). Some of these reasons are more practical, but others are quite deeply entwined with one's sense of self from which agency flows. The relationship itself, and the community within which the relationship is embedded, are important sources of power and identity for the woman that cannot be jettisoned without serious harm to her life plan. The tension between competing gender and racial imperatives is lived through women's bodies. Where the physical harm is not severe and unending—and where personal resistance strategies are working to some degree—staying is the most agentic thing some women can do to care for themselves as whole, community-embedded beings.[38] Resisting domestic violence is not a question of leaving or staying. It is a question of implementing a variety of staying and leaving tactics that intervene in the violence while building on one's resources and contributing to one's life projects.

The Agency in Victim: Staying, Leaving, and Women's Resistance

Although for most advocates and theorists the sine qua non of agency in domestic violence has been leaving, there are a number of reasons why leaving might not be the best choice for a particular woman at any given moment. At other times, it might be the optimal choice, but not one she can reasonably exercise. Thus, here I want to explore and argue for seeing the agency that women can and do enact when they stay with abusive partners. The point in doing so is twofold. First, I argue that because different demands are placed on women, agency must be seen as a more complex phenomenon than making one objectively right choice. Rather, agency has to be weighed in context, in part because it coexists to varying degrees with victimization. That is, the political possibilities constructing one's situation make possible different kinds of agency. Further, not only do I reject an either/or construction of agency and victimization in situations of domestic violence, in some cases—as I discuss below—it appears that agency is enhanced through the acceptance of the identity of (partial) victim. Second, locating agency in particular, identifiable webs of constraints helps to pinpoint how and where interlocutors can intervene to make better choices possible, to enhance freedom within the swirl of competing desires and social expectations. To share in the production of more open possibilities, we have to see how and why different means and ends are desired among different groups of women.

It is important to stress that leaving is not always permanent. It is not always synonymous with ending a relationship but may instead signal a temporary break while the terms of the relationship are renegotiated. In addition, even if the goal is to end a relationship—to leave it for good—this ending is usually a process and not a discrete act. Women separate from their abusers an average of five times before making a final break, and this process takes eight years on average (Goetting 1999, 15). The efforts to balance conflicting needs contributes to the length of this process. Being in violent relationships alters one's sense of the world and her place in it. As it takes time to become oneself, it takes time to "re-become" and recreate one's sense of self in relationship. One's relationship with an intimate partner is the core of the field within which one acts. As Norman K. Denzin explains, "Violence places persons and their assailants outside the taken-for-granted structures of the world. Such conduct produces a sense of the bizarre, the unusual, the frightening, and the unknown. Violent conduct transforms family intimates into the categories of victims and assailants" (1984, 496–97). It takes time to reorganize one's relationships with others to adopt the label "victim," and especially additionally to reconcile "victim" with the agency that one already knows oneself to have. One is continually reconstructing the interplay of resistance and iteration as she weaves this new status into the life plans and self-conceptions that are the habitual ways she has of being in the world and thinking of herself. Given that developing strategies of resistance that are coherent with one's subjective sense of self takes time, as one has to reevaluate one's goals and options, it should not be surprising that the first line of defense for many women is trying to placate their abusers or simply to avoid them by going for a walk or sleeping in another bed. Such seemingly passive responses buy women time to figure out what to do now that one of their most intimate relationships has radically changed (see, e.g., Abraham 2000, 135). Resistance strategies are often launched without knowing what the final outcome will be and whether the desired outcome can be achieved, which means that one's goals will be reevaluated as each resistance strategy is more or less successful, and this reevaluation requires rebalancing the competing interests outlined above.

Ending abuse is the ultimate goal of domestic violence work and women's responses to their partners. Some abuse—physical, mental, or both—is so severe that the woman's life is in danger and severing the relationship is the only way for the woman to save herself. But relationships do not always need to be severed for the violence to end. Where the battering is infrequent and controlled,[39] there is a greater chance that the goals of ending the violence and maintaining the relationship can be achieved. Six-month follow-up studies of heterosexual women who reunite with their batterers show that 60 percent of women who return to abusive partners find that the abuse resumes. But this means that 40 percent are able to get the violence to stop (Mahoney 1994, 77). Thus, sometimes the resistances enacted out of a strong desire to maintain a relationship but end the abuse are quite effective—perhaps the best, most agentic choices one could have made, given the balance of needs and wants.

So while "leaving" has become the holy grail of domestic violence intervention because the legal model has become so dominant, there are significant problems with positing a clean break as the ur-strategy of agency and resistance. First, for many women, leaving is not possible because of material resources or personal needs. Even if leaving is the only way to get the abuse to stop, a focus on leaving that materially, culturally, or psychologically does not take into account what is required to leave fails women. Second, staying is often part of leaving, and by reconceptualizing leaving in this way, we can better see the agency women have and the resources they still need. Finally, getting the abuse to end should be the goal of the anti–intimate partner violence movement. In many cases, what women want—and what they can achieve— is ending the abuse without ending the relationship. Leaving is the right answer for some women and thus needs to be facilitated, but it is the wrong answer for others, so leaving needs not to be mandated.

A woman cannot know from the moment she launches an intervention into the violence what the outcome is going to be. She can know what she hopes for, and she can try to make that happen. This is an assertion of agency—of attempting to bring to fruition her life plans as shaped by the intersecting norms and sources of power noted above. This resistance is agency, regardless of whether she is successful in achieving her goals; that is, it is the evaluation of goals and options in light of the normative competence and resistance to violence that is the mark of agency, not the result of, or her partner's response to, her actions. And her goals may shift as she is more or less successful in stopping or ameliorating the abuse. Through the course of responding to violence, women can be both victims and agents in their relationships. It is important to remember in assessing agency that one can do everything right and still end up dead or further abused. Women's agency needs to be evaluated and facilitated in terms of working within the structural conditions of their lives and the way they negotiate the norms within which they must operate. Agency should not be judged primarily by how successful or not one is at changing the behaviors and attitudes of others.

Two tragic examples from Kathleen B. Jones's work debunking the false simplicity caught up in reducing decision making for battered women to an easy, obvious choice between staying with and leaving a batterer help to illustrate the points I am emphasizing here about, first, the relationship between class, race, and subjectifying norms constructing desire and self; second, the continuum between staying and leaving as one copes with abuse; and third, the way that incorporating the identity "victim" into one's self-understanding can be the cognitive shift required to more fully facilitate the deployment of one's agentic resources. In the first case Jones relates, a white San Diego State University women's studies student (and student coordinator of the women's studies resource center on campus), Andrea O'Donnell, was murdered by her black boyfriend, Andrés English-Howard. In the second case, told fifteen years after the relationship ended, a prominent professor in the department ("Dr. C") was battered to the point of near death by her lesbian partner, a student who was the same race and almost the same age as the professor. In each case, the batterer was empowered or dominant according to some identity markers, but disempowered by others. The battered women were contending with their own social power in the context of feeling stunted power in a relationship and wanting to be responsible in the way they yielded their social identity power relative to their partners.

Dr. C felt silenced because she was abused in the context of a lesbian relationship. Her abuser used homophobia and Dr. C's (tenuous and untenured) position in the university as tools to keep her silent about the abuse. She also used the then-popular discourse of egalitarianism in women's studies to argue that they (women, lesbians) were all equal in the fight against oppression, essentially accusing Dr. C of failing to take responsibility for her role in the abusive dynamic. Dr. C noted that she felt "trapped" by the situation, "hamstrung by the very idea of power that she always reminded me that I had had and she lacked. But, just like Andrea, all the power that I had was rendered completely unavailable to me by the intensity of her violent rage. And my own embarrassment" (Jones 2000, 157). For her part, Andrea seemed to be keenly aware of the social power differences between herself as a white woman and Andrés as a black man, as well as the disapproval of others in San Diego of their interracial relationship. Not only did she genuinely care for Andrés, she seemed to want to avoid being responsible for getting a black man labeled a batterer. Further, thinking back to Richie's work and the tentative conclusions about women of higher social standing being less likely to go public with the abuse, it is significant that Andrea was middle class and believed herself to be capable and strong, able to "fix" people and her own problems. As Jones writes, "Andrea cannot be described, except in a distorting way, as having 'chosen' to stay or 'chosen' to leave. She 'chose' both. When confronted with deeply conflicting demands, most women do choose both" (7). Andrea was working to extricate herself from the relationship with Andrés while still taking care of him (by helping him find employment and deal with his drug addiction). She stayed in the relationship because she loved him, but she was also distancing herself in important ways to try to escape his abuse. For Andrea, as for so many other women, leaving was a long process, in part because she believed Andrés to be someone going through a rough time rather than someone who was an abusive partner.

Because of the time and cognitive shift required to orient oneself to being in an abusive relationship rather than just a relationship, a range of responses are on evidence as women figure out what they want to happen. Early interventions into the violence may include placating the abuser or talking back, or even hitting back, although this is the strategy employed most by women who have few other options for challenging the violence they face (Goodmark 2008, 77). The woman may leave for a shelter to give the abuser time to calm down and for her to plan how best to address this situation. If she cannot leave, she may refuse to cook, or she may spit in his food before serving it (Venkataramani-Kothari 2007, 20–21).

In the context of staying, women often take many brave and ingenious steps to try to end the abuse with the limited resources they have available. The details of their stories are unique, but they all resonate with the ingenuity Mallika demonstrated in her efforts to use the strength of her small community to slowly build a plan, first for ending the abuse and, then, when that didn't work, to leave her husband. Mallika's story is revealed in Margaret Abraham's book on intimate partner violence among South Asian immigrant women in the United States. Mallika explained to Abraham that she knew almost no one in the United States, except for six families, all of whom were relatives of her husband and thus would not help her. But, she says,

> By God's grace, I thought up this idea. I took the telephone directory of my area, and made a list of all the Indian families listed there. I thought I would call them and somebody could help me. I talked to Mr. S. I told him that I don't know anybody in America. I don't have any relatives and I am not aware of all the things here so I need some help and could he help me? He said that he empathized with me, and he would talk it over with his wife and call me over to their house and discuss the ways that they can help me. So I went to his house. (Abraham 2000, 145)

The man worked to keep the couple together in large part by introducing them to more people so they would not be so isolated. He thought this would minimize the abuse. This was the first step to Mallika finding her way to a South Asian women's organization that was eventually able to get her the community and material resources she needed to get out of the abusive marriage. Through this process, Mallika both stayed with and left her abuser, using the collective power of her immigrant community to validate the importance of many aspects of her identity and building and using the survival tools that worked best for her particular needs, which eventually included severing the relationship. Mallika's access to a culturally sensitive anti–domestic violence organization became the external resource that eventually opened up her conditions of freedom and autonomy.

Sometimes women will leave their partners but then return not because they are particularly invested in saving the relationship, but because of failures of freedom (structural failures). These failures often are misread by criminal justice providers and other outsiders as failures of autonomy (personal weakness). One example of this lack of freedom includes failures of welfare policy to account for the sometimes causal relationship between domestic violence and welfare use; that is, "women may utilize social services benefits as their means of support in the process of escaping their abusive partners" (Josephson 2005, 92). Time limits on benefits can make women feel more trapped in their relationships as they need to be able to support their children, get a place to live, and get their finances back in order—perhaps even needing education or job training after dealing with legal separation issues—in order to be able to sever a relationship. This type of structural entrapment is different from normative gender entrapment but no less constraining of one's situation.

Further, as part of the coercive control batterers engage in, some abusive partners harass women at work or interfere with their ability to get to work on time as a way of further isolating them and keeping them from being independent. The work requirements of Temporary Aid to Needy Families fail to account for some women's inability to work given the harassment and abuse they are facing from their partners (see Josephson 2005, 94–95). Other examples of failures of freedom that thwart agency include race discrimination in housing and employment practices that can leave some women of color feeling like they have few survival options except to return to a batterer they were trying to leave, and culturally incompetent social service providers, such as shelters that do not or cannot provide services in the battered woman's language, legal advice about the immigration issues she faces, or living arrangements that can support women's cultural identities—for example, engaging in specific religious practices, cooking in traditional ways, or washing utensils in different ways (see Abraham 2000, 160–68; Crenshaw 1994, 107–10; Goldfarb 1996, 593; Grewal 2007).[40]

Thus, women who want to salvage the relationship but stop the violence, or mitigate the violence until they have a workable exit strategy, can and do use many tactics, such as leaving temporarily and making return conditional on assurances of safety, hiding away money as it becomes available, copying important documents, calling the police, enlisting the help of others to get her partner to stop hitting her, getting a job, getting her partner into counseling, hitting back, obtaining a temporary restraining order, threatening divorce or separation, or perhaps engaging in criminal activities either as a means of getting resources to leave an abuser, or as a way of bonding with the abuser in the hopes that this bond will diminish or end the abuse.[41] "Continuing the relationship may therefore be part of a pattern of resistance to violence on the part of" abused women (Mahoney 1994, 73; see also Ristock 2002, 88–89). Abraham breaks resistance strategies into three types: personal strategies (talking, hiding, promising, avoidance, passive or aggressive defense), using informal sources of help (family, in-laws, neighbors, friends, shelters), and using formal sources of help (police, social service agencies, lawyers) (Abraham 2000, 133–34). Studies of other groups of women find a similar range of strategies engaged, often simultaneously and building on each other to increase bargaining power and exit options.

These interventions, which all get clumped together as staying with an abuser, are strategic choices women make for themselves, and they are informed by what it means to be a "good wife," a "good black woman," even a "person who can pay her bills or afford to raise her children." These are all socially valued roles that take on more or less importance depending on how cognizant one is of the sources of power creating the imperatives to fill these roles and on the particular communities within which one lives. If she is successful in asserting her agency to effect her will in this particular part of her world, if the violence ends and the relationship survives, the woman will be dubbed "a successful strategist. She will be seen as an agent in her life if his violence has stopped *even if these same acts in another woman would be called 'staying' and treated as lack of agency*" (Mahoney 1994, 76, emphasis in original). This is part of the problem of judging the agency of the woman as though this agency were something other than a political prerogative. Whether or not her acts count as agentic only ever gets judged by the outcome, rather than also by the web of conflicting demands and constraints that led to her choices. If we judge by the efforts to put the pieces of a life together in a rewarding and normatively competent way, then far more women look like agents—compromised agents, as we all are in some way, but agents nonetheless.

Further, expecting one to walk away from a relationship—to make a clean break—imposes a public model of relationships on private relations. Although personal relationships are structured by political ones, intimate relations are phenomenologically different from public relationships. Criminal justice and social service providers must deal with this difference if they are to be useful in cases of domestic violence. They must "see" intimacy; marriage or marriagelike partnerships are not the same as law partnerships or friendships with members of a sports team, where one can walk away without losing something profoundly constitutive of one's self in the process. Private relationships are less fungible than public ones. Even when they are dysfunctional, they are unique and essential in a way that public relationships are not. To say that one must simply walk away to be an agent worthy of respect does not merely miss the contextual ambiguity of women's lived situations: it indicates a fundamental misunderstanding about what is at stake in private life.

Ultimately, the discourse that constructs women's only options as staying and being a victim or leaving and being an agent, assumes a level of emotional and economic independence that many women do not have. This construction of the problem also overlooks the many roles that partners fill in people's lives. Emphasizing exit "reflects a concept of agency as the functioning of an atomistic, mobile individual, and this concept of agency also reflects a binary opposition between agency and victimization" (Mahoney 1994, 74). Women opt to stay in abusive relationships for many reasons: there was probably a time when the relationship was good, and she has some reason to think it can be again; she loves her partner, or at least they have children together and she wants them to have a two-parent home; her partner is the only real family she has; she feels she has no economic alternative; she is under pressure from family and friends to keep her marriage and family together; or she is uncertain "about other options or her ability to subsist or care for dependents, because of depression and dislocation that come with intimate loss and harm, or because she is afraid that leaving will trigger lethal danger—because, essentially, she is held captive" (Mahoney 1994, 73).[42] As Angela M. Moe found when she interviewed nineteen women of various ages and races currently in domestic violence shelter, "all had returned to their abusers for reasons such as having no money; being threatened, stalked, sabotaged or harassed by their abusers; being encouraged by their families to reconcile; feeling guilty; being lonely; and still loving their partners" (2004, 122).

Obviously, the strategies women use are open to interpretation, but their meanings derive from specific contexts. Women's actions might appear to be provoking an attack when in fact they are simply trying to control the place and severity of an inevitable assault. Similar actions would have very different meanings if she engaged in them at a time when she was not expecting to be beaten. Further, particular types of resistance are only likely to arise under specifiable conditions, as we see with Linda Gordon's analysis of the rise of the claim to a right not to be beaten.[43] Rights talk assumes absolute claims about bodily integrity that were incompatible with the economic and social realities of many women's lives until very recently. The issue of interpretation, resistance strategies, and context arose in Richie's study, as well. As she examined the role that battering played in her study subjects' criminal activity, she found that the white women used crime as a means of getting out of the violent relationships, whereas the black battered women were trapped in the criminal activity in the same way that they were trapped in the abusive relationships. They were drawn into crime as a way to try to end the violence but not the relationship, because their partners promised the abuse would stop if she committed the crime for him; because she tried committing crimes with him as a way of bonding with the partner; or because she took the blame for crimes he committed because of her concern that her partner not be abused by a racist criminal justice system. Again we see that gender and racial norms produce the very possibilities one can conceive and plausibly act on.

In addition to resisting the staying/leaving dualism, another kind of interpretative shift is also central in facilitating agency. Richie, Goetting, Jones, and many others have found in their work with battered women that one of the cognitive shifts that often allows women to challenge the violence in their lives and enact greater degrees of agency is in seeing themselves as victims, as battered women, and further coming to understand that this label does not have to become the entirety of their identity.[44] One of the fundamental points Jones develops throughout her 2000 book *Living between Danger and Love* is that it can be the unwillingness to claim the (denigrated) status of victim that will keep people in battering relationships and prevent them from engaging all of the social resources she might have available to her to end the abuse (see Jones 2000, 155–57). Ironically, it is quite often in the acceptance of the identity "victim" that one can gain some critical perspective on why she has made certain choices and how she can engage outside help to open up future possibilities for enhanced freedom.

It is true that there is some danger in adopting these labels (victim, battered woman) because they can feel totalizing, due in no small part to the too frequent construction of agency and victimization as mutually exclusive categories, and because it is or can feel like an admission of failure in one's role as spouse or partner. Further, the label "battered women" is problematic to the degree that it defines women only by the abuse that is inflicted on them by others (see discussions in Mahoney 1994, 60–63; Russo 2001, 28; Schneider 2000, 60–65). Understanding that one can act agentically under conditions of oppression helps women gain a greater sense of control and fosters the development of an exit plan or relationship interventions. When the only definition of "victim" that a woman has available to her "is so stigmatizing that it is impossible to reconcile with perceiving agency in oneself or in others," then she will usually refuse to adopt the label, resulting in denial about the severity of the abuse, shared experiences with others, and resistance to involving others in attempts to change one's situation (Mahoney 1994, 62; see also Mahoney 1992). But seeing that women are victimized without being solely defined by that victimization, and understanding the ways in which women assert themselves in situations of victimization and oppression, not only helps battered women muster their resources, but also helps others (activists, lawyers, judges, police officers) to see the other things the woman is and to look at what she does rather than only what is done to her.

Despite the pitfalls, part of what adopting the label "battered woman" accomplishes for women's agency is the provision of a construct that comes equipped with categories and analyses, and outside services, that women can then apply to their situations, helping to make sense of where they have been and where they are going. Being able to put a narrative on her situation that includes a sense of how to utilize outside services in a systematic way can increase a woman's chances of being able to protect herself and make better decisions for her future. Rather than wallowing in victimization, battered women who claim that identity can and often do use it as a starting place for increasing the freedom in their lives to whatever degree is possible rather than resigning themselves to a lack of structural options. For some, claiming the status or identity of victim ("battered woman") is one step in developing a critical consciousness about the ways in which systemic and discursive power works. Although this might not completely denaturalize the gendered, raced, and sexed norms one is committed to, it can at least begin the process of allowing alternative ideals of being into one's consciousness. Further, moving beyond seeing oneself as deserving of the violence, or the "violence as individual pathology" model, and developing a critical consciousness only comes through somewhat active participation in shaping the contexts in which one lives and makes choices. This is a crucial element of Foucault's "care for the self" that I discussed in chapter 1, which he described as part of the deliberate practice of liberty. Recall that such care for the self requires the active participation of others serving as counselors and guides to support and challenge people in their conceptions of self and situation. This is a critical component of the criminal and social service responses I advocate below.

One cannot underestimate the role that others play both in supporting the agency that women already possess and enact and in helping battered women find further resources for coping with the violence and imagining (and achieving) a safer, more expansive life.[45] We often hear that violence can happen to anyone, and this is true. Yet "it's not because all women are potential victims or all men potential batterers, but because choice is a full-time responsibility that cannot be undertaken all alone. No matter how empowered any one of us feels, no matter how aware, how informed, how knowledgeable, being in control of our lives and being informed are not individual acts. They are public projects" (Jones 2000, 177). In this way, agency is not only individual or collective; it is shared. Respecting another's suboptimal choices does not preclude trying to help her see that other realistic possibilities exist (if they do); nor, more importantly, does it preclude critiquing the political and social conditions that limit, sometimes severely, the openness of some women's agency. A life without abuse is clearly better than a life compromised by physical or emotional cruelty. We have a social responsibility to construct a world where fewer people are trapped in violent situations. Social discourses of—and economic inequalities that attach to—class, citizenship status, and race intersect with gender norms to influence a women's real and perceived exit options. Even if some women want to stay and work things out, they need the credible threat of exit options in order to have their demands for change hold any persuasive power (Crenshaw 1994, 95; Okin 1989, 134–69). Framing agency in this way opens up a political space for talking about what we owe each other socially in order to foster the agency and human flourishing of others in addition to that of ourselves.

Engaging Discursive and Material Construction

Because of the varied nature of violence and the number of coincident normative, productive forces of power that go into creating the subjects who are the perpetrators, victims, and survivors of intimate partner violence, a range of approaches to stopping domestic violence is required. These approaches must combine the individual-level interventions that can keep a woman safe with the collective production of consciousness that reshapes how we see ourselves and how we engage with the world, as well as producing inroads into changing dominant institutions. Feminist interventions must continue to include the option of police and criminal justice intervention, but they cannot rely on a narrow criminal justice approach to stop violence or change identity-producing norms and freedom-constraining material structures. Although the number of interventions and legal and social changes needed are vast, I will focus here on a few that most directly engage the way we think about gender in relationships and that enable women to restructure their relationships while still respecting the gender and racial norms that produce their subjectivities. These options see staying as an option but also facilitate leaving. The more collective strategies can be developed, the more the conditions producing subjects—and their subjective desires—can be reiterated and reworked toward a more gender-equitable future. Staying in a relationship while resisting the violence is more effective at actually *resisting* the violence if exiting the relationship is a real option. The more options we can create for women to leave if necessary—and end the relationship in a way that meets the myriad needs comprising their choice structure—the greater is any individual woman's agency, regardless of what she decides to do. To facilitate agency, all of these options must exist, but without being mandates. Donna Coker reports that women who report being "highly satisfied" with the police response to their calls are the women who are given a range of options and types of information about where they can seek help, how the court system works, what will happen if they pursue an arrest, and so on, and were then allowed to decide for themselves which of these avenues of intervention to pursue (2000, 1038). The interventions I focus on here are meant to work together as much as possible rather than being either/or options.

Two kinds of institutional assistance can aid the most women: legal and economic aid (housing, employment, and child care).[46] A recent study out of Virginia shows that having access to a lawyer—regardless of whether women stay or leave, or press charges or not—decreases violence. According to Aries Keck (2009), domestic violence in Southwest Virginia dropped over a five-year period when access to legal aid to domestic violence victims was increased. The legal aid workers were there to pursue legal cases if that is what the women wanted, but they also were willing to work as advocates outside the courts, setting up safety plans and putting the women in contact with shelters and other programs in the area. This supports Cris Sullivan's research comparing women who received an advocate's help in obtaining a range of material resources versus those who did not. The women who received the advocates' help were empowered to improve their lives and decrease the battering: "One out of four women in the experimental group experienced no abuse during the twenty four month follow up, while this was true for only one out of ten women in the control group" (cited in Coker 2000, 1023). Given this, anti–domestic violence workers need to think creatively about how to use the legal system, both to be a fail-safe backup plan to aid women in getting out of relationships when they want and need to, and to provide resources to women to increase their bargaining power in relationships—resources that in fact empower them in relationship and increase their credible threat of exit.

The legal reform that could meet the most needs discussed in this chapter is a change in civil protection order law. Although the most common civil protection orders are "stay away" orders, there is another form of protection order that prohibits future abuse but allows future contact. Currently, these orders are available in only a few jurisdictions in the country, but they can be quite effective in getting women the legal help they need without demanding actions that they are unable or unwilling to take. Limited civil protection orders are not appropriate in cases of severe abuse, but they can be highly effective in many cases by allowing women to invoke outside approbation of the abuse with potentially serious penalties for violating the order and by allowing women to stay in whatever kind of contact with their partners they deem necessary or desirable without risking becoming a criminal themselves. As Sally F. Goldfarb argues, these contact but no-abuse orders serve as a way of giving women some bargaining power in the relationship without requiring her to take any particular step at any one time: "For many women, obtaining a protection order is deeply empowering because it entails asserting one's own needs, standing up to the abuser, and enlisting a potent institutional ally. This empowerment can be a major step in the process of ending the abuse" (2008, 1515). The survivor of violence can then continue to have contact with her partner if it is her desire to try to repair the relationship, or if she simply needs to continue some contact with him for purposes of, for example, child support or help with rent. These kinds of protection orders bring the courts to women's assistance without necessarily bringing in the police. As a civil response, they can help women by providing them more tools and affirmation that they have help, without mandating that they take actions they cannot or are not willing to take. Even though they are not a panacea for violent relationships, limited protection orders can help many of the women like the ones I cite above to change the dynamics of their relationships, to intervene in the coercive control that their partners are trying to tighten around them while still allowing them to be true to their gender and racial identity and community commitments.

In cases where the abuse is not severe and escalating, these contact-permitted protection orders can meet many of the material and psychic needs of women who do not want separation or who face impoverishment if they no longer have access to their partner's income.[47] If these types of orders are available, many women would be more likely to seek legal help, especially those who currently avoid the courts because "stay away" is not an order they view as a viable or desirable option. Because seeking legal help in and of itself can help women intervene in the violence, any reform that encourages legal help seeking should be encouraged.[48] Such interventions can support women in their relationships while condemning the abuse in a way that stay-away orders do not. That is, Sally Goldfarb is exactly right when she says that "stay-away orders convey the message that women have a right to leave violent relationships, but they do not convey the related but distinct message that women have a right to remain in relationships and demand that they become non-violent" (2008, 1536).

These interventions further provide the kind of support that women need to begin to unravel the web of coercion their partners have spun around them. Goldfarb reports on a study of one thousand battered women who were able to maintain their relationships but end the violence: "Legal intervention was among the factors that women identified most frequently as helping to stop the abuse. The legal intervention was effective in large part because it carried the threat of future negative consequences for the batterer. Thirty percent of the women who were interviewed for this study said that the batterer stopped the abuse because he was afraid of divorce; twenty percent said that he stopped because he did not want to be arrested or charged with a crime" (2008, 1536). Limited protection orders can meet women's needs in part by allowing them to exploit their batterers weaknesses, and they can be amended to become stay-away orders if the batterer fails to uphold his end of the bargain. By intervening in the time of violence, limited protection orders can engage some temporal elements of agency, embedding the iterative aspect of agency in a new practical-evaluative context. By changing the contingencies of the moment, an alternative future can be imagined. That is, the projective aspect of agency—that which is most obviously the resistant element of the time of agency—becomes real in a materially significant way. If these limited orders were more readily available—and were always an option that could be supplemented if necessary with a stay-away order—then more women might gain access to the resources they want without having to call the police or separate.

Even with their potential to alter the structural and temporal conditions of women's relationships, limited civil protection orders are still primarily an individually focused intervention. However, to challenge the normative structures that both produce violence and limit women's autonomous response responses to violence, communal responses need to be a more prominent part of the mix of freedom-enhancing reforms as well. As Anannya Bhattacharjee (1997) has argued, the more individualized the approach to domestic violence, the less likely domestic violence organizations are to threaten the very structures that support battering in the first place. The conditions that support battering and the solutions that are deemed appropriate come from an understanding of how group identities function in the world. To really change the conditions that permit battering, we need to change the structural conditions within which we become desiring, thinking adults; such change is a collective, political project. Agency is shared in that the conditions that give rise to our agentic capacities are public—shared—ones. That is, social institutions create the shared space within which we make possible more or less agency, and better and worse choices; the way in which we act together as a community marks elements of agency. Agency is shared also when we enlist the help of others to control the conditions of our lives and make positive changes. One way in which community resources can be pooled is through culturally specific anti–domestic violence aid groups such as Sakhi in New York City, Apna Ghar in Chicago,

Manavi in New Jersey, Kiran in Durham, North Carolina, and Congreso in Philadelphia. These groups can provide resources themselves or can serve as conduits to culturally sensitive and legally appropriate interventions for women who are ill-served by the more mainstream shelter services or simple police interventions.

The reason that ethnicity-specific aid groups are so important is that they understand the cultural contexts from which women are coming and through which they are interpreting—and presenting—their situations. When we talk about a "language barrier" in access to services, it is sometimes quite literally true that women needing assistance do not have the English-speaking skills to articulate their needs and be understood within Anglo organizations. But language goes beyond the words used. For example, many Indian immigrants speak perfectly fluent English, but their cultural modes of expression and ways of interpreting and living within cultural expectations are quite different from the U.S. context. This is where having service providers who understand their clients' context of meaning-making is invaluable. For example, Mandeep Grewal's (2007) study participants were shy about naming the abuse that had happened to them because they were ashamed; thus, the words they used did not convey to the police the kind of help they needed, and they ended up not receiving the counseling and other services they could have gotten. Saying that they were in a "bad situation" or a situation that was "not good" or that their husband used "bad words" did not convey to the mainstream service providers the rapes, beatings, and verbal abuse that they were enduring (Grewal 2007, 170–71; see also Abraham 2000, 167).

The women in Grewal's study said that the opportunity to work with a group of advocates who shared their cultural background was very important in helping them get out of violent relationships because they did not have to explain cultural and familial expectations to them; there was a level of cultural understanding that enabled them to focus on explaining their specific situations and needs and getting the immigration and community assistance they needed to address their specific problems (Grewal 2007, 173–74). Sonali said: "I went to the American shelter, I felt like I was so subdued. I could not speak English [properly] so all my feelings were suppressed." Parneet was even more blunt: "Without Manavi, there is nothing for me" (174). In this case, it is the normative competence of the organization that facilitates the freedom—opens up the material possibilities—of the women they work with. In demonstrating this normative competence, these organizations reach women in a way that can help them reinterpret the race-gender norms that have produced their subjective sense of self and desire, thereby more effectively generating a resistant resignification of how to live these norms. An ethos can be produced because the culturally adept material resources are in place.

These community-based groups can thus intervene in essential moments of resubjectification, thereby changing the nature of one's agency, developing the structural and interpersonal links that help to create new norms and new ways of achieving old norms that are still important. They can also serve as an essential link between abused women and mainstream resources. For example, support groups like Sneha aim to help abused women without assuming that they will want to stay or leave their relationships. They model their group on the extended family because they work with South Asian women, and the extended family model is central to one's sense of place and one's identity (see Ayyub 2007, 32–33). As an advocate from Sneha said, "[We] listen unconditionally; if required, we provide information about mainstream agencies and begin a referral process. We are both of the community and harbingers of change. . . . We view our work as a collective process of empowerment" (Purkayastha, Raman, and Bhide 1997, 101). A group like Sneha is then in a better position to help women like Aisha, who came to the United States through the sponsorship of her brother and then was able to bring her husband here. Her husband began to drink more and more, then stopped supporting her while also beating her. As she became more desperate for help, Aisha called a mainstream domestic violence service organization and asked them to talk to her brother to get him to intervene. This made no sense to the traditional agency, but "the expectation that a husband would change his behavior because of the reactions of his wife's brother, even after a 35-year-long marriage, resonates among South Asians" (Purkayastha, Raman, and Bhide 1997, 103). Thus, like Manavi and Congreso, Sneha has a cultural understanding of why women prefer the kinds of interventions they do and can help them achieve some of the those interventions in the context of U.S. cultural and legal requirements and norms (Purkayastha, Raman, and Bhide 1997, 103).[49]

Not only can community-based groups put women in contact with other survivors and legal and economic advocates and provide safe spaces to figure out next steps but they also can bring together the power of a group of women in the community to call men out on their violence as a means of protest. That is, they can bring the violence to public light in order to shame the men for their behavior without necessarily calling in the police or other legal interventions. Such community responses have the benefit of not allowing the men to hide behind the cloak of family privacy and directly challenging gender constructs of female passivity and family constructs of hierarchy and suffering that are some of the subjectifying norms shown above to limit women's agency in terms of the construction of desire and perceived options. For example, solidarity could be shown if a group of women who are being abused "engage in a publicly advertised 'strike,' whereby they would temporarily or permanently leave their abusive situations together" (Bhattacharjee 1997, 34). If a group of women harasses an abusive man and continues to confront him about his behavior, the abused woman has support for her claims that the violence is wrong and must stop. Other men might hear about the gang of support too and be less willing to beat their wives (34). Bhattacharjee also reports on another successful community strategy: a woman in a domestic violence shelter wanted to move back into her own home and turn it into a shelter. So she and seven women went to her house, removed her husband's belongings, threw them into the street, and moved into the house (35, citing Judith Stevenson). But I would emphasize along with Bhattacharjee (1997) and Abraham (2000) that these kinds of strategies only become viable if they are part of the routine arsenal of (collective) resistance and not aberrations. Public shaming to show that abuse must not be tolerated needs to be followed up by community group support throughout the social and legal services processes (Bhattacharjee 1997, 35; Abraham 2000, 186–87). Perhaps one way to avoid marginalizing these forms of protest is to have them routinely facilitated through community-based anti–domestic violence groups such as Manavi and Kiran.

The interventions I offer here are not meant to be exhaustive. They are preliminary suggestions for how to engage the myriad constraints on and opportunities for developing the agency of a wide range of women. They are also illustrative in their trivalent approach, combining recognition with a demand for material redistribution and political inclusion of a wider range of perspectives. By targeting the ambiguity of phenomenologically diverse situations, these types of interventions engage the temporally and subjectively diverse modes of agency development.

CONCLUSION

In this chapter, I have tried to respect both "the agency in victim" and the "agency in staying" without conceding that all choices are optimal ones or that agency is everywhere. Rather, I have attempted, when examining the internal (individual) components of agency, to see how one can begin to wrest some control from a compromised situation, positing that the capacity for reflection, critical consciousness, and the development of a life plan consistent with normative commitments and oriented toward a greater degree of freedom can sometimes be extremely stunted. This is so in part because of the social construction of desire—the way in which the nexus of power in which individuals are located constitutes a sense of meaning, purpose, and opportunities for them. The governing conditions of one's habitus have to be examined in any attempt to see or judge the agency that women enact. The meanings of one's choices, and the possibilities one can imagine, vary by context. Thus to judge the agency of the individual, one must focus first on her context.

The interventions I endorse are political in that they are a form of recognition. They see women's identities as they see them, and they meet their needs in ways that enable them to act on the identities that they have while also challenging the hegemonic constructions of gender and the heteronuclear family that enable battering in the first place. We need to see ourselves reflected positively in culture and laws to develop our abilities to engage positively and productively with public institutions, to get the things that we need to increase our freedom. Likewise, we need to be recognized in our homes as valuable and valued members of the household unit to achieve our intimate goals. Intimate partner violence is a denial of subjectivity, a failure of recognition (see Denzin 1984, 499–500). Thus, interventions that restore or provide recognition of the battered women's subjectivity and her needs are required. She must be recognized in ways that make sense to her and value her self-expressed needs rather than externally imposed ones; imposing someone else's preferred outcomes on her is yet a further failure of recognition. This is the problem with mandatory interventions, which is why I have focused on responses to violence that set out to increase options and provide meaningful choices.[50]

As one is working on improving the violent relationship, one is constructing new skills and new conceptions of self-in-relationship. If this relationship is important to the woman—and presumably it is— then her identity is in fact shaped in part by being part of this unit. The more resources we can make available to more women to intervene in violence and insist that it or the relationship end—and make these credible threats—the more we can intervene in the imagery of heterosexual familial relations. Increasing the ways to respond effectively to violence— through social, cultural, and legal service provision—without requiring that women make use of any specific measure so that we take them seriously is a form of gender norm protest and reiteration. Rather than requiring women to conform to liberal jurisprudential terms of rational

action in order to be seen as agents, courts, police, social service providers, and interested others need to meet women on the political terms
available to them, given the subjectifying forces they have developed
within. I have pointed to some of those forces and the political possibilities for agency that have resulted, considering how women take up
these political possibilities—ways that do not always conform to our
current legal models for addressing intimate partner violence, but ways
that must inform how we construct future interventions into violent
relationships.

CHAPTER 3

Mum's the Word

Assisted Reproduction and the Ideology of Motherhood

In 1970, Shulamith Firestone argued that reproductive technology would be the key to a radical feminist future, severing the essential conflating of "woman" with "mother." Forty years later, new reproductive technologies have hit the mainstream, solidifying pronatalist ideals rather than severing them from the definition of "woman."[1] Indeed, perhaps even more than in 1970, pronatalism profoundly shapes gender identity development in women; what has not changed is that the material possibilities for maternity are marked by stark race- and class-based differences. Although all women imbibe pronatalist discourses, the opportunities and encouragements for motherhood differ depending on where one sits in relation to public polices and private investments in promoting—or discouraging—maternity. In the United States, both pro- and antinatalism are shaped primarily implicitly through health care, environmental, and welfare policies and cultural norms of family life and gender identity. Although there are some explicit natalist policies (such as the Family Medical Leave Act, FMLA) and religious dictates about motherhood, in the United States these tend to be weaker or more diffuse than in many other countries. As I will discuss below, the implicit nature of many motherhood norms and policies may help explain their persistence.

In addition to the subjectifying force of norms about good mother-hood and public policies supporting or thwarting the achievement of motherhood in shaping one's life plans, I examine the role that assisted reproduction technologies (ARTs) play in both supporting and under-mining extant norms about mothering and motherhood's place in mature female identity.[2] My question here is not whether women are victims of technology but where ARTs sit in relation to norms about motherhood. I consider ARTs because of the different ways they can enter the discursive and material space within which women become normatively competent relevant to motherhood and family norms, thus not only shoring up but also reshaping those norms.[3] Rather than see-ing ARTs solely as exploitative of women's bodies, or primarily as fan-tastic tools opening up more choices for women, I read ARTs as less agency enhancing for some women and more agency enhancing for others. ARTs can inhibit autonomy in that they serve to buttress patri-archal norms about the relationship between womanhood and mother-hood, thus reinforcing the social construction of desire for biological motherhood. Yet they can also enhance freedom, opening up the mate-rial conditions within which embodied ideals are lived out. That is, they can circumvent some of the very policies that have the effect of limiting the motherhood options of women who symbolically reside outside of the "cult of motherhood" discourse that is alive and well in the United States. The problem, as I explain below, is that the women for whom ARTs offer the greatest potential for increasing freedom are the ones least likely to have access to them. I end this chapter by considering what it would mean to use these technologies to foster women's agency in the context of pronatalism.

Pronatalism and Mothering Norms

Pronatalism is one of the subjectifying discourses that shapes the situa-tion of all women in the United States. Although women grow up in a situation marked by pronatalism, the particular forms that pronatalist messages take and ideas about why and how women should mother differ considerably along race, class, and sexuality lines. That is, women absorb pronatalist ideas in different ways because these imperatives take on different forms depending on one's particular situation, but motherhood as central to feminine identity is a hegemonic norm that must be confronted to some degree by all women. As I will discuss below, for less privileged women, pronatalism exists in a situation also marked by stark antinatalist public policies, but the pronatalist cultural imperatives are still ripe within that situation.

Drawing on Alena Heitlinger's (1991) and Kristin Park's (2002) work, I want to explore how pronatalism can operate on at least four different levels, through means both obvious and implicit, material and rhetorical: *culturally,* pronatalism naturalizes motherhood as central to a woman's identity, with childlessness perceived as abnormal or suspect; *ideologically,* motherhood is constructed as women's duty to the nation for patriotic or eugenic reasons; *psychologically,* childbearing is linked with both rational and irrational personal aspirations and beliefs about maturity; and *politically,* population policy regulates fertility through access to abortion, sterilization, contraception, sexual education, and immigration.[4] Thus, even if only some of these pronatalist forms target specific groups, women cannot escape each of these forms of pronatalism. I first look at pronatalism as constructive of women's sense of self and desire generally before moving to consider specific forms of pronatalist messages.

The idea that motherhood is central to the development of women's adult identity has its roots in and is reinforced, naturalized, and fossilized (to use philosopher Diana T. Meyers's term) by religious teachings, myth and folklore, Freud's theories about femininity and "normal" women's desire to bear children, the social ideology of "true womanhood" and the "cult of domesticity," and the many and ever-updated cultural images thrown at consumers "depicting motherhood as the only creditable form of fulfillment for women. . . . This vast system of representations collapses womanhood into motherhood and idolizes the mother" (Meyers 2002, 48). Meyers calls this pronatalist discourse *matrigyno-idolatry,* an idea I borrow here to think about women's subjectification. In the imbricated definitions of woman and mother, "negative stereotypes of childfree women match and buttress idealized matrigynist figurations" (2002, 49; see also Ireland 1993, 6–8, 13). In this way, women are immersed in pronatalism, and to a significant extent, they absorb this imperative subliminally (Meyers 2002, 24–26).

Because of the pervasiveness of the matrigyno-idolatry and the web of constraints on women's agency generated by the cultural, economic, and political discourses in which women are steeped, women's autonomy and agency are diminished. "Whether because imperious desires about motherhood exert a seemingly despotic power over women's lives, because women's feelings about motherhood are so repressed or so conflicted that they cannot figure out what they want, or because social expectations, personal privations, or cultural myths stifle women's self-reflection, self-determination is elusive" (Meyers 2002, 39–40). Women internalize norms of gender identity, such as "good women are mothers." Although this internalization does not mean that every woman will adopt the norm uncritically and in exactly the same way, it does mean that the norm must be confronted, because women's other choices are measured against it. Motherhood is an unavoidable aspect of women's subjectifying situation, where embodied potential becomes normative imperative.

Motherhood is what Helena Michie and Naomi Cahn define as the "reproductive master narrative: that a girl naturally grows up wanting to marry and to become a mother and that the most accepted form of female development involves marriage and (subsequent) motherhood" (1997, 167). They call this a "master narrative" because of its cultural centrality and effect on "more local" narratives. In the way that this reproductive master narrative takes hold in the culture, both Foucauldian domination and governmentality work through individuals and social groups. The effects of ossified and consolidated power relations (domination) are evident in the degree to which femininity is made synecdochal for motherhood even before our capacities for resistance develop. But Foucault also points us to the possibility for govern-mentality, by which he means ways in which individuals exercise self-development in negotiation with conflicting norms and power relations (1994 [1984], 283, 300). Because pronatalist ideology—and, specifically, pronatalist politics—has a specifically embodied and materially situated woman in mind (as I will develop below), the rupture between the preva-lence of pronatalism and its narrow ideal help to create the potential for resistance, for governmentality. What will become clear in my discus-sion of ARTs is that they serve both ends: domination and resistance.

Although matrigyno-idolatry makes motherhood the dominant and dominating force in many women's lives, there are, of course, "counter-narratives" that challenge both motherhood as women's ideal adult form and the particularly white, middle-class, heterosexual, nuclear family, consumptive model of motherhood that dominates motherhood narra-tives. That is, "culture can and does produce a variety of stories, some of them in direct opposition to [dominant] cultural narratives" (Michie and Cahn 1997, 167). These counternarratives do not escape the influ-ence of the master narratives, but they exceed and challenge them.[5] To clear a productive space for truly agentic decision making about parent-hood, effective counternarratives would need to be raised to the same level of prominence as the master narrative. This would mean produc-ing supporting political, economic, and legal structures to make dif-ferent kinds of affective relationships and different models of family equally legitimate and easy to fit into public life and modes of discourse. Indeed, women who have chosen to be childless often talk about the im-portance of role models as sources of inspiration and validation. These role models can include, for example, drama coaches, older cousins, childless aunts, and nuns.[6] Role models work well individually; to rise to the level of counternarrative, these complex, happy, and nonstigma-tized women need to be incorporated into more modes of discourse and made available to far more women.

Because of its pervasiveness and hegemonic status, the socially con-structed desire for motherhood thus directs, even impedes, women's agency to the degree that motherhood becomes the female gender norm despite other, often contradictory, desires with which it coexists (see Meyers 2002, 35).[7] Those who absorb and shape their life plans around such disciplinary forms uncritically—or subconsciously—are in that regard less autonomous because the imaginary possibilities of their lives have been choked off and normative competence stunted. Once this happens, material possibilities are constructed around a life plan that makes future resistance less viable or imaginable. For example, Michie and Cahn's research on pregnancy and infertility guides revealed that "many younger women, who have not even tried to become pregnant, are concerned that they will be unable to do so once they begin trying. The myth of an infertility epidemic has taken over their lives, influencing their lifestyle choices as they seek control over their fertility" (1997, 152, citations omitted). Additionally, Elizabeth Hervey Stephen and Anjani Chandra discuss the new problem of "impatience to conceive" that captures the increasing "subjective perception of being unable to conceive [that] has grown over time. Couples are inclined to pursue treatment sooner than had been observed in the past, more medical oversight is available, and couples are more focused on carefully timed intercourse during a woman's fertile period than in the past" (2006, 522). The question still outstanding is whether the counterfactual infertility epidemic would be so powerful if motherhood were not seen as fundamental to being a woman. Thus, the sheer ubiquity of pronatalism renders subjectively unavailable many options that might be practically feasible and psychically desirable (see Bartky 1990, 63–82; Meyers 2002, 52). Pronatalist discourse, as Meyers argues, "harnesses highly directive enculturation to unconscious processes and protects the resulting psychic structures from change by codifying and consecrating them in standard-issue self-portraits and self-narratives" (2002, 47).

While most women personally value the role of mother, the social imperatives to be a mother also affect the *degree* to which women individually prioritize this identity. Part of the problem with the saturation of the culture with pronatalist imperatives is that "desires about motherhood are generally formed well before women are equipped to make autonomous decisions, and, implacable as these desires are, they are subsequently insulated from open-minded reflection and modification" (Meyers 2002, 37). Thus, self-conscious reflection on choices and reasons for desires is harder to induce in the area of reproduction, making motherhood seem natural and therefore the choice to forego motherhood unnatural, a rejection of feminine identity. One mark of agency is the ability to articulate reasons for the choices one has made, with some sense of the available options. Or, where appropriate, an agent exhibits an awareness that, in a particular case, other options were not available, and the agent has some sense of why they are not available. That is, agency grows as one's self-conscious reflection on one's life circumstances and the ways that one's place in the world shape those circumstances grow. Because agency requires weakly substantive autonomy, agency would be reflected not in the acceptance or rejection of motherhood per se but in the denaturalized critical reflection on the role that motherhood plays in one's individual life plans. Additionally, as one's capacity for agency increases, these introspective and evaluative agency skills will be combined with communicative skills. Yet women get highly defensive about their own choices concerning motherhood and are derisive of others who have chosen differently. "If women were autonomously becoming mothers or declining to, we would expect to hear a splendid chorus of distinctive, confident voices, but instead we are hearing a shrill cacophony of trite tunes" (Meyers 2002, 40). But neither having nor not having children is, a priori, the most agentic choice for any woman.

Aside from its cultural and psychological influence, pronatalism is often measured politically, so that countries defined as pronatalist, such as Sweden and France, are those that have state-sponsored programs such as subsidized child care, direct payments for children, extensive paid parental leave policies, or other family-friendly programs that encourage women to produce more citizens. The United States has few of these policies. Yet cultural, ideological, and psychological pronatalism are rife in the United States, which may help to explain why it is one of only two industrialized Western nations with fertility rates above the replacement level.[8]

Ideological pronatalism has a long history in the United States, with the intensity of appeals rising and falling in response to both women's political activism and external threats to the nation. In the former case, as women have more successfully, or at least vocally, challenged traditional sex roles and expectations, pronatalism has served as a backlash or counterbalance to the cultural shift. In the latter, because pronatalism is a central element in nationalist discourses, the most palpable invocations of pronatalism in the United States have been evident during the Red Scare of the 1950s and after the September 11, 2001, terrorist attacks (May 1995, 129–31; Park 2002, 22–23; Scott 2007, 71; Story 2005). These ideological appeals are implicitly raced, exhorting white, middle-class women specifically to fulfill their duty to the nation while challenging their efforts to expand norms about women's "proper" roles in political and social life.

For example, as reported by Elaine Tyler May, in the 1950s a range of government, social, and academic forces (including J. Edgar Hoover, *Newsweek,* and the *American Journal of Sociology*) raised the specter of race suicide—a theme itself resurrected from the early twentieth century—if women worked outside the home rather than having children and staying at home with them. They all argued in various ways that because employment outside the home was correlated with having fewer children, as more women worked, the birthrate would go down. This did not happen. Additionally, they argued that women's educational achievement was detrimental to their reproduction—a lie contradicting the data readily available at that time. As May reminds her readers, "Even as late as the peak of the baby boom in the mid-1950s, *U.S. News and World Report* echoed the same concern: 'America's college women . . . are failing to keep up with the baby boom. It is the relatively uneducated women who keep the U.S. population on the rise.' The report was inaccurate; the sharpest rise in the birthrate was among the most highly educated women. Nevertheless, distorted claims like these kept eugenic fears of race suicide alive and brought public shame upon women who were childless" (1995, 134). This was the same period during which the marketing of early infertility treatments was beginning to take off, with magazines and journals regularly touting "miracle babies" in their pages (May 1995, 87–88, 147–48).

Pronatalism waned during the 1970s, but after the successes of second-wave feminism, pronatalist appeals increased again in the 1980s and have been on a steady upward trajectory ever since (Douglas and Michaels 2004). One notorious contribution to this renewed pronatal-ism was the disputed study published in the *New England Journal of Medicine* in 1982, which claimed that a woman's chances of conceiving a baby dropped suddenly and precipitously after age thirty. Although the study's authors later retreated from their findings, and the U.S. National Center for Health Statistics reported in 1985 that the infertil-ity rate for women aged thirty to thirty-four was 13.6 percent, not the 40 percent cited in the *New England Journal of Medicine* study, the orig-inal findings fueled a media frenzy about an "infertility epidemic" that gave a boost to both the market in ART and the discourse of pronatal-ism (see Faludi 1991, 27–29). Unsurprisingly, this period was also marked by an outpouring of baby-themed books and movies; a pronatalist mes-sage was perfectly encapsulated by feminist icon television character Murphy Brown crooning "You Make Me Feel Like a Natural Woman" to her newborn in a 1992 episode.

In *The Mommy Myth,* Susan J. Douglas and Meredith W. Michaels chart the increase in cultural pronatalism and "intensive mothering" imperatives across mass media forms targeted primarily at women from 1970 through the early twenty-first century. They label this increasing pressure not only to become a "mom" but to be the best mom you can be the "new momism." The new momism is marked by "the insistence that no woman is truly complete or fulfilled unless she has kids, that women remain the best primary caretakers of children, and that to be a remotely decent mother, a woman has to devote her entire physical, psychological, emotional, and intellectual being, 24/7, to her children. The new momism is a highly romanticized and yet demanding view of motherhood in which the standards for success are impossible to meet" (2004, 4). The increase in pronatalism in general and the new momism in particular can be traced through, for example, the fact that "over eight hundred books on motherhood were published between 1970 and 2000; only twenty-seven of these came out between 1970 and 1980" (8–9), the near absence of news about motherhood, working moms, or child care in the 1970s, and the explosion of nightly news and news-magazine stories in the 1980s and beyond, the rise of celebrity journalism, which became a recognizable phenomenon in the 1980s and exploded in the 1990s, and which in turn led to the rise of the celebrity mom profile that has become a ubiquitous staple of women's magazines, and the change in advertising tactics in women's magazines, which in the 1970s "focused on the mother and her alleged needs—whether for hand cream, hair dye, toilet cleaners, or tampons. . . . Rarely were mothers and children pictured together as some beatific unit. . . . But by 1990, images of children were everywhere, and there was a direct address from the ad to you, the mom, exhorting you to foresee your child's each and every need and desire" (Douglas and Michaels 2004, 17).

There are an ever increasing number of media outlets to help reinforce not just the woman–mother connection, but the ever more stringent imperatives about how to mother. In the 1990s, there was an explosion in the mainstream women's magazines of monthly advice columns dealing with motherhood, and in addition, the genre of child-rearing magazines took off. From the choice between *Parents* and *Parenting* magazines, the options have broadened into at least twenty different niche parenting magazine alternatives (Douglas and Michaels 2004, 229–30). This does not include the countless Web sites devoted to parenting or overcoming infertility. Broadcast and print media, both entertainment and news oriented, present together an ever-increasing convergence of the identity of woman to mother and mother to child, so that fulfillment of one's female gender identity becomes complete once the mother completely identifies with the child and his or her needs. This is especially true according to these sources for white, middle-class women.

Both psychological theory and many religions support pronatalism by equating motherhood and female identity, and they mark maternity as a developmental stage that is essential for emotional maturity, even though women, like men, can develop healthy personalities without being parents (Safer 1996, 122; Ulrich and Weatherall 2000, 324). The medical establishment promotes a pronatalism that bridges the psychological and the cultural. As Jeanne Safer so succinctly put it, while "the technical term for a woman without a child is still 'barren,' . . . there is no equivalently pejorative term for a childless man, and nobody, himself included, questions his masculinity" (1996, 17–18). That childlessness is primarily a problem of women's failure is also evident in the way statistics on childlessness are collected: childlessness is measured in terms of women; data are not kept to count childless men, and rates of childlessness are not measured through men (May 1995, 11).[9] Constructions of infertility and childlessness are part of the discourse of pronatalism and motherhood ideology. How we understand the "problem" of infertility stems from this ideological and cultural construction, and how we cope with infertility also depends on the forms that pronatalism and ideal motherhood norms take. Involuntary childlessness is often thought of as failure. Consider the medical jargon surrounding infertility: "barren," "sterile," "hostile mucus," "blocked Fallopian tubes," "incompetent cervix," and "failure to conceive." Furthermore, childlessness and infertility are often conflated in the popular imagination and in literature on childlessness. This may be because although involuntary childless is perceived as failure, "not wanting children has been viewed as unnatural and pathological" (Ulrich and Weatherall 2000, 324).[10] Safer reported on a number of surveys of attitudes toward childless people. In one, social psychologist Sharon Houseknecht looked at attitudes from 1916 to the mid-1990s. Throughout the twentieth century, the childless have "been perceived as misfits who are 'infantile, self-indulgent, and materialistic.'" In another study, psychologists Pollyann Jamison, Louis Franzini, and Robert Kaplan asked a large sample of subjects to rate the mental health of two couples who were described identically in every way except that one couple had chosen to have children. The "nonmother" and her spouse were perceived as less satisfied at present than the "parents" and were predicted to be less happy at the age of sixty-five. The childless couple were described as lonelier and more emotionally maladjusted, as well as less sensitive and less loving, than their counterparts with families. (1996, 121–22)

Sociologist Kristin Park also found that women who opt not to have children are stereotyped as materialistic, selfish, and cold (2002, 24). Such norms help to perpetuate cultural pronatalism and make not-motherhood a more difficult, fraught, and "unnatural" choice. Many women who opt for childlessness mention how frequently they are called on to explain (or even change) themselves and their choice, a choice almost always constructed by the questioner as a rejection of the natural (Park 2002, 26; Morell 1994, 141).[11]

The master narrative of motherhood as identity extends to motherhood as an institution with clear expectations for women's behavior and priorities. Good mothers are always available to their children; always supportive, caring, nurturing, ready with love and guidance; in addition, good mothers keep their homes neat and clean. A good mother is unselfish and always puts her children's needs ahead of her own. A mother should have responsibility for her children at all times. And finally, a good mother operates in the context of the heterosexual, patriarchal, nuclear family that is based on the assumption of a privatized female dependence and domesticity (see Kline 1995, 119–20; Douglas and Michaels 2004).[12] This is not to say that this is the reality of motherhood, but that this is the ideal to which women are held, and they are often found wanting. Douglas and Michaels extensively document these prescriptions in a variety of media outlets. As they make clear, "all these media suggest, by their endless celebrating of certain kinds of mothers and maternal behavior and their ceaseless advice, that there are agreed upon norms 'out there.' So even if you think they're preposterous, you assume you'll be judged harshly by not abiding by them. In this way media portrayals can substitute for and override community norms" (2004, 18–19). Further, the more these ideal motherhood norms are approximated by infertile women, the more legitimate their maternal aspirations are assumed to be, and the more likely they are to be granted access to fertility clinics.[13]

As Douglas and Michaels (2004) point out, although these prescriptions for intensive and perfected mothering are impossible to meet, they are also becoming more specific and inescapable across mass media forms that shape so much of the cultural and ideological understanding of womanhood and parenthood. In shaping what motherhood as an institution entails, there have been a few central cultural touchstones that have been particularly explicit and widespread that help shore up classed and raced expectations about who should mother and how she should do so. The juxtaposition of the laudatory celebrity mom profile with the demonization of the welfare mother has been particularly effective in promulgating these norms.[14] On the one hand, with the beginning of the standard trope of the perfect celebrity mom profile in the 1980s, celebrity moms came to serve as role models for average women.[15] These profiles "are carefully packaged fantasies, but they ask readers to approach them as if they were real" (Douglas and Michaels 2004, 123). And while early instantiations of this genre allowed celebrities to remark on some ambivalence about motherhood and the sacrifices it requires, by the early 2000s, the trajectory of these articles had "moved toward suggesting that once the celebrity mom discovers motherhood, she sees the pursuit of a career as a much lower priority" (134). Stories no longer featured any ambivalence. "Celebrity moms loved their kids unconditionally all the time; they loved being mothers all the time; they yearned for babies if they didn't have them and yearned for more if they did" (116). These profiles, along with the explosion of news stories about the potential dangers in the world around kids—in their food, their toys, their environments—meant that mothers had to be eternally vigilant,

devoting themselves tirelessly to providing the safest, cleanest, most en-
riching environment they possibly could if they hoped to rear children
who could grow up to be anything resembling successful adults. All of
this devotion takes a great deal of time and money.

To help make these prescriptions more than just laughable forms of
excess, the media helpfully provided a simultaneous warning about what
happens if women break the rules about mothering, and good mothering in particular. Douglas and Michaels document the simultaneity of
the white, heterosexual "mom" deification and the warnings provided on
the nightly news by welfare mothers (always illustrated by pictures of
black women, even when the content of the story was about the fact that
more white than black women are on welfare) (2004, 180), as well as
sensational stories about failed motherhood: crack babies, the lawsuit
surrounding the custody of surrogate-born Baby M, and Susan Smith,
the South Carolina woman who drowned her children (140–202). They
note that "one of the most important trends that [they] found during this period was that the attacks on the maternal qualifications of
welfare mothers increased, over the years, in direct relationship to the
increased emphasis on the new momism" (199). The more the celebrity mom profiles (almost always of straight white women) humanized
them, the more the profiles of welfare mothers dehumanized them.
With the celebrity mom, interviews focused on her individual, subjective thoughts and feelings. Stories about welfare mothers used individual women as an "exemplar of a trend . . . and suggested that her inner
life was devoid of thoughts, except where to score her next hit of crack
or how to dupe her landlord out of a month's rent" (182–83). Although
in the 1970s news stories on welfare focused on problems with the
system, by the 1990s, the problem became women on welfare. Only
women who were wealthy enough to have professional jobs that they
could afford to leave, at least temporarily, once they had children were
cast as deserving mothers.

In the United States, the cultural and ideological rhetoric of pronatalism is often directly at odds with state policies for family support.

The pronatalism targeting middle-class white women emanates primarily from the private and social sectors, which is where ARTs are located. With few state-sponsored pronatalist policies, the United States both encourages and privatizes motherhood, making the combination of work and family more difficult and producing one kind of infertility in the group of highly educated professional women known as "postponers."[16] Postponers attempt to establish education and career credentials before embarking on parenthood, and they often find that by the time they have reached a point in their careers where they can try to devote time to parenting, they have aged out of their prime fertility years. Such socially caused infertility is not a medical condition per se. It is created by an economic model that posits the ideal worker as a male breadwinner who has a wife at home and so can commit tireless hours to the needs of the office (see Slaughter 1995, 78–82). It is also created by the lack of any systematic private or public policy to align early career demands with women's (and men's) most fertile years. Again, the Family Medical Leave Act (FMLA) is the only broad pronatalist policy that might seem to support parenthood before age-related infertility becomes an issue, but the fact that FMLA leave is unpaid, short term, and limited in scope (to companies with more than fifty employees and to employees who have worked a minimum of 1,250 hours in the previous twelve months, for example) means again that its target is primarily middle-class professional women. "The cause of these women's infertility is not biological; rather, it is a workplace that makes it virtually impossible for women to combine employment and child-rearing. These women can avoid this social problem by seeking expensive fertility treatment after achieving some status in the office. In other words, they can afford to bypass the structural unfairness to mothers through technological intervention" (Roberts 1997, 292). By privatizing the solutions to the problem of balancing work and family demands, the state implicitly endorses a market-based approach to reproduction, in effect saying that only those who can afford to hire help with children, pay for infertility treatments necessary if one waits to have children until past her most fertile years,

or who have a two-parent family and can afford to have a sole breadwinner should be aided in having children.

Even such state-mandated support for infertility treatments as exists
targets middle-class women while ignoring the needs of the infertile
poor. Some states now require private insurance to cover infertility
treatments—without attendant mandates to cover contraception methods—while public welfare (Medicaid and Title X) covers contraceptive technologies but not infertility treatments. Not surprisingly, in the
fifteen states that have mandates compelling health insurance companies either to provide or to offer some form of infertility treatment
benefit, there is "no evidence of expanded access" for "women with
varying levels of education" or for women who are "not white" (Bitler
and Schmidt 2006, 864). This is because these mandates improve access
only for women who have private health insurance coverage, and those
women tend to be older, white, and highly educated. The combination
of matrigyno-idolatry, workplace structures assuming a male breadwinner with a wife at home, rigid directives for "good mothering" behavior,
and the medicalized model of infertility socially construct women's freedom—and hence their agency—at the level of both materialization and
the discursive construction of social meaning of motherhood.

To some degree, norms about family life are slowly changing. Sociologists Arland Thornton and Linda Young-DeMarco summarized several
longitudinal studies and found that both childlessness and single parenthood are becoming less stigmatized while, *simultaneously,* marriage
and parenthood are becoming more important (Thornton and Young-
DeMarco 2001, 1028–30). As the authors report,

> [T]here is very little evidence that the commitment of Americans to chil-
> dren, marriage, and family life has eroded substantially in the past two
> decades. In fact, there is some evidence that these familial dimensions of
> life may have increased in perceived importance in recent decades. As
> compared to the 1970s, young Americans in the 1990s were more commit-
> ted to the importance of a good marriage and family life. . . . Furthermore,

both motherhood and fatherhood are generally viewed as more fulfilling today than they were in the mid-1970s. (1030)

It seems that the imperative of parenthood is still strongly felt, even if the ideas about who makes appropriate parents are slowly becoming more open. We are in a period of discursive shift with liberalizing attitudes toward who can parent combining with technology that underwrites the compulsion to parent and increasingly unrealistic strictures on the intensity of surveillance that parenting requires. If the opening up of norms about "good parents" can help change laws and material supports for different kinds of families, then ART can fill a niche in enabling more women to become mothers on their own terms and be agency-enhancing to that degree. But if the ideal mother norm is opening up, then true material support for this expanded norm would include the kinds of laws and economic policies that would help prevent infertility for all groups of women, rather than just treating childlessness in some groups of women.

The pronatalist ideal mother norm figured through cultural, ideological, and psychological discourses is not just a gendered norm; it is also a raced and classed gender construction meant to separate "good" women from "other" women and to police resistance by creating a hierarchical ordering within the gender category "woman." Although pronatalism has been politically implicit—primarily through state inaction to combat the mother–woman construct in general—antinatalism has been more politically explicit in order to sever the reality—if not the psychology—of the mother–woman connection for specific groups of women.

Historically, both welfare and sterilization policies have been hugely detrimental to poor women's reproductive autonomy (see discussions in Roberts 1997, 56–149, 202–45; Solinger 2001, 139–82). In the early to mid-twentieth century, involuntary sterilization was directed against the poor and "feeble-minded" (a designation often ascribed to "willful" and/ or sexually active young women). As sterilizations moved from the West (primarily California) to the South and Southeast through the mid- to

late twentieth century, poor women of color became the target popula-
tion. Black and Latina women suffered from coerced sterilizations, but
Native Americans confronted near-genocidal rates of fertility control (see
Smith 2005, 80–88; May 1995, 96–124; Silliman et al. 2004, 53, 111–12).
In a few cases, all pure-blooded women of certain tribes were sterilized,
making their generation the end of the line for the tribe and laying
starkly bare the eugenic and nationalist goals of reproductive policies
(Smith 2005, 82; May 1995, 119). In the 1970s, both the American College of Obstetricians and Gynecologists and the U.S. Congress changed
their policies on voluntary and involuntary sterilization. But "even after
the federal guidelines were strengthened in 1978, 70 percent of the
hospitals did not comply with them. In 1981, the *Boston Globe* reported
that states were still sterilizing poor Medicaid recipients, many of them
minors, without properly obtaining their consent" (May 1995, 123).

Sterilization abuse is no longer rampant, but other forms of coercive
contraception persist. In the 1990s, welfare policies included provisions
that capped or ceased payments if women had more children while receiving aid or paid for (or insisted on) Norplant or Depo-Provera (long-
acting contraceptives with a number of serious health risks) but not for
abortions, which would enable a woman to end a pregnancy without
jeopardizing or foreclosing her future fertility.[17] In some states, Medicaid
covered the costs of implantation, but not removal, of Norplant, leaving
poor women stuck with the health and financial costs of the drug (Smith
2005, 94). Norplant and Depo-Provera also took the place of sterilizations
in the Indian Health Service; and again, Native women were pressured to
use these methods of birth control without being told of their side effects,
or in some cases being told there were none (Smith 2005, 95; Silliman et
al. 2004, 112–13). Thus we see the return from the 1950s of a juxtaposition
of fears that white women are not producing enough babies (cultural
pronatalist appeals) with fears that women of color may be producing too
many (coercive contraception; lack of access to infertility treatments).

The point of highlighting certain gross abuses of poor women's health
and reproductive autonomy is to draw attention to the historical and

ongoing attempts to limit the fertility of poor women of color along-side the simultaneous promotion of the fertility of middle-class white women. This is the background from which norms and images about motherhood and ideal mothering arise. Women of childbearing age have grown up steeped in this discursive and material nexus of under-standing of motherhood. Except in cases of sterilization or coerced abortions, these policies and cultural norms neither mandate nor pre-vent any particular woman from bearing or not bearing children, but they shape both the desires and the means (psychic and material) she has to pursue these desires. This is also the nexus within which ART emerged in the United States. ARTs arose to treat infertility, which is a problem if motherhood is desired or deemed essential (either by the potential mother or the norms about motherhood). But as a matter of ideology and public policy, infertility is apparently not a problem if it is a condition for someone whose motherhood is to be thwarted. Pro- and antinatalist ideas inform who gets targeted for ART use and how. ARTs are not available to all infertile women. Importantly, as I develop below, ARTs do not treat infertility per se; they treat childlessness, or the childlessness of some. Thus, although ART could become a form of resistance against ideal motherhood norms—but not a resistance against pronatalism itself—because of the way they are distributed, these tech-nologies more often than not serve an iterative or recuperative func-tion rather than a resistant one. That is, although they may potentially enhance choice, ARTs can be ideologically and culturally pernicious because of the way they can be—and have been—narrowly made avail-able. Below, I look briefly at what causes infertility and who experiences it, as compared to who is able to make use of ARTs. I then discus how all of this is a question of women's agency.

INFERTILITY AND THE USE OF ASSISTED REPRODUCTION TECHNOLOGIES

There are women in all demographic groups who are infertile, but the highest rates of infertility occur among lower-income women of color and poor white women, not among the groups targeted by the media infertility hysteria, doctor's advice to have babies as soon as possible, or the ART industry. From 1982 to 2002—the period over which advanced ARTs have developed and their use become normalized—there was a statistically significant drop in rates of infertility.[18] Although infertility rates have dropped, childlessness rates have remained stable. This combination means a couple of things. First, voluntary childlessness is on the rise for certain groups of women, and involuntary childlessness (infertility) has increased among some women and decreased among others. Remember, rates of childlessness alone are not the same as rates of infertility. Joyce Abma and Gladys Martinez of the National Center for Health Statistics have found that "Black, Hispanic, and White women do not differ notably with regard to overall childlessness (19%, 13%, and 19%, respectively, among those aged 40–44 in 2002)" (2006, 1047). The difference is in rates of voluntary childlessness versus childlessness due to infertility. Those who are most likely to be *voluntarily* childless are white women who have higher educations and work full time in high-prestige and relatively highly remunerative jobs who also are less religious and hold less traditional views of the family (Abma and Martinez 2006, 1046, 1050, 1052). Meanwhile, *infertility* is more common among nonwhite women (especially those with less than college education) and among older women (Bitler and Schmidt 2006, 861). Although black and Hispanic women have higher rates of infertility, Anglo women have greater access to infertility treatments (861). Not only are the high-tech ARTs primarily available to the group of women with relatively lower infertility but also, as Gay Becker and colleagues from the National Institutes of Health and Aging have found, "as new reproductive technologies have come to dictate practice trends and dominate reproductive medicine, attention to low-technology infertility treatment has all but disappeared, and low-income women and men face increasing difficulty in obtaining even the most basic evaluative services. For poor women and women in racial or ethnic minorities, access to these services is limited or nonexistent" (2006, 882).

Although actual levels of infertility have not increased, "since the birth of the first U.S. infant conceived with ART in 1981, use of these treatments has increased dramatically. Each year, both the number of medical centers providing ART services and the total number of procedures performed have increased notably" (Wright et al. 2007). This rise in use of infertility treatments, despite little improvement in success rates,[19] is occurring at the same that that, according to Kristin Park, voluntary childlessness is rising for ever-married women and decreasing for never-married women. Yet although the numbers of those who are childless by choice increased somewhat during the 1990s and 2000s, it is still a rare decision, and one that, in the aggregate, is no more common now than in 1988 (6.2 percent in both 1988 and 2002).[20] Thus, the increase in pronatalist appeals after September 11, 2001, cannot be attributed either to rising infertility rates or to rising rates of childlessness by choice (as neither rate is actually rising in the aggregate), but to the specific increase in married, educated white women opting not to have children—the one subgroup of women for whom voluntary childlessness is increasing. That is, for those women who are the targets of cultural and ideological pronatalist messages, ARTs provide the means to keep trying to achieve the goal whenever the repeated barrage of pronatalist appeals are effective. Here is where ARTs assist traditional pronatalist forces without putting pressure on market and political practices that continue to make it difficult for women to combine career and family building during their most fertile years. Because infertility treatments are targeted at those who are relatively the least infertile and not those who could, as a group, most benefit, there is, I am arguing, an ideological and not merely medical mechanism at work. This ideological mechanism works both at the level of autonomy (the social construction of desire) and freedom (the choices structuring one's situation).

While pronatalist appeals and marketing of new reproductive technologies to white, middle-class women were on the rise at the end of the twentieth century and the beginning of the twenty-first century, as infertility among this group was decreasing, the government and medical researchers assiduously avoided dealing with the causes of the rise in other groups' infertility rates. For example, legal scholar Dorothy Roberts reports that "the infertility rate of young Black women tripled between 1965 and 1982. The reasons for the high incidence of infertility among black women include untreated chlamydia and gonorrhea, STDs that can lead to pelvic inflammatory disease; nutritional deficiencies; complications of childbirth and abortion; and environmental and workplace hazards" (1997, 252). According to Chandra et al. (2005) and Wellons et al. (2008), rates of infertility for African American women still remain markedly higher than rates for Anglo women.[21] Similarly, Native American women have higher rates of infertility partly as a result of a rate of chlamydia six times higher than among white women, and Latinas' infertility risks are higher at least in part as a result of their overrepresentation in labor market categories with the highest levels of exposure to teratogenic chemicals: clerical, service, and agriculture jobs, and work as laborers (Silliman et al. 2004, 115, 218).

Workplace and environmental hazards are linked to infertility, but studies on these chemicals have been slow in coming, and despite indications that many chemicals used in a range of nonprofessional jobs can contribute to infertility, only four of these chemicals are regulated by the U.S. government ("Environment and Infertility" 1996, 136; Hruska et al. 2000, 824–27). The environments in which poor women live are more likely to be toxic because their homes are generally closer to polluting industries and waste sites, increasing their exposure to known— but largely un- or underregulated—contaminants, and their rates of infertility reflect these desecrated environments. For example, the Mohawk community in upstate New York has been battling the contamination of their food, air, and water by companies like General Motors and Alcoa and their release of polychlorinated biphenyls (PCBs) (which have adverse effects on male and female reproduction) into the water and contaminated smoke into the air. General Motors left a Superfund site that has been the source of illness for the Mohawk Nation and resulted in years of legal, political, and grassroots struggle in an effort to get the environment cleaned up (Sengupta 2001; Silliman et al. 2004, 123–25).[22] Similarly, the Nez Perce Native community in Washington State has experienced the brunt of radiation poisoning from the waste from the Hanford nuclear reactor dumped in the Columbia River. Higher rates of endometriosis, miscarriages, and male sterility are just some of the results (Smith 2005, 65–66).

These facts and figures lead me to two claims that should be relatively uncontroversial at this point. First, childlessness is the result of both infertility and voluntary abstention from motherhood. Although the two are often conflated, they are quite separate phenomena. Second, rates of infertility are higher among poor women[23] and women of color, while voluntary childlessness is higher among highly educated and more affluent white women.[24] If the goal of the medical community, the government, and social service providers was to combat infertility, either ART would be marketed and distributed across all income and racial groups but would target poor women, or resources aimed at combating infertility would be funneled into environmental clean-up, studies on hazardous chemicals with the goal of eliminating from the workplace those that cause infertility and birth defects, preventing the spread of sexually transmitted diseases, and finding better treatments—or even a cure—for endometriosis and fibroids. The latter would positively affect both the women who experience higher rates of infertility and the health of all women, regardless of their childbearing (and child desiring) status. The former would seek to overcome childlessness among the group who are involuntarily childless. Neither of these is the approach we currently have. Instead, pro- and antinatalist policies and discourses work together to create an environment where ART marketing and use can thrive not to solve the majority of existing infertility problems but to solve the "problem" of ideal mothers not having enough children—of exercising too much self-governing resistance agency in the face of matrigyno-idolatry or risking childlessness due to a "late start." The mere existence of ARTs does not oblige their use, but they do serve an important ideological and material function in the context of matrigyno-idolatry.

Further, because the medical model of infertility reigns—that is, because infertility is subsumed first and foremost into the model of a medical problem as opposed to either a problem caused by social factors, or not a problem but one possible outcome of one's reproductive life—infertility stays individualized. This individualization of infertility allows the woman-as-mother trope to continue to reign in the social discourse of the identity "woman." This medicalized individuation also helps to perpetuate the focus of infertility discussion on those less effected by infertility—that is, those women of economic, educational, class, and racial privilege who are the unstated norm or focal point of discussion of the infertile patient. The groups of women who experience higher levels of infertility are ignored in this model because much of their infertility is caused by social and environmental factors that are not easily assimilated into the privatized and medicalized model of treatment through ART (see Ulrich and Weatherall 2000, 331).

In the context of pronatalism, infertility becomes a serious problem, a sort of identity crisis or failure of embodied agency for which ART is a potential solution. This tie between motherhood and womanhood works ideologically even if one's status leaves one targeted by antinatalist political policies. That is, one's gender identity develops in relationship to the mothering norm, even if one's opportunities to fulfill that norm are discouraged by public policy or thwarted by infertility. Thus we would expect the existence of ART to effect how all women think about and try to cope with infertility, yet a resource-intensive, individualized solution such as ART is only available to certain women, and not the most infertile women. As Roberts points out, "One of the most striking features of the new reproduction is that it is used almost exclusively by white people" (1997, 250–51). More Anglo Americans than black Americans, for example, use ART for a mix of reasons related to financial disparities, cultural differences regarding ideas about genetic heritage and the transmission of cultural values, and the professional manipulation of the availability of service and types of marketing that are engaged. Even African American couples who can afford advanced treatments are not seeking them in great numbers. One reason may be that they have bought into the cultural stereotype of black women as overly fertile, making infertility especially embarrassing.[25] In addition, use of these treatments "reflects a confidence in medical science to solve life's predicaments" (Roberts 1997, 159). Given the history of coercive and abusive medical experimentation on people of color in the United States, "many Blacks harbor a well-founded distrust of technological interference with their bodies and genetic material at the hands of white physicians" (260).

Cultural norms and political history could explain black women's underrepresentation as infertility patients relative to their infertility rates. But social and economic exclusion seem more likely explanations for the underrepresentation of Native American women and Latinas. Genetic parenthood is a significant concern for Native women whose tribes have been decimated through genocide and forced sterilizations. Latino culture frowns on adoption, and *marianismo* (the idea that a woman's self-esteem is manifested in her ability to be a generous mother and maintain strong traditions of family) elevates motherhood to exalted status, the combination of which would lead one to expect to see more Latinas among infertility patients (Becker et al. 2006, 886).[26] But Becker and coinvestigators found that low-income Latinas have little access to infertility treatments in Title X clinics, aside from some diagnostic procedures and prescriptions for clomiphene and metformin (Becker et al. 2006, 884). Latino culture is highly pronatalist, yet Latinas' infertility is not widely aided by the increasing prevalence of ART. This is perhaps not surprising because ART can potentially solve the problem of childlessness, though it cannot cure infertility. Child-free Latinas are far more likely to be so as a result of environmentally caused infertility rather than postponement.

That ART help to shore up ideal race and class motherhood norms in many ways is thus evidenced by the way they are distributed. They are targeted at the infertility of the least infertile group of women because those women are "ideal mothers." The imbrication of ARTs in pronatalist, ideal motherhood discourse is in evidence by what they solve, which technically is childlessness. Solving *infertility* would mean targeting the range of social, economic, and medical causes of impaired ability to conceive. To a large degree, ARTs are a medical cure for a social problem: the difficulty in conceiving among a select few, primarily postponers. Given their current distribution, ARTs work within existing normative discourses rather than opening up the ideal motherhood norm. Privileged women's mothering options are increased (although their parenting—and not-parenting—options are not); underprivileged women's mothering options remain limited. And childlessness by choice remains a deviant category, even if less stigmatized that it used to be. ARTs thus work within the revival of republican motherhood against certain liberalizing ideas about childlessness.[27]

ASSISTED REPRODUCTION TECHNOLOGIES AND WOMEN'S AGENCY

Because motherhood is seen as central to women's identity, infertility is often perceived as a personal failure. Although the failure is experienced as personal or individual, it is only a failure because of the social standard that measures what a woman is. The desperation that some women feel when they cannot meet the cultural definition of womanhood by becoming pregnant is to some extent a cultural artifact, which does not make the experience of loss any less real. As Ulrich and Weatherall say of their infertile interview subjects, because "the mandate for motherhood was compelling . . . distress was a reasonable rather than a problematic response to infertility. . . . Motherhood was overwhelmingly constructed as important for women's social, psychological, and physical sense of adequacy and completeness. For this reason, infertility was seen as a failure" (2000, 334). This social standard often becomes so engrained in the female psyche by such an early age that it becomes part of one's female identity. That is what makes the failure seem like a personal failing, but the source of that standard is decidedly external—at least originally.

Although infertility might lead one to consider the range of ways to inhabit womanhood, to refigure and resist compulsory motherhood, the option of ART to fulfill a desire generally seeded early in life offers the chance to stay well within not only the motherhood norm, but also the *biological motherhood* imperative. Because of the pervasiveness of matrigyno-idolatry, the desiring subject is thereby disciplined in such a way that what she "really" wants often cannot be separated from the ideological imperatives of what she should want. If she is hegemonically normatively competent—and she fits the ideal mother mold—then ARTs become a form of what Foucault called biopower: "tools for governing our selves through, not against, our wish for freedom" (Valverde 2004, 77). That is, once the desire for motherhood is uniformly and firmly enough embedded in one's self-consciousness, ART just become a way of giving some women what they want.

In embracing this element of normative womanhood, one begins to reiterate other aspects of the gender script as well. As Charis Thompson found, in her study of infertility clinics, "infertility patients display exaggerated stereotypical gender attributes at appropriate times during treatment—perhaps to signal their fitness to become heterosexual nuclear parents and probably also to rescue gender and sexual identities that have been compromised by the lack of fertility. Patients had to act out these roles emotionally, economically, and legally to have access to treatments, which, if successful, allow them to reassert their station in this normative social order" (2005, 71). To be accepted as an infertility patient, one generally must conform to "norms of heterosexuality, ability to pay, appropriate comportment, and compliance" (85). The more central motherhood is to women's gender identity, the more difficult it becomes to refashion other elements of normative gender if women want to receive help in achieving their maternal goal. Although one of the agency-enhancing promises of ART is in the reworking of motherhood norms to include more and different kinds of women—and not just married heterosexual women—this potential is undermined in many clinics by the gatekeepers who also have also been steeped in ideal motherhood norms and have some investment in continuing to promote those ideals. The demand for gender norm compliance here—

along with the still-limited distribution of ART resources—disciplines any radical potential to "trouble" gender offered by ART.[28]

Efforts to enact one's agency are efforts to impose one's will on or wrest control in a situation. ARTs are sold as a way of giving infertile women control over their bodies, of increasing their agency by offering them more choices. Despite the rhetoric of "choice" (which implies control), control is a slippery concept in the realm of ART. For example, in Susan Lang's work, we meet Denise, whose experience exemplifies one way in which women become alienated from their bodies and their life plans through rounds of infertility treatments. She and her husband sought fertility treatment when they had trouble conceiving. Although about 40 percent of the couples who try fertility treatment get pregnant (and about one-third carry to term), Denise and her husband did not. Denise said she began to feel helpless and hopeless. As she "kept failing to get pregnant, she had to grapple continually with loss—loss of privacy, loss of control over her reproduction, over her daily life as medical procedures invaded her mind and body, and loss of her dreams" (1991, 127).[29] Additionally, although the dubious rhetoric about ART is that they give more women more control over their ability to have children, this is a pitch used in part to counter the growing trend of educated, economically privileged, and married women not having children, a type of reproductive control that women of privilege are not supposed to exercise.

Michie and Cahn's study of infertility advice books revealed a clear theme of promoting women's subservience to, rather than self-mastery through, technology. All of these advice books are written for women rather than couples, and they tell women to keep reading, to learn as much as possible in order to be in control of their infertility. The infertile woman

will be told that she can "overcome" infertility, "overcome" the odds, "overcome," in many cases, her own reluctance to proceed further with treatment and into the infertility maze. She will read over and over again that she can put up with discomfort; with pain; with interrupted work days, weeks, and years; with a mechanical sex life, with financial sacrifice. She will learn to put up with these things because these are choices: she will have chosen these things in the name of a greater, a canonical, reproductive choice—the choice to become pregnant. (1997, 138)

One popular exercise involves "redrawing the line" at which a woman believes she must stop treatment. She is given scripts for talking herself through ever more invasive and expensive treatments. Readers of these books are repeatedly assured that if they try hard enough, they will get pregnant. "These books encourage infertile couples to see control in terms of negotiation of further treatment and not in the larger sense of understanding and challenging the pervasive cultural images of infertility" (Michie and Cahn 1997, 160). In the end, all of this information is about decreasing resistance to the extraordinary lengths infertility patients must go to and is not about resituating parenthood in the hierarchy of one's aspirations and self-definition.

Control in the case of infertility is a double-edged sword: it suggests on the one hand "the potential for empowerment while, on the other, it reiterates a deeply rooted cultural desire to blame women for failing to have children" (Michie and Cahn 1997, 139). Many of the advice books and popular news stories aimed at helping women deal with infertility pick up on the cultural sense that if women were better women or were better organized or adequately pursuing the options that ART presents, then they would be pregnant. In these accounts, they are infertile because of choices they have made to delay childbearing while establishing careers, or they are told they are overweight, or underweight, or not relaxed enough, and so on, ad nauseum.[30] The message of infertility guides is that women can overcome infertility if they choose to do so, if they are willing to police their bodies appropriately. This discourse of autonomy—of choice of reproductive outcomes—is specious. Although arguing that women can autonomously choose the right lifestyle to get themselves pregnant, the vaunted choice is not in the outcome. There is only one right outcome: pregnancy. The choice is expressed in the ways in which a woman regulates herself so that she may achieve the desired result: a child.

In discussing the common charge that ARTs are detrimental to women's agency because they are objectifying, Thompson argues that rather than being detrimental, this objectification can be essential to women's agency:

> As long as the activities in question promise to lead to pregnancy, synecdoche between the objectified patient and her long-term self is both enabled and maintained. In these cases, she exercises agency through active participation in each of the forms of objectification. However, if the synecdochal relation fails and the ontology of the educed treatment trails is not sustained long enough to overcome the infertility, then the different dimensions of objectification come apart from their associated kinds of agency. (2005, 201)

That is, so long as the objectification leads to a child, the woman is an agent. If the woman remains childless, then, by Thompson's account, her agency has been thwarted. But such a reading of the infertile patient means that her agency has nothing to do with her own decision making, her own evolving sense of self. Once the desire for motherhood becomes consummate, only motherhood makes her an agent. Such an understanding makes her a dupe of technology and a victim of pronatalism, not an agent. Where control was promised, control was again taken away. One becomes alienated from her embodied capacities through both objectification by technology and a thoroughgoing pronatalism. Actual control in the context of technology would offer more resources for actively negotiating the possibilities for confronting infertility and developing an expanded sense of oneself in relation to governing norms of identity and political possibility.

The individualization and medicalization of the problem of infertility combined with a pronatalist discourse that renders motherhood essential to women's identity is what makes ARTs significant in questions of women's agency and identity development and makes normative competence regarding motherhood and the place of ART in reproductive decision making difficult to develop. Where women are driven (by social, ideological, and psychological forces) to pursue motherhood at ever-increasing costs, self-determination becomes a phantasm. Women can end up spending many years and thousands of dollars trying to fulfill a role that might not seem so vital to self-determination if other discursive imagery were as readily available and as valued.[31] Rather than increasing women's choices in some meaningful sense, ART can often serve to sharpen the disciplinary effect of pronatalism and narrow the imaginative field. Consider, for example, Diane, one of Mardy Ireland's research subjects. Although she eventually went to graduate school after years of failed fertility treatments, she said that infertility "consumed [her] whole life." Before graduate school, "all I was was my infertility" (Ireland 1993, 35). That motherhood is a deeply felt gender identity is evidenced in Diane's sense of being a "failure as a woman" (37). For women who dearly want children but cannot have them, there is a long period of mourning before they can work to reorient their female identity. For women like Diane who go through years of infertility treatments, "it is as if each new fertility treatment, each attempt to conceive, is a new experience of loss" (18). Rather than offering more control, in the more common case where ARTs fail to deliver a child, women often get caught in a spiral of less and less control.

In the case of motherhood norms and gender identity, ideological and disciplinary powers conflict on the site of women's bodies. Consciousness and embodiment are tied together through the social and economic discourse of pronatalism and the "ideal mother" norm. Because the capacity for pregnancy "is a feature which is consistently constructed as salient, and . . . bears a critical relation to the needs and concerns of 'women' as embodied subject," pregnancy becomes one critical site of the development and political deployment of women's agency (Webster 2002, 201). Thus, technologies that promote and encourage certain groups of women to experience pregnancy in particular ways—while

simultaneously ignoring or outright discouraging other women's pregnancies and motherhood—ought not to be viewed as unrelated to the
development and deployment of their political subjectivities and their
capacity for agency. The phenomenological understanding of the lived
body here sutures together the autonomy and freedom of the subject,
actively producing the agency of the woman as ideological and disciplinary powers conflict on the site of women's bodies (Ziarek 2001, 22). As
subjects are produced through both competing and mutually reinforcing discursive structures, these powers contend with, and help subjects
make sense of, the knowledge of the world gained through their embodiment and the expectations and possibilities that are generated by
particular bodies. The body itself serves then as a location of historical
struggle over the meaning of what, for example, "woman" and "motherhood" mean. The meaning and significance of these social categories—as
well as relationships to each other—are worked out through the regulation of women's bodies in, for example, the legislation and social practices surrounding ART in conjunction with patterns of employment,
marriage, welfare policy, and contraceptive policies.

Thus, reproduction and infertility are questions of agency not only
because of the norms about gender identity, but because of norms about
gendered embodiment. We come to develop life plans through our embodied knowledge of our capacities and pleasures interpreted through
the lenses of the political prerogatives creating our identities and material opportunities. Pregnancy and motherhood are not just physical
potentials but privileged sites of meaning about what a woman is and
how one moves from being immature (a girl) to mature (a woman). Following from Merleau-Ponty's concept of the lived body, we can think of
the body that seeks meaning from the world and creates meaning in the
world as the "basis from which personal projects, decisions, volitions,
and judgments are differentiated" (Heinämaa 2003, 79). The various
capacities that our bodies have help set our plans, our horizons within
which we work, and our ways of apprehending and gaining meaning
from the world around us. The (potential) capacity for reproduction is

one of the means through which we construct meaning and judge which courses of action we desire to take. The lived body absorbs and becomes a repository of social discourses surrounding the capacities and desires we have. If our bodies do not behave "properly," or if the political situation we inhabit thwarts that potential, there are a limited number of ways of re-knowing one's body and reconceiving one's life plans, partly because of the effects of pronatalism. When we think our bodies can do one thing and then discover that they cannot, cognitive dissonance is likely. ARTs step into that space.

If disciplinary power is a specific relation of forces that are both violent and ideological, then ART is a good example of how this interplay of physical force (medical practice) and ideology (motherhood) plays out through women's bodies. Where ideological constructions are most in flux, and when new technologies arise that need to be given social meaning through use and regulation—meanings neither obvious nor settled because of their newness—one can see disciplinary power working in its most obvious ways in these contexts through the changing sense of an imperative to mother, the public acknowledgment of but disdain for voluntary childlessness, and the use of technology to shore up motherhood on new—as well as on very old—terms. These moments help clarify how the body serves as a stable holder of cultural meanings that still is not *fixed*. The white female body in legal matrimonial relation to a white male body is coded as "mother." And "mother" is essential, so that the other relations and identities follow from that parental index. As the race and martial status of that body in the motherhood norm is either challenged or reinvoked, technology can either aid or impede discursive rupture. ARTs are settling into and helping to solidify in some cases, contest in others, the social ideology of "mother."

Challenging ideological and cultural pronatalism would leave motherhood still an important potential for women as embodied subjects, but the weight of that embodied potential could be ordered and evaluated differently. Making infertility less of a "failure" and more of "another way that bodies operate" would still leave motherhood as important but

would, one hopes, make infertility less devastating, which is more likely
to be the case if infertility were less political (distributed more in proportion to racial and ethnic group's representation in the population)
and if motherhood were an important, but not the central, construction
of ideal femininity. Recoding the place of motherhood in female identity and revealing the social construction of the desire for motherhood
does not require rendering motherhood unimportant; it simply resitu-
ates it as only one means of female fulfillment. As sociologists Leslie
King and Madonna Harrington Meyer found, "Many infertile women
see themselves less as victims of biomedical experimentation and more
as individuals forced to choose between a set of disagreeable alternatives"
(1997, 22). But perhaps if motherhood were more equably weighted in
relation to other identities and goals one could achieve as an adult, then
childlessness would not be so disagreeable.

ARTs are currently more effectively, and more accurately, described
as a tool of cultural and political pronatalism than a means for enhancing women's agency for two reasons. First, the use of ART is increasing
as infertility rates are declining, and the use is increasing specifically
among the groups of women with lower aggregate rates of infertility—
women who also happen to be those targeted as ideal mothers. ARTs are
not here problematic because they somehow disrupt women's natural
state or fail to respect the integrity of women's bodies; they are problematic because they reinforce specifically raced and classed pronatalist ideals. Second, the last thirty years have seen a slight increase in the
rates of voluntary childlessness among some women; this, too, is occurring more frequently in the women targeted by ideal mother pronatalist
ideology. The form that pronatalism takes in the United States includes
the gender normative ideal that having children is essential to one's
womanhood or femininity, along with a concern that the "right" women
are not having enough babies and the "wrong" ones are having too
many. Hence we see increasingly frequent cultural reminders that children are essential to race and class normative female gender identity and
the near-unregulated provision and advertising of ART to treat infertility

(and the fear of infertility) among ideal mothers to defend against the feared tide of voluntary childlessness. This occurs simultaneously with the failure to address the preventable causes of infertility in all groups of women, in addition to the active steps taken to limit their reproduction.

That said, technology itself is not inherently oppressive, although the socioeconomic conditions within which it arises may lead to its use for oppressive or inegalitarian ends. Science develops within a nexus of power relations, and it is at least influenced by those power relations (in the assumptions about what technologies are needed, how the technology ought to be used, and who ought to control it). Political, social, and economic discourses impinge on the freedom that is gained by any technological advancement. Although scientific and technological advancements also shape and alter the political, social, and economic realities in which we live, the ways in and degrees to which particular advances can alter power relations are ultimately limited by these contexts. My argument is thus not that assisted reproduction technology is inherently bad or wrong or damaging to women; rather, I contend that the liberating potential of these technologies is rarely realized; the ways in which they are marketed and made available prey on women's social indoctrination into the ideals of motherhood as women's fulfillment and deflect attention from the political and economic causes of infertility in all groups of women. To this end, rather than opening up women's agentic possibilities, ARTs further constrain the imaginary and material domains in which agency develops, despite the rhetoric of increased choice and control. Yet the technologies are not going to disappear. The question, then, is how to harness the potential for ARTs to open the discursive fields within which women develop and motherhood ideals are evaluated while mitigating the dominating effects of ARTs.

As a matter of freedom, ARTs can open up the material possibilities for more women to become mothers, but they also constrain freedom by being so narrowly available. (And with success rates still well under 50 percent, they are not a panacea for infertility, even for the women who can afford the treatments.[32]) As a question of autonomy, ARTs reinforce the biological motherhood component of normative gender identity for women, doing little to open up or help women resist the ideology of woman as mother. If the decision to remain child-free were not so clearly marked as other and deviant—that is, if motherhood could be reindexed in relationship to other goods women might achieve for themselves—then ARTs would be less constraining to women's autonomy, and thus their agency. ARTs hold out more potential to increase the material conditions of freedom for women as they become more normalized and democratized, but their relationship to women's agency will remain ambiguous until mothering and not-mothering are more equally valued as part of normal adult womanhood. Said differently, ARTs hold more potential for increasing women's freedom than their autonomy. That the stigma attached to childlessness seems to be slowly receding, according to Thornton and Young-DeMarco's study (2001), is a sign that this discursive shift may slowly grow over the next few decades, but the increasing desire of the young people in the studies they examined to fit into the heteronormative ideal of marriage and children may make the child-free choice a continually fraught one as the voluntarily child-free counternarrative will continue to be underrepresented among cultural role models who serve to bolster women's sense that childlessness is an acceptable option for them.

To confront disciplinary power productively, alternatives have to be not only available, but also feasible and valued before they can challenge the ubiquity of pronatalism. These alternatives must be both material and psychic in nature. Not only must women have viable education and career and personal options available, but they must also at an early age be exposed to a range of positive examples of childless adults. If childlessness is viewed only as the way one thumbs one's nose at social convention rather than as a good in and of itself, then ARTs can and will continue to work as tools that prolong many women's feelings of inadequacy. Rather than increasing freedom and choice, ARTs would here result in further buttressing matrigyno-idolatry.

The models on which individuals build their life plans "are proposed, suggested, imposed" on them by culture, society, and social groups (Foucault 1994 [1984], 291). So while resistance always takes place "from within power relations, . . . at the same time it shifts those relations" (McLaren 2004, 223). What counts as resistance to existing relations of power depends very much on where one is situated within those discursive forms. In the case of ART, utilizing the same technology can be either an act of resistance or a reiteration of expectations and a shoring up of existing normative ideals precisely because ARTs are situated in a paradoxical relationship to discourses about motherhood, simultaneously reifying the mother–woman synecdoche while denaturalizing the process of reproduction in such a way that motherhood can be, although does not necessarily have to be, rethought. Furthermore, just because resistance is possible, embracing the "proposed, suggested, or imposed" course of action is not necessarily the wrong course of action. Rather than rejecting motherhood, for example, agency might be developed through the resignifying of the natural by achieving it (motherhood) precisely through defying the material limits on the impediments to one's desire.[33]

For example, the use of ARTs by lesbian and single women (of any sexual orientation) is on the rise. Such use can increase the material and imaginative possibilities of these women, provided that they are not legally prevented from accessing these technologies. The subversive potential is made possible in large part in the United States because ARTs are not nearly so heavily regulated as they are in most European Union states. Precisely because ARTs are intervening in the private sphere, overtly political forces have less influence on how they are disseminated, although economic considerations loom large. While U.S. legislation has focused on circumscribing women's fertility options through abortion, sterilization, and contraception policy, the government has largely left ARTs to market forces. This does little to serve the needs of poor women, but it does relieve in some small way the narrow specificity of pronatalist rhetoric where single and lesbian mothers who are not poor are concerned. Agency is here enhanced not simply because more women find it easier to become pregnant, but also because the master narrative about what behaviors constitute good mothering is expanded. That is, "woman as mother" is not simply cited by more groups of women; the meaning of motherhood is here resignified.

Yet this form of resistance also shores up the mythology of motherhood in its own way. Consider lesbian parenting. "Some feminists question whether the focus on reproduction in gay partnerships has the unintended negative consequence of relegating women to traditional roles of taking care of others at the expense of their own individuality. Thus, while the emergence of new family forms undoubtedly changes cultural assumptions about affiliation and power relationships, it does so in fractured ways that carry multiple meanings" (Ertman 2003, 37). Lang's study (1991) revealed that as more lesbians are becoming mothers, the pressure to parent for lesbians is almost as strong as it is for heterosexual women (Lang 1991, 158). Some child-free lesbians argue that lesbians who have children, particularly in the context of a committed relationship, are to some degree using motherhood as a way to feel and appear "normal." Their primary identity shifts from being a lesbian first to being a mother first.[34] So while expanding the notion of the proper family and encouraging the dismantling of a narrow definition of "mother" are social shifts that can productively open the discursive situation for some women, there is an attendant danger that pronatalism will be reentrenched in the process. Simply put, the definition of "mother" can be stretched without radically interrupting or undermining matrigyno-idolatry per se. As Meyers reminds us, "Figurations are open to interpretation, and this elasticity enables them to stretch to cover new situations" (2002, 27). Pronatalism and matrigyno-idolatry will truly be placed in a more reasonable relation to other socially normative forces when women who currently fit the mold of the ideal mother can deliberately choose not to have children without confronting pronounced social stigma, and poor women and women of color find their motherhood no longer circumscribed by hostile legislation. ARTs will be in service of increasing agency when they are available to the women who need them most and when they are developed in conjunction with social policies to prevent infertility rather than treat it after the fact.

CONCLUSION

Increasing women's agency is partly about increasing the material goods available to them, but it also requires engaging in discursive resistance. Having more choices alone is not enough; choices must work with the discursive possibilities women already have access to and those they are trying to create. Further, having choices is as much about making judgments as it is about getting things, about developing an ethos of desire. Making judgments means being able to articulate why we want what we do and how we go about getting what we want. Given current gender norms and embodied meanings, it is rather obvious why so many infertile women want so desperately to conceive their own biological children. Thus the emphasis of feminist social and political activism committed to increasing women's agency needs to be on rearticulating and recalibrating social norms that place an inordinate emphasis on motherhood for particular groups of women and social policies that misdistribute new ARTs with a singular focus on individual childlessness rather than the social causes of infertility. Both broadening and decentralizing the motherhood norm will require collective social, cultural, and political action from coalitions of feminist and related groups working for reproductive, environmental, and workplace justice.

There are at least two things that must happen to resituate ART and motherhood in the context of the subjectifying discourses and material structures of women's lives. First, ARTs must be more widely distributed. To the degree that assisted reproductive schemes can facilitate liberating changes in the ideologies of family life and gender norms, then they should be encouraged. As part of this shift, socially caused infertility, rather than individual childlessness, must be the target of medical research and economic policy. Both public policy discussions and grassroots activism must more explicitly intervene in and highlight the connection between, on the one hand, the economic and cultural resources spent on ART for privileged women, and on the other, the antinatalist policies directed at nonprivileged women. Money spent on research, development, and distribution of curative approaches to infertility is money not available for preventative measures such as environmental cleanup or improved public health services. Focusing on the latter would make motherhood one possible choice for more women without encouraging the manic quest for motherhood that new reproductive technologies treatment often becomes.

Second, as Morell writes, "Unless nonreproduction and reproduction are both envisioned and supported as viable options, women are not liberated" (2000, 321). While the desirability of motherhood for many women must not be overlooked, the choice to remain child-free must continue to be destigmatized as well. Because these technologies continue to be marketed to the public, the public in which they are marketed needs to be transformed. The recuperative effects of ARTs on idealized motherhood norms and pronatalism can be reined in only when the discourse that posits motherhood as women's primary means of fulfillment is more successfully challenged. There are ways to deemphasize motherhood via public policy, but much of the work will need to occur at the level of social norms and cultural scripts that could raise non-mother models up to the prominence of motherhood messages. Raising the prominence of counternarratives is one step in this direction, and the Internet has been a boon for subversive parenting and child-free by choice networking.[35] But the Web sites tend to collect highly self-selected audiences, making them less useful as broad measures against culturally entrenched master narratives. Additionally, given the importance of role models in helping women conceive of potential futures, glowing exposés of the delightfully child-free need to be featured as widely and as prominently as the standard-issue celebrity mom profile, for example.

On the question of distribution, because the women who are currently shut out of ART services are the ones who experience the highest rates of infertility, then a focus on providing more of the high-tech services to these women should be a top public policy concern. To redistribute ART resources, mandating insurance coverage is insufficient, because most of the people who have access to private insurance are not the same group of people who are most infertile. Rather, this redistribution will require publicly subsidizing at least some of the costs of the reproductive services so that exploitation and exclusion of poor women is less of an issue.[36] Of course, resources are finite, and providing coverage of highly expensive procedures that are not aimed at life-threatening or severely disabling illnesses and that have a very poor success rate is more a concession to the inevitability of the continued prominence of ARTs than to the more useful ways of fighting pronatalism and increasing reproductive agency.[37]

Truly to give women even more control over their fertility and to broaden the ideal of motherhood more fully, public and private medical resources should be targeted toward the causes of infertility rather than selective after-the-fact childlessness. If either matching grants for dealing with causes and effects were put in place or some funds were diverted from high-tech ART research toward finding causes and cures for endometriosis, cleaning up the environment, and strengthening workplace health and safety regulations, then all women would benefit, regardless of whether they ever desire or attempt to become mothers. Such a shift could also help to begin the recoding of infertility as a social problem rather than an individual medical problem. This discursive move would intervene in the idea that infertility is an individual woman's failure. Where infertility is not a failure of embodied potential, and where childlessness is not vilified, the (potential) "mother" aspect of women's identity can develop, or not, more reasonably, in line with other possible goals. To speak of reproductive freedom, we "must acknowledge that we make reproductive decisions within a social context, including inequalities of wealth and power. *Reproductive freedom is a matter of social justice,* not individual choice" (Roberts 1997, 6, emphasis in original). This is why the individualized medical model is so damaging: it mischaracterizes the problem, thereby allowing the impact on the development of women's psyches—their imaginative possibilities and thus their agency—to remain invisible and unchallenged.

CHAPTER 4

Working It

Prostitution and the Social Construction of Sexual Desire

Prostitution engages questions of freedom and autonomy as it is undertaken by some women with severely limited options and by other women with many options, and the confluence of their analyses of what they are doing and why helps to lay bare the constitutive effects of external options on the social construction of sexual desire. That sex work is engaged in by women from across the economic spectrum—although much more frequently by poor women—is significant in the way it illuminates how sexuality undergirds the economic relationships between men and women as well as between different classes of women, and the role of embodied labor (and embodied knowledge) in opening up avenues of agency and freedom. In this chapter, I pick up on the themes of victimization and agency, as well as the social construction of desire attending to the identity "woman" in the context of sex work. I examine three different feminist arguments about agency in sex work in order to think about what needs to change for a more open legal and economic discourse within which women's sexual agency can develop. I argue here, with many emendations, that prostitution could be part of a more open sexual discipline producing both male and female desire.[1]

There are many forms of sex work, and these different sites and types of work exist on a hierarchy of respectability and legality in the dominant cultural and legal frameworks of the United States, as well as among sex workers themselves. Exotic dancers make it clear that they are not prostitutes, and phone sex operators make it clear that they are neither dancers nor prostitutes (see, e.g., Rich and Guidroz 2000; Morgan 1998; Frank 2002, 57–58). The primary hierarchy here is between looking (or hearing) and touching. And within the various types of sex work, there are more and less stigmatized versions of that type of work, depending on where it is done and who is doing it. In the case of prostitution, for example, call girls exist at one end of the prostitution hierarchy, streetwalkers near the other end, although even within streetwalking there is a difference between those who work primarily for drugs and those who work primarily for money. Race is the other major hierarchy within sex work, with white women and lighter-skinned black women generally able to earn more money than darker black women. "White" strip clubs will limit the number of black and Latina dancers they have on the floor at any one time, just enough to "exoticize" the stage, not enough to turn a "gentleman's club" into a "black" strip club. As I discuss in more detail below, these hierarchies of sex workers and sex work tend to correlate with the level of physical danger one faces; the higher up the rung, the less the physical danger (see, e.g., Lever, Kanouse, and Berry 2005; Lewis et al. 2005; Brooks 2007; Chapkis 1997, 98–106).

Although I initially tried, I found that I could not wrest into coherence an adequate exposition on the questions of agency across the various hierarchies between and within each kind of sex work in one relatively short chapter. A cross-sex-work venue comparison would require a separate volume. So, in this chapter, I limit my discussion primarily to prostitution—with a short comparison with pornography to highlight some of the salient issues of the embodied ethos of prostitution that I am trying to develop here—and solely to sex work in the United States. Prostitution is the form of sex work that is illegal in all forms in the United States, with the exception of a few counties in Nevada, and the most stigmatized among the culture at large and within the sex work domain.

Yet it offers greater potential for opening up the subjectifying discourses of sexuality than any other form of sex work. Perhaps this is why it is illegal.

THREE MODELS OF PROSTITUTION

Sex as Violence (Abolitionist Feminism)

Abolitionist, or radical, feminists argue that all sex work is inherently a form of violence against women. In prostitution (and pornography), women are selling *themselves;* this is so because the act of sex is a fundamental form of self-expression and self-knowledge. As sociologist Elizabeth Bernstein explains, "It is both the inextricability of sexuality and self-identity as well as prostitution's stake in maintaining systemic gender inequality that have led [radical] feminists to argue for its 'market inalienability'" (1999, 96). For example, Carole Pateman argues that,

> [like manhood,] womanhood, too, is confirmed in sexual activity, and when a prostitute contracts out use of her body she is thus selling *herself* in a very real sense. . . . When women's bodies are on sale as commodities in the capitalist market, the terms of the original contract cannot be forgotten; the law of male sex-right is publicly affirmed, and men gain public acknowledgement as women's sexual masters—that is what's wrong with prostitution. (1988, 207–8)

Similarly, Catharine MacKinnon argues that

> what is called sexuality is the dynamic of control by which male dominance—in forms that range from intimate to institutional, from a look to a rape—eroticizes and thus defines man and woman, gender identity and sexual pleasure. It is also that which maintains and defines male supremacy as a political system. Male sexual desire is thereby simultaneously created and serviced, never satisfied once and for all, while male force is romanticized, even sacralized, potentiated and naturalized, by being submerged into sex itself. (1989, 137)

So, for Pateman, women become *women* through sexual activity with men. For MacKinnon, "man fucks woman; Subject verb object" (124). This relationship structures all other social relations. When men command sex through prostitution—which becomes then the sale of control over women's saying "no" to sex acts that are demanded in a specific period of time—then men become women's masters. On this account, prostitution is domination, not representation or sexual negotiation. It is a way for men to exercise power over women's bodies and minds.

Nancy Fraser (1993) has offered a sympathetic and insightful rebuttal of Pateman's argument about the master/subject model inherent in the prostitution contract. On Fraser's reading, which I think is persuasive, the master/subject model is deployed at both the literal and the symbolic level in Pateman's analysis. It fails at the literal level, but it is powerful at the symbolic level:

> Prostitution encodes meanings that are harmful to women as a class. . . .
> Contemporary prostitution is gendered; it is overwhelmingly men purchasing sex from women. . . . In heterosexual prostitution, the "buyer"
> belongs to a higher-status gender than the "seller," and the "service" is
> often permeated by symbolic associations that link masculinity with sexual mastery and femininity with sexual subjection. (1993, 179)

But because men are not buying actual command but the fantasy of a male sex right, what needs to be transformed are cultural meanings (about sex, dominance, gender, and labor) and structural relationships between men and women, rich and poor. But Fraser contends, and I agree, this does not necessarily mean that prostitution needs to be abolished for sexual equality to be achieved.

Notice that in the abolitionist framework the harm of prostitution is not just to the individual prostitute, but to women as a class because its existence promotes and enforces "the belief that all women are whores by nature" (Stark 2006, 47). That is, sex work is part of the process of social construction, and what prostitutes are helping to construct and reinforce is the view of women as always available to service men. Even if some women freely choose to engage in sex work, their actions limit the autonomy of others and limit their ability to challenge the sexualized view of women that permeates our pornographic culture (see Brison 2006, 195–97; Whisnant 2004, 23–24). Rather than redefining what sexual relations can be and should look like, prostitutes need to stop what they are doing in order to begin redefining what women are. When radical feminists think about how to increase women's sexual agency, they argue that the only approach that makes sense is the abolition of prostitution because it is a system that perpetuates and reinforces women's subservience to men and the definition of women as sexual beings for men. To intervene effectively in the social construction of desire, it is appropriate to use the constraining effect of the law in addition to cultural interventions both to make sex pleasurable only under very different terms—nonhierarchical and non-gender-role-differentiated ones— and to remove all sex (acts) from economic life. Sex is special, never to be instrumental.

Finally, to call prostitution *labor* is wrong because sexual labor has no inherent value in that it does not produce anything of value and it does not meet any social need. Sociologist Julia O'Connell Davidson argues that prostitution is not labor because no one needs sex and no one has a right to sex (2002, 92). Because humans do not have sexual needs—rather, they only have socially constructed desires, and because the enactment of these desires through prostitution physically and emotionally harms women—no service should cater to sexual desires (92–93). As prominent abolitionists H. Patricia Hynes and Janice Raymond write, "An economic analysis is necessary but insufficient for explaining the business and the buyers of prostituted women. It leaves unaddressed the tolerated and/or accepted 'natural law' of male sexuality—that men's alleged innate sexual needs must be satisfied and, therefore, that prostitution is inevitable" (Hynes and Raymond 2002, 206). Thus the institution of prostitution should be abolished in part through changing the predominant understanding of—or the actual content of—male sexuality.[2]

But if labor is only valuable if it caters to needs rather than wants, it is unclear whether most labor that humans engage in would pass this test. Further, all of our desires are socially constructed. If the argument is that the current social construction of sex needs to be altered—and I think that is O'Connell Davidson's argument, given that she argues for a new model of sexuality that places masturbation at the highest level of sexual fulfillment (2002, 95–96)—then this is a different argument than that sex work has no worth. It clearly has a high value in the current sexual economic system, given the upward of $40 million spent daily on prostitution in the United States, and it bears a heavy ideological load in perpetuating a falsely naturalized version of male and female sexuality in the patriarchal system of gender relations we currently have (Spector 2006a, 1). So the problem is not that prostitution has no value but that it often has the wrong symbolic value, and most of the many meanings of prostitution—and sex—need to be recoded. The problem, as legal scholar Noah Zatz has pointed out, is that radical feminists like MacKinnon, Pateman, and O'Connell Davidson focus "attention on the dangers of transgression rather than on creating spaces in which it is less dangerous" (1997, 289), but clearly transgression is what is required if the current state of heterosexuality is as dire as MacKinnon and Pateman claim it to be—and it does seem clear that at least some of the sex in heterosexual relations is dangerous to women: it is sometimes violent and too frequently nonconsensual. If this is the case, then it is unclear why sexual labor is singled out for abolition—unless one relies on a labor critique, rather than the sex critique that abolitionists offer.[3]

In the abolitionist discussions, male sex workers are not considered relevant to the analysis of sex work.[4] Perhaps one reason why they are neither pathologized nor deemed germane is that abolitionists (and others) simply assume that men can separate self from sex without being deficient in some way. It is the cultural code of what a woman is, of woman as sex, that makes women seem so pathological when they "sell themselves." It is perhaps also why it is difficult for many to take seriously the boundary maintenance between public and private sex acts that prostitutes claim as part of their job skills. Rather than accept the definition of woman as defined through sex, I would argue that a feminist theory of sex work should distance itself from the patriarchal view of women's worth and identity. Although one's sexual desires are obviously an important aspect of who one is and how one sees and understands the world, desire is not why most women go into prostitution. Further, to argue, as MacKinnon does, that gender is fully constituted through and by sexuality is to ignore the ways that race, class, and ability, for example, bring different meanings to sexuality, as do the contexts in which sexual interactions take place. "Gender" is never unmodified, is never only sex. To argue otherwise is to mirror the patriarchal view of women as only for sex, only for men's sexual gratification, not to challenge that construction of them (see Brown 1995, 77–95). That is, as Wendy Brown has observed, the abolitionist position—particularly as articulated by MacKinnon—conflates subjectivity (identity) and social position, which leaves no room for agency (Brown 1995, 93). Agency arises in part because of the tension between one's subjectivity and the denial of its full political and social expression. Agency comes through the tension between the norms to which one has to be competent in order to acquire social standing and social intelligibility, and the desires that one has as a result of her unique social position. (Recall from chapter 1 that subjectivity is the generative site of agency precisely because it is produced by *but exceeds* the intersecting norms and power relations producing it.) Resistance is born of trying to overcome the tension between subjectivity and social opportunity and private life. The abolitionist position is quite helpful in pointing out and taking seriously the violence that marks too much of women's sexual experience, but it cannot account for the pleasure women need, seek, and have as they struggle to produce a more open sexual world.

Sex Radicalism

The sex radical position is promoted primarily by a subset of relatively privileged sex workers. Although this position should not be dismissed simply because many of its proponents are economically and education-ally well-off compared to other sex workers, it is important to under-stand that this position is produced from what could reasonably be called the "gold standard" of sex work positionality, from those who have the most choices going into sex work and therefore the most exit options. These workers thus have some bargaining power and can choose to work in the "best" sites: indoors and in situations where they have more control over which clients they see, what they will do with and for clients, and how much to charge each client.[5] Not surprisingly, those who inhabit the higher echelons of prostitution start out with a number of structural advantages. Lever and Dolnick's large-scale study compar-ing street walkers to indoor prostitutes found that "nearly 70% of the street sample was African-American, whereas nearly 80 percent of the off-street sample was white. The average educational [*sic*] was 11.6 years in the street sample, a little less than required for a high school diploma, and 13.5 years, or some college, in the off-street sample. Median age, on the other hand, was the same, between twenty-nine and thirty years old in both samples" (2000, 88). There is a clear difference in the clients too: nearly all of the call girls' clients were white (82 percent), then Asian (7 percent). The street prostitutes "host a more democratic array of clients of different races and ethnicities" (89). Money paid is starkly different: the median amount for call girls was $200; for street prosti-tutes, $30.[6]

From this relatively privileged position, sex radicals argue that sex work is a site of multiple meanings and structural inequalities that need to be engaged directly rather than refused (through attempts to abolish prostitution). Sex radicals further argue that sex is

> a cultural tactic which can be used both to destabilize male power as well as to reinforce it. . . . Practices of prostitution, like other forms of com-modification and consumption, can be read in more complex ways than simply as a confirmation of male domination. They may also be seen as sites of ingenious resistance and cultural subversion. . . . The position of

the prostitute cannot be reduced to one of a passive object used in a male sexual practice, but instead can be understood as a place of agency where the sex worker makes active use of the existing sexual order. (Chapkis 1997, 29–30)

By embracing rather than being shamed by their sexuality and displaying and practicing it in ways not rewarded or approved by dominant cultural norms, sex radicals argue that they are challenging views of who women are and what women want. I will unpack this argument a bit.

First, sex radicals argue that sex work serves a therapeutic function in society, serving sexual needs for clients that otherwise might not be met, and engaging in sexual healing and sexual openness, allowing people to grow in their self-knowledge and to approach sex in a healthier way.[7] This healthier approach to sexuality is about lack of shame, but it is also aimed at teaching men how to be more in tune with and better caregivers of women's bodies (see Hartley 1997, 63; Queen 1997; Metal 1998). Those who argue the therapeutic point contend that sexuality is not some natural state or set of acts needing to be liberated, but that sexuality is socially constructed and, as it currently exists, needs to be reconstructed. Sex radicals do not argue that no women are harmed by sex work, but rather that there are women who can and do choose this kind of labor for the positive benefits it brings them and society and that women are harmed by current configurations of sexual power in private too. Where prostitution can be chosen, allowing it to be so is to permit women sexual autonomy and sexual experimentation while acknowledging that "dominant male sexual practice is . . . in dire need of therapy" (Schwarzenbach 2006, 237).[8] One goal of such therapy is a reduction in the levels of sexual violence against women. This therapeutic argument is related to the second good that sex radicals argue their work brings to society: a new kind of sexuality, "whore sexuality."

Sex radicals argue that whore sexuality can help to liberate women and men from the repressive effects of a puritanical heritage, specifically patriarchal notions about women as "good" only when they inhabit the

narrow space that is the Madonna side of the Madonna/whore dichotomy, defining women as pure and deserving of male protection. They
argue that this protection comes at a high cost: women are expected to
sublimate their own sexual needs and desires to those of a husband, and
they are confronted with sexual harassment as part of their "respectable"
jobs, as part of reminding them of the dangers of transgressing the
boundaries of femininity. The whore sexuality that sex radicals promote
tries to erase the distinction between good women and bad women that
is based on sexual behavior. They argue that women who are sexually free
to engage in the sex acts that they find pleasurable with whomever they
choose are truly valued as autonomous agents.[9] Requiring women to be
sexual only with men that they are related to in legally and culturally
sanctioned ways (husbands or boyfriends) is no less a denial of agency or
instrumental view of women than stripping or prostitution; it is simply
less honest about the economic and power dynamics that are being
enforced between men and women (see Kuo 2002, 53–57). Further, they
frequently point out, many of those state-sanctioned relationships fail to
protect women, but the harm marriage, for example, inflicts on victims
of domestic violence has yet to serve as a call to end marriage for women's
health and well-being. Hence, calls to end prostitution for women's own
good are really about trying to control women's sexuality, not protect it.

   Bernstein (1999) contends that sex radicals are to some degree transgressive in their work precisely because they refuse to meet expectations
about who they are ("good girls") and what they will do ("respectable
work"). Sex radicals often come from the middle class and have at least
a high school diploma, if not some college education. By opting to be
"bad girls" when they have other options, their acts can be interpreted
as a challenge to the Madonna/whore dichotomy and the sexual status
quo. For them, "being a sex-worker is about taking pleasure in sex,
unleashing repressed energies, or exploring the socially-deemed dangerous border zones of eroticism. Often, there is an explicit rejection by
women of romance and the 'good girl' marriage contract for which they
have been socially slotted" (112–13). But, according to Bernstein, "there

is nothing transgressive about one who has been socially born and raised to be a 'bad girl' and remaining one" (112). This, I think, is an only partially accurate assessment of sex workers from the working class; poor women in sex work argue that they have opted to take the best-paying job they can rather than remain poor but on the socially acceptable side of the law and culture. They are challenging the legal and economic system that works to keep them poor and under state control. So Catharine MacKinnon is right: in a sexual order that defines women as being sexually available to men, we should not be terribly surprised that the best-paying job many women can find is in prostitution or stripping. But it is also true that refusing to remain poor and to work at "acceptable" minimum-wage jobs because that is what respectable women do is a way of contesting the nexus of economic and gender power and is, in effect, an exemplary form of weakly substantive autonomy. The options on offer—and the reasons for them—have been clearly seen and explicitly assessed. These women are exercising the best agency they can given their particular structural constraints, even if their empowerment comes at high social and physical costs.

Finally, sex radicals agree with their critics that much sex work as currently practiced is abusive, but insist that abuse is not inherent in sex work itself but is instead a function of how power currently works in a patriarchal culture.[10] Part of the role of the sex worker is to challenge that configuration of power both within and outside sexual relations. That is, sex is not the only arena in which men exercise the power to abuse women. And it is the power to abuse, rather than sex or sex work, that needs to be criminalized and eradicated. This view is expressed explicitly by Maryann, a nurse and former prostitute interviewed by Chapkis:

> When I worked as a prostitute, I often got the feeling that the men felt they had a right to whatever they were getting, and I did resent that. The most difficult moments were when I had to deal with a guy who had the attitude of "I'm the man. I have the power. You do this for me." Sometimes that was an attitude they walked in with, sometimes it was

what they left with. I used to wonder if it wasn't because I was too clearly in control. It was the attitude, not the sex, that was abusive because I can tell you I see a lot of the same thing from doctors: you're there to serve them and whatever they need they should have. Nurses are there to carry out doctors' orders and to intuit their needs. It's something we're always battling. . . . My point is, don't battle prostitution; go deeper than that. Abuse is about power and the intentions behind it. It's that attitude we have to battle wherever it appears. (1997, 86)

Additionally, as women's studies professor (and former exotic dancer) Merri Lisa Johnson writes, "Sex workers remain outside the boundaries of those who can reasonably expect safe work environments, much less respect or right wages. The persistent link between sex work and danger comes across as natural, but this expectation mystifies the ideological work of the link. It is a load-bearing wall in the social construction of proper femininity" (2006, 177–78). Because "feminine" has been coded to mean "weak" in relation to masculine, sex work is seen as dangerous.[11] But by changing the law and engaging in cultural protest, sex workers hope to normalize and refigure women's many desires. The desired long-term effect of such challenges is to change what it means to be female in relation to male and to challenge feminine sexuality as submissive or imperiled. This would then focus attention on the dangers of sex work and women's sexuality on abuse rather than on sex—on the aberrations as such, rather than assuming or naturalizing the violence as normal.

Sex radicals are clear (and here they are united with the sex-as-work position) that the illegal nature of prostitution contributes to its stigma and restricts women's sexual freedom and property in their persons. Sex radicals argue that sex has multiple meanings depending on the context, and the restricting force of the law tries to impose one meaning on all citizens' sexuality. Certainly sex acts can have multiple meanings, although they cannot mean just anything, given the historically and culturally specific contexts in which they take place. In this vein, we need to take seriously the sex radical critique of the juridical limits on sex and the cultural norms of "good womanhood," but we must also remember, as legal scholar Jane Scoular notes, that sex work should be viewed with ambivalence: "It is an activity which challenges the boundaries of heterosexist, married, monogamy but may also be an activity which reinforces the dominant norms of heterosexuality and femininity" (2004, 348). Because sex and sex work have many meanings but those meanings and the ability to deploy them are restricted by the material conditions under which prostitutes labor (and clients and outsiders come to understand sexuality), the sex radicalism perspective is best used in conjunction with the sex-as-work analyses.

Sex as Work

Although sex radicals define sex work as a therapeutic service, a distinct sexuality, and/or an empowering intervention in the production of gender relations, abolitionist feminists define prostitution as violence against women and the production of female subordination. But the sex-as-work position stakes out a different set of claims about the ontological and political status of prostitution. Sex worker feminists argue that sex work is defined by its social relations and its illegal status, and not by some inherent relationship between sexual acts and one's essential self. The sex-as-work argument also claims that most labor is exploitative, and that for sex workers, poverty and the low-paying jobs that they can obtain are more alienating than providing sex to strangers. Why, they ask, should poor women not be able to make a living wage? Taken together, these two arguments lead sex-as-work feminists to argue that what needs to be challenged are the conditions under which sex workers labor, not the legitimacy of sex work or sex workers themselves. Those like abolitionist feminists and conservatives who would rather attempt to eradicate prostitution than improve women's existing working conditions through proposals like decriminalization misunderstand the problems with the job and are making the perfect (gender equality) the enemy of the good (job protection). I will explain each of these arguments briefly in turn.

If asked, most prostitutes will say they entered prostitution for the money.[12] Former prostitute and current activist Gloria Lockett's comments summarize the vast majority of first-person accounts from sex worker feminists:

> Prostitution to me was a way of making a living, I was solely in it for the money. All the other stuff about power came along with it after a while, not in the beginning. I and most African-Americans who get into prostitution are in it because of the money. If we had another way that would make us $50,000 and $60,000 a year, then that's what we would be doing. Prostitution is very difficult; it's a job. . . . I've heard some of my white friends say that they're in prostitution because of the power. Well, for black women it's for the money. We are powerful people, we don't need to get power by standing on no corner. (Brooks 2007, 154–55)

Sex work thus is not just a means to an end; it is, as sex worker Janelle Galazia writes, "a means to a different end" (2007, 87)—an end that isn't abject poverty and the different forms of indignity that attend to underpaid menial labor.[13] Sex-as-work feminists see economic exploitation as a greater concern than changing men's conception of sex, thereby altering the demand side of prostitution, which is a goal more in line with abolitionist feminists, and to a lesser degree sex radical feminists. Sex-as-work activists see economic oppression and poverty as more sexist and as more "primary" than sexualized practices of normative femininity (Kuo 2002, 142). Galazia is clear on this point: "The wage gap, welfare 'reform,' sexist and racist hiring practices, the decline in the real value of the minimum wage, lack of universal access to healthcare or rehab services, and the widening disparity between the rich and poor: these are the things that undermine the social fabric and degrade the status of women more than me tramping around in heels could ever hope to" (2007, 89). Thus these women view their jobs as work and not primarily as sex.[14]

On this view, women's agency would be greatly facilitated by changing the laws that turn prostitutes into criminals and that help maintain the stigma of prostitutes as dirty women undeserving of legal protection or personal respect. Laws against prostitution make women's working conditions more dangerous—by subjecting them to police harassment, feeding clients' beliefs that whores are appropriate targets of violence, and impeding their survival strategies, such as taking time to assess a client before getting into a car with him or traveling in groups. They also make it more difficult for women to leave prostitution and enter the legitimate professions.[15] Further, "by denying prostitution the status of legitimate work, criminalization helps patrol the boundary between the sex/affective labor routinely assigned to and expected of women and practices deserving of the financial and status rewards of 'work'" (Zatz 1997, 287). Thus, although abolitionist feminists argue that the legalization question is separate from the politically relevant features of sex work, sex workers see the criminalization of sex work as one of the primary features constructing what prostitution is and how it is experienced, if not the single most important feature. Its illegality creates it as the stigmatized, violent, and othering phenomenon we know today. "These forms of state regulation articulate prostitution within a cultural realm of marginalized sexuality and isolate it from the status of work" (284). Illegality keeps sex workers from articulating what they do as a form of work, forcing it into the realm of sexual act and denying it the status of labor, all while reifying women's caretaking work. "Many prostitutes attempt to resist this construction by articulating their practice as a form of service work structured as a sex *act,* a performance in which the client's experience of participation in a *sexual* act is an illusion created by the sex worker, the sex actress" (284).[16] *Sex worker* is the term preferred by most prostitutes (and pornography actresses) because it makes clear that there are women who earn their living through sex and that the sex work that women do—like the cleaning and care work that they do—is work and not some natural, essential capacity. It takes skill and effort to do it well, and it involves a number of risks—

not just violence, but repetitive stress injuries, allergic flare-ups, in-
fections, and emotional burnout (McIntosh 1996, 201; Alexander 1998,
211–15).

Sex workers Peggy Morgan, Donna Marie Niles, and "Debra" have
found that all jobs sexualize women, so for them, the choice was between low-paying jobs where they were harassed but were expected to
pretend it was okay or ignore it, and jobs where any sexualized treatment was remunerated and not a freebie. Morgan writes,

> In my own experience with "square" jobs, I've put up with condescension
> and sexual harassment that either would take complicated grievance pro-
> cedures to redress—with no guarantees—or was too "subtle" to confront
> without arousing accusations of oversensitivity and craziness. Besides, I
> had to worry about being fired if it was discovered that I'm gay—all of
> this for a wage I could not live on. . . . The fact is, there's a livable wage
> to be made in the sex business, and *we* decide when, where and with
> whom we'll do what. Money talks, bullshit walks, and we don't have to
> put up with anything we don't want. (1998, 25)[17]

In the "straight" labor market, women are controlled via their sexuality as they are in the home. At work, women are kept in their place
through inappropriate objectification and sexual threats. At home, they
provide sex for one man who protects them from the rest. The prostitute threatens this control of female sexuality—control aimed at promoting and protecting gender hierarchy (Nussbaum 1999, 286–87).
Prostitutes, in fact, insist that they are in control of the transaction, not
the clients. As Bernstein found when she went on the stroll with different groups of prostitutes, "they can and often do refuse to perform sex,
or indeed, to even talk to men they are not interested in" (1999, 105–6).

The hierarchy and stratification of the labor market continues to the
licit, but still gendered, labor market, so that the range of appropriateness shifts subtly with each step out of the licit and toward the illicit markets, with no clear line demarcating them. "In its contemporary format,

striptease can be usefully situated within a broad gendered service industry—ranging from flight attendants to Hooters girls to strippers—in
which women provide both erotic fantasy and emotional support to
customers in addition to their visual displays and performances" (Egan,
Frank, and Johnson 2006, xviii). Shared across the labor markets is the
expectation that women will serve men's various needs and provide the
emotional labor that is central to so much economic activity. This presents yet another form of gendered labor hierarchy: less remunerative
work is more respectable. It allows one to fit nicely in the caretaking/
wife/good girl mode of normative femininity, but it also assures dependence and limited self-directed, projective agency. Sex work is lower down
on the rung of respectability but higher up the ladder in terms of economic agency, leading to certain kinds of structural and discursive distance from the norms of the "straight" world. Bernstein makes the point
here quite explicitly when she writes that "what is key for all streetwalkers (and for most prostitutes generally) is that there is no other job at
which they could make anywhere near a comparable wage. Indeed, even
the most successful women professionals would be hard-pressed to match
their hourly earnings, let alone women of class, race and educational
backgrounds similar to their own, for which the most likely alternatives
would be a minimum wage job or marriage" (1999, 104).

Both sexuality and sex work are exemplary cases of an ambiguous discursive situation leading to forceful resistance in the face of freedom-
limiting material (and discursive) structures. There is no one meaning
of sex, whether in public or in private. The context within which the sex
takes place helps to create the meanings of sex—love, intimacy, exchange,
and so on. A single sexual act can even have different meanings for the
participants in it. Sex radicals want to redefine what sex and prostitution
mean while often attending too little to the ways in which we cannot
control the meanings others impose on our actions. Abolitionists argue
that prostitution is not really about sex or money, but instead is about
power and subordination. But as Noah Zatz rightly reminds us, these
are not separate things, and this totalizing theory crushes "conceptual

complexity and cultural variety" and "encourages us to forget the variety of meanings that participation in a 'single' practice can have for different individuals or groups" (1997, 279, 280).[18] Further, although MacKinnon and other abolitionists are clearly right that "social hierarchy is at the root of the deformation of desire. . . . Puritanism and the repression of female erotic experience" also deform sexual desire into forms of objectification and commodification. In fact, sexual desire might not be central to these problems of prostitution any more than "economic norms and motives that powerfully construct desire in our culture" (Nussbaum 1999, 239).

The most radical, subversive thing about prostitution and the sex-as-work position is "its open challenge both to the identification of sex acts with acts of desire and to the opposition between erotic/affective activity and economic life" (Zatz 1997, 279).[19] Because of this conceptual and contextual multiplicity, sex-as-work proponents talk about labor, but they do not necessarily engage in debates about what the sex itself actually *means*. The abolitionists argue that the sex is violence; the sex radicals argue that the sex is empowering and transgressive. But the social meaning of the sex acts are outside the scope of the sex-as-work framework. As political theorist Heike Schotten observes, "Prostitution may in some cases be exploitive, and may in some cases challenge the gender or sexual status quo, but neither of these is due to anything about sex work itself as sex work. As labor, prostitution may be exploited or it may be unionized, and workers may have more or less bargaining power, freedom of movement, and desirable working conditions. But sex workers do not, as sex workers, carry the burden of determining the meaning of sex and gender relations on their shoulders" (2005, 223). This determination comes through the status of marriage and the economy, the law of sexual relations and religious norms at play in public life, among other things. Differently situated people will bring their experiences to interpreting or participating in sexual labor and see sex as many different things in different contexts.[20] The commodified context can help to denaturalize sex acts and desires, but this will come only through resistance to dominant norms in many realms structured by sexual discourses.

The abolitionist perspective does not leave room for the possibility that the act of paying for a sexual service is a form of separation—a mediating step—in the creation of the meaning of a sexual act. In the negotiating of what is being paid for, women can help to define what the sex is going to be for them—for example, work and not desire—even if they cannot define it for the men involved. If Pateman's and MacKinnon's argument that what women are is determined through the sex act has any purchase, then women should be given more control, rather than less, over areas where they can and are expected to negotiate the sexual acts involved. It is true that to be reduced to a body is to be denied agency, but this is different from saying that using one's body in the way that one does in sex work is the denial of agency. If we deny prostitution the status of labor and insist that it defines the self of women—and that women's selves are being sold in prostitution—then the feminist argument is as essentialist and totalizing as the misogynist one. This is not to say that some women are not horrifically abused within the system of prostitution or that prostitution as currently practiced by many prostitutes is the idealized version of femininity, but it is to deny that such horrific abuses are all that prostitution is. Prostitution is about both sex (as the abolitionists and sex radicals would have it) and economics (as the sex-as-work prostitutes would have it).

In order to see the agency sex workers currently enact and to increase all women's sexual agency, sex radical and sex-as-work analyses both need to be used as the bases of interpretation and footholds for political intervention into increasing women's agency. The problem highlighted through sex work is the simultaneous production of women's (and men's) sexual desires with women's economic options. To be truly an agentic practice, prostitution would need to be restructured politically, legally, and culturally, all of which in turn would produce highly different subjectifying discourses for women's and men's sexual identities and social relationships.

The sex radical position on prostitution offers promise for helping to refigure the meaning of sexual interactions and women's sexuality by questioning the necessity of the connection of sex with intimacy, by providing spaces where nonnormative sexual desires can be enacted or negotiated, and potentially by positioning women on equal or more powerful footing with their sexual partners in determining exactly what acts will, and will not, be engaged in. Sexual desire is denaturalized, and social construction is not only recognized but potentially positively, consciously engaged. However, the sex radical position simply ignores the reality that most prostitutes enter the profession out of economic necessity, not because they desire to engage in or develop alternative sexualities (see Delacoste and Alexander 1998). Most of them view the sex they engage in as *work* separate from their private sex lives and sexual desires, with working conditions that suffer because of its stigmatized and illegal status. As Noah Zatz has pointed out, the sex radical position can undermine the efforts of many sex workers to get respect for their work as labor deserving of respect and the protections provided to other laborers. The demand for worker's rights is diminished—as is the potential for resistance to sexualizing identity norms—if prostitution is just another form of (private) sexuality (Zatz 1997, 293–94).

The idea of (private) "whore sexuality" carries two additional risks. First, normative femininity remains unchallenged and prostitutes remain marginalized if "normal" female sexuality and "whore sexuality" are considered two separate and distinct categories of self-expression. Second, arguing for the acceptance of sex work because it is central to women's identity or subjectivity risks turning sex radicalism into the mirror of abolitionism: either sexuality is so central to women's identity as women that it cannot be commodified without existential harm, or whore sexuality is so central to some women's identity that it cannot be criminalized without existential harm. Here the sex-as-work view of prostitution and pornography is superior as well: sexuality is central to one's subjective sense of self, but the ways in which that sexuality gets expressed, is experienced, and holds meaning for individual women varies widely. Sex worker Peggy Morgan makes clear the important point of convergence in radical feminist and sex radical analyses of female sexuality: "Society decrees sex a moral issue—especially for women. Beneath this façade, we find that this is really a political tool, designed to maintain the social order" (1998, 26). The question is thus how to intervene in the politics of sexuality without mandating or producing ever-narrower definitions of women's sexual self-expression and subjectivity. Commodification (a market in sexual acts) is neither the problem nor the solution. Rather, lack of control over when, with whom, and under what circumstances one expresses one's sexuality is the problem. That some women are harmed by sex work is not a reason to abolish sex work; it is a reason to punish the harm. Where women can develop and share (or not) their sexual selves without fear of arrest or rape or other physical assault, they will be sexual agents. Thus, if the sex radical position is to be helpful to the majority of prostitutes, the analytical focus must include the labor analysis of the sex-as-work position in addition to the value of providing a service that can productively disrupt the Madonna/whore dichotomy and the rigid confines in which "respectable" women must operate.

Women (and men, for that matter) do not have the kind of agency to make sex work mean whatever they want it to mean. They have to operate within the norms and interpretative frameworks available, even as they push the boundaries of those normative categories and interpretive structures. But sex workers are not simply victims of an oppressive economic and gender system. In choosing to adopt stigmatized roles like "whore" over stigmatized roles like "poor" (or welfare dependent), women are demonstrating exceptional normative competence and normative resistance. By insisting that stigma and poverty are the problem, not sex outside desire, women take the position of victim and reveal both the agency within it and the structural conditions that limit further agentic development. This revelation is resistance; it is agency as political prerogative and political critique.

THE AMBIGUITY OF BECOMING A SEXUAL AGENT

Building on chapter 1's discussion of the work of Michel Foucault and Maurice Merleau-Ponty can help us see how to achieve the shared goal of the above three approaches: increasing women's agency and improving women's options. The combined aspects of Foucault's concept of power producing agency through intersubjective relations along with Merleau-Ponty's arguments for an understanding of life as ambiguous and embodied, and for sexual knowledge as central to making sense of the world, can, I believe, reveal how sex work might be practiced and socially located in ways more conducive to women's individual and collective agency. When the work of Foucault and Merleau-Ponty is situated in the context of a combined sex radical and sex-as-work framework, prostitution is then positioned as one means of enacting the agency available in victimized social positions and increasing the subjective and objective nexus of power relations producing women's agency.

Recall from chapter 1 Foucault's discussion of becoming, for example, heterosexual or homosexual, rather than obstinately *being* a heterosexual or homosexual. In this argument, he is at least partly recasting an ontological question as an epistemological one, specifically embodied epistemological becoming in line with Merleau-Ponty's concern with becoming as a temporal aspect of agency. When Foucault explains the question of becoming homosexual, he says that in that "becoming" is the quest to develop certain forms of social relations. For homosexuals, these relations are ones of friendship (Foucault 1994 [1981], 135–36). That is, the problem of sexuality is one of creating relationships, not identities. Because homosexuality is a nonnormative relationship, Foucault's language here helps to highlight that becoming a homosexual can be done—constructed—in a number of different ways. There is no naturalized mode of relating as homosexuals. Whether or not friendship is the relationship "toward which the problem of" heterosexuality tends as well, it seems true that heterosexuality as much as homosexuality needs to be understood as a practice—as becoming, rather than being. Foucault here reminds us to focus on how heterosexuality, while overdetermined in the current sex/gender lexicon, is still deeply socially constructed, as various forms of power work together to create sexuality.[21]

It is imperative to focus on the social construction of heterosexual practices because they configure so much of social relations. This becoming of and development toward relations of friendship is easier to conceive as the problem of homosexuality—even if it is just as hard to do—because homosexuality is not everywhere, and every social institution is not built on the presumption of homosexual relations. But to reimagine all social relations, the sexual relationships between men and women must be laid bare and then clothed anew. As Foucault says, the question we must ask is, "'What relations, through homosexuality, can be established, invented, multiplied, and modulated?' The problem is not to discover in oneself the truth of one's sex, but, rather, to use one's sexuality henceforth to arrive at a multiplicity of relationships" (Foucault 1994 [1981], 135). So, too, with heterosexuality. Where prostitution mimics the abuses and violence of too much noncommodified heterosexuality, it helps not at all in this project. But to the degree that prostitution makes us rethink the relationship of sex acts to sexual desire, and of the erotic to the economic, it is one component of this much larger project of redefinition and reordering of social relations. Further, thinking about sexuality as the construction of relations helps illuminate the weakness of both abolitionist views of sex work as selling of the self and the aspect of sex radicalism—specifically libertarianism—that posits sex work as "liberating" an extant, repressed sexuality.

Sexual identities and sexual practices are normalized and produced through processes of marginalizing and medicalizing some behaviors and not others. As Jana Sawicki explains, "Foucault claims that deviancy is controlled and norms are established through the very process of identifying the deviant as such, then observing it, further classifying it, monitoring and 'treating' it" (1991, 39). In the context of my discussion in this chapter, the "deviant" in question is the prostitute who sells sexual services rather than uses her sexuality only in private and romantic relationships with individual men. Feminists should be suspicious of

aligning themselves with juridical projects that continue to marginalize (through stigma and criminalization) and medicalize (through the
treatment of whores as vectors of disease) prostitutes. What is at stake
for patriarchal power structures is the continued power to dominate
and produce submissive and controllable female sexuality and the need
for women to align themselves with individual men for sexual respectability. What is at stake for feminism in the "politics of refusal" is an
effort to rid sex of domination and objectification. But it is unclear
whether ending all forms of objectification is a desired end among
many women, or whether criminalization is an effective means to this
end if it is desirable.[22] Support of criminalization means supporting
the juridical domination of women's sexuality. This does not mean that
feminists have to support violent prostitution practices, but that these
violent practices should be fought through means other than state domination, that women's political possibilities need to be opened up rather
than closed off.

Like the domestic violence victim/survivor who insists on repairing
her relationship through the use of various legal and social strategies
rather than ending it, and like the single woman who uses reproductive technology to embrace motherhood on nonnormative terms, "sex
workers embody one of the most contradictory locations in our society,
simultaneously aiding in the production of, but also resisting features
of, gender inequality" (Spivey 2005, 417). The politics of abolitionism
mirrors the politics of insisting that women leave relationships in which
there is violence. If we require women to leave sex work to be good
women, we are narrowing the discursive and material fields of agency,
just as we are if we require women to leave bad relationships rather than
repair them. Particular values become generalized and essentialized. But
middle-class values about sexual respectability should not be allowed to
be universalized as all that women are allowed to be sexually.[23]

The problem with venerating prostitution as a practice of freedom—
as an act of resistance aimed at insisting upon seeing of the economics
of the erotic—is that most prostitution is engaged under conditions

closer to domination than of power relations producing ruptures of resistance. Foucault was clear about this possibility too: "Of course, states of domination do indeed exist. In a great many cases, power relations are fixed in such a way that they are perpetually asymmetrical and allow an extremely limited margin of freedom" (Foucault 1994 [1984], 292). This is the case with prostitutes whose pimps abuse them and take 80 percent of their money; with brothel prostitutes who have to pay 50 percent of their earnings to the house in addition to tipping the staff; and with streetwalkers who begin hooking at age fourteen because they have had to leave abusive homes and have no other way to survive. Prostitution under these conditions can tell us little, if anything, about creating a new gender order. Power and domination here produce not only poverty and desperation in some cases, but also desire, specifically the desire to purchase sex or the desire to be master of another. But criminalizing poor women helps to reproduce an ideology about the proper place of sexuality in one's life and an economic order that relies on the availability of a pool of poor women to work in underpaid jobs while not addressing incest and drug use, the two main reasons driving younger women into the most abusive forms of street prostitution.[24]

If there is no outside of power, then the only way to challenge the production of particular desires is to refigure them from within. Abolishing prostitution is an extremely long-term solution, if it is even possible, and continuing to criminalize it has only exacerbated prostitutes' lack of power. Rather than accepting that this is what prostitution must look like and that therefore it must be abolished, one option is to try to change the juridical and cultural order that creates and makes sense of prostitution. There will always be power relations. So, as Foucault says, "The problem, then, is not to try to dissolve them in the utopia of completely transparent communication but to acquire the rules of law, the management techniques, and also the morality, the *ethos,* the practice of the self, that will allow us to play these games of power with as little domination as possible" (1994 [1984], 298). One way to begin to open up the ambiguous possibilities for sex workers in many different positionalities—and not just the most privileged ones—is to change the structures of domination that gird the terms in which they work. One of these dominating forces is criminalization. When one's status is illegal, the power of the state can be used to enclose one in multiple, overlapping double binds, making all options fraught with danger. The argument for decriminalization that I develop in the final section of this chapter is one small part of an effort to acquire a better juridical stance and ethos to permit women and men themselves to become, in various relations, different kinds of heterosexuals. This becoming is part of what it means to enact and inhabit a (complicated, compromised) state of agency.

Because of the complicated ways in which power constructs the positions or identities from which we act, prostitution has different meanings for different actors. We simultaneously inhabit positions of more or less power. It is the dissonance or tension between the interests that adhere in each of them that helps produce moments of rupture or resistance to dominant norms. This is why sex radical sex workers who inhabit some positions of relative privilege have a different relationship to the resistance and empowering discourses in sex work than do sex workers acting out of a different set of identity positions. They are engaged in similar acts, but the structures within which they engage them give different meanings to those acts. "There are no inherently liberatory or repressive sexual practices, for any practice is cooptable and any capable of becoming a source of resistance. After all, if relations of power are dispersed and fragmented throughout the social field, so must resistance to power be" (Sawicki 1991, 43). The political conditions of possibility of sex worker subjectivities and resistance strategies are produced through the intersection of discursive modes of sexual ideology and an economic order that reflect the bifurcation of women's sexuality (Madonna/whore) and the devaluing of women's labor. Neither can be productively engaged unless both are. What this means is that the sexual practices of sex workers can be resistant and productive of competing sexual norms, but only if there are exit options. And even if women have exit options, this does not mean that everyone who encounters this sex worker will read her as flouting sexual norms, although they will have to confront her refusal to be ashamed of her sexuality. Likewise, poor women sex workers are flouting the dominant norms of proper womanhood by choosing sex work over poverty. This resists the figure of the victimized sex worker and the piety of poverty as well as the necessary connection between sexual desire and sexual acts. When sex work is the only option for making a living wage, however, it is also victimizing because it is overdetermined as the only way out (except for marrying up—another problematic option) while simultaneously being an act of agency. There is still a choice to be made: poverty or sex work. There is no feminist reason to make painfully limited options worse by criminalizing one of those options and further limiting women's exit options and life choices, and her ability to make her working conditions more respectful of her person.[25]

Agency is thus conflicting and ambivalent. Sex workers (like the rest of us) are acting despite the lack of assurance of the exact meaning or relationship they are trying to create or will be creating. Agency without certainty combines what we know with what we seek. It is made possible because of the ambiguity of embodied knowledge and the social life in which we try to interpret it. In making this case for agency in sex work, I am also drawing on Merleau-Ponty's argument that the ambiguity of sex and the body are not present so much in the thinking about them as in the doing—in the enacting of sex. He goes so far as to say that social knowledge (metaphysics, "the coming to light of something beyond nature") is gained through sexual activity. Not all of this activity is liberating, but where consent to touch is involved, social knowledge is gained.[26] This knowledge is produced through sexuality as a way of "situating oneself in terms of one's intersubjectivity. . . . Sexuality is both reflexive and corporeal and signifies a relation between the embodied subject and others" (Butler 1989, 89). As I discussed in chapter 1, Merleau-Ponty's idea of the body as holder of meaning and tool of changing social relations is deeply influenced by existential ideas of freedom and becoming. Here his work is particularly amenable to Foucault's argument: where Merleau-Ponty helps us understand the *how* of the becoming, one of the means through which we simply do (become), Foucault helps us think through the *why*, toward what ends. Sexual acts cannot be interpreted as natural expressions of bodily knowledge or meaning; our bodies can be used to create new meanings as well as hold and express existing ones. Thus what is particularly useful about Merleau-Ponty's work in this context is that he makes clear that all sexuality is ambiguous but comes with a history; there is a sedimented weight of understanding from our personal history and the meanings of the positions that we inhabit in the social world. In Marxist terms, we make history—or here, meaning—but not under conditions or terms of our own choosing.

The ambiguity of the prostitution encounter is created through the differences in what each person needs to get from an interpersonal exchange as well as the historical and social conditions producing the site of the exchange. I am drawn here to Noah Zatz's proposal for avoiding an essential theory of sex or prostitution by imagining the prostitution encounter as a "bifurcated event, meaning different things to each participant. . . . Consider, for instance, Carole Pateman's statement, 'Prostitution is the use of a woman's body by a man for his own satisfaction' [1988, 198]. This figures prostitution as about a man's pleasure. What of the following redescription: 'Prostitution is about the use of a man's desire by a woman for her own profit'?" (Zatz 1997, 295). Here men's desire becomes a tool women can exploit to improve her economic condition, which is how sex-as-work feminists often claim to understand what they are doing. Prostitution is ambiguous precisely because it is both of these things at once. Only if sex is inherently demeaning is the sale of sex by women demeaning to them. But as Laurie Shrage points out, "If a woman's sexed body is part of her humanity, then to desire it is not to reduce her to a non-human thing, and when she yields her body sexually she does not give up her status as a human subject" (2005, 54). Allowing women their sexuality as part of their humanity is, in fact, a highly radical act; that is, conceiving women's sexuality as theirs to live in and shape over the course of time and relationship is to permit a productive engagement of power that is currently lacking in most laws that regulate the uses to which women may put their sexuality (and, by extension, their reproductive capacities). In fact, the less constrained and formally codified women's sexual expression is, the more rights women tend to have in a given society. Allowing this coextensive development of mind and body—the embodied mind—goes a long way toward recognizing the subjective development of women's agentic capacities.[27]

If men abuse women in the exchange of sex acts for money, the abuse is still criminal, but the sex does not have to be. The question is how to relearn what significance to give to the act of sex—and the act of exchange—in a social context that shames sex and the women who sell it. Decriminalizing sexual labor may help destigmatize sexual exchange, but family and economic life more generally will also need to be reconfigured if women's and men's sexual relations are going to be reimagined. The discursive construction of women as "nothing but whores" because some women engage in sex work is facilitated in part through providing sex work as the only living wage option available to them. To expand ideas about and possibilities for who women are, the conditions for who they can be must change. To realize sex radicalism's revision of prostitutes as being (simply) "women of unrestrained sexuality," the labor critique of sex work has to be rendered irrelevant through the revision of the economic conditions of private and public sexual life.

In attempting to remake social, sexual relations through extant sexual institutions, all of us are limited in the degree of change or of resignification we can effect. But we cannot refuse to act at all, and we cannot refuse existing relations simply because they are poorly constructed. In fact, we cannot help but engage them in efforts to create new ones. Perhaps prostitution is the venue through which sex radicals attempt to resignify sexual/gender relations because it is the tool that most obviously exists. They are, again, acting within power. The context and constraints of our lives create the realm of the possible, including those actions we can conceive of, think possible, and find desirable to change the constraints on our freedom.

Although sex workers coming to prostitution from a sex radical perspective are better able consciously to interrupt standard readings of commodified (and noncommodified) sexual relations, in demanding direct payment for sexual services, all prostitutes bring into question the presumably settled relationship between sexual acts, sexual identities, and sexual desire. The reflections of Ans, a window prostitute in Amsterdam interviewed by Wendy Chapkis, highlight this point: "There was a kind of power play in the whole transaction that I enjoyed. I lured the men in and I controlled most of what happened once they were inside. What I didn't want to have happen, didn't happen. That was different than having sex with men in my private life" (1997, 116). Prostitution can thus help refigure and not just mirror normative heterosexual relations.

Susan Brison argues that in some cases we have more freedom—and therefore more autonomy—when our choices are more, rather than less, constrained (2006, 195). This is the case specifically for prostitution, she says. In thinking about agency as constructed collectively and not just individually, she reminds us that the actions of some women effect the life opportunities and agency-enhancing structures (e.g., discursive construction of "woman" or employment conditions) for many women. "*Even if* having the option of legalized prostitution enhances the freedom of some women, we need to ask whether it diminishes the freedom of other women" (Brison 2006, 196; Whisnant 2004, 23–24, makes a similar argument). Because no action is completely self-regarding, all actions we take shape the possibilities for agency—specifically the social construction of identities—for others. Although true, Brison's objections to sex work assume unitary constructions, a lack of rupture within hegemonic normative discourses in addition to a lack of insurgent responses to the norms to which we are socialized. As both "women" and "sex" are multiply constructed—and need to be more so, rather than less so—it is collectively agency enhancing to have prostitutes who insist that women can separate their erotic desires from their economic activity—even within sexual labor—and that women must have the final say over the sexual uses of their bodies (e.g., sexualizing women in any field of work outside of prostitution is inappropriate). Inappropriate economic sexual objectification is what drives many women into prostitution. Rather than be sexualized in the law firm or construction office when they are trying to accomplish nonerotic labor, the women decide that because the eroticization is inescapable, they will insist on the time, place, and manner of the erotic interactions. Where women are defined so that sex is not all that they are, women's economic conditions are more likely to improve, and fewer women will enter sex work out of inappropriate objectification in other realms of life.

Sex workers open up the sexual imagination and engage in normative rupture in ways similar to how child-free women challenge hegemonic norms about proper womanhood. In constructing alternative norms of femininity, women's sexual identities, and the role of sex and motherhood in women's lives, sex workers and child-free women work to contest subjectifying norms producing women's identities and desires, thereby working to restructure the terms on which women become women, and, by extension, men become men. As gender identities are reworked, more possibilities for living autonomous lives are envisioned and enabled as the rigidity of dominant norms is chipped away at. The stigma attached to certain roles is contested, and thus the social construction of desire is engaged. As it becomes possible to inhabit "woman" in myriad ways without experiencing social stigma, more political and social opportunities begin to open up for women as well, thereby expanding the conditions of freedom within which people come to know themselves and engage with the world. What is most significant about the agency of sex workers and child-free women is the ways in which they engage what it means for women, as a class, to be agents. We do not have to agree that these choices (to forego children or to make a living selling sexual services) are ones we would choose for ourselves in order to agree that the more they are normalized, the wider the range of the definition of "woman." And the wider the range of the definition of "woman," the greater the possible deployment of one's skills and desires can be. Agency can be conceived as a political possibility in a greater number of ways than it could when stigma carved out more impermeably who counts as "good" women and who therefore gets the benefit of political inclusion.

PROSTITUTION VERSUS PORNOGRAPHY

To highlight both what is wrong and what is potentially right with prostitution, I want to compare it briefly to pornography. These are two very different kinds of sex work, phenomenologically, discursively, and legally. A comparison of the two forms of labor as discursive productions of power relations helps to highlight the dominating effects of patriarchal legal systems and the need to re-see sex work and reposition it structurally if women's collective sexual and economic agency is to be improved. The legal treatment of sex work has profound implications for the degree of stigma the work entails as well as the risks women face on the job. With the exception of ten rural counties of Nevada, prostitution is illegal throughout the United States, whereas pornography enjoys broad First Amendment protections. I want to look first at the conditions of production and the messages conveyed by pornography and then put this in the context of the legal treatment of the two forms of sexual labor.

Pornography is obviously different from prostitution in that it is a mediated experience for the consumer, but there is actual sex that is being sold. The talent making the movies engages in sexual acts for pay, making part of the transaction quite similar to prostitution.[28] But the pornography actress or model is not negotiating the sexual exchange or interaction with the customer, thereby making him confront the realness of her body and subjectivity, so she cannot respond in any way to the viewer's (the client's) response to her. The pornography talent has far less control over the ways in which her sexual acts are taken up than does the prostitute, and she has less control over the context in which the sexual representations are used or interpreted (having little to no input into where the porn is viewed), and thus she is not really remunerated for the client's/customer's use of her image (her body) for his sexual satisfaction.

This distance between the sex worker and the client is clear in the pay structure of pornography. Pornography talent do not get paid by the customer; they get paid by the act and see no more or less profit from their images whether the movie sells well or poorly (or whether the image is downloaded often), because they are paid a flat rate per scene filmed or photo shoot completed. (There are no royalty payments to those on screen; see Abbott 2000, 29.) Ironically, while her image can be used by customers for years, nearly all pornography actresses and models have shorter careers than prostitutes, given the emphasis on youth and the speed with which the industry uses up women (see Amis 2001; Abbott 2000, 26).

In most pornography, men behind the camera control the content, distribution, and profits of the images or film, while the talent have little creative control over content and see little profit from the sale of the work, although an actress usually will get to negotiate what she will and will not do for the camera. There are two primary forms of video pornography, features and gonzo. Features have some pretense of narrative, some effort to explain why the actors are having sex. Gonzo pornography, which is becoming the more common variety, is simply a series of sex scenes with no narrative. As Martin Amis (2001) found in his exposé of the move toward more extreme sexual acts in mainstream heterosexual porn, "Features porno is much, much dirtier than it used to be, but Gonzo porno is gonzo: way out there. The new element is violence."[29] Porn producers keep upping the "extreme" ante, in two ways, first with the industry generally and the move to gonzo, and second with individual women in porn, who are pressured to engage in a wider variety of more extreme acts to stay interesting to their audiences. According to one of the mainstream porn directors that Amis interviewed,

Some girls are used [*sic*] in nine months or a year. An 18-year-old, sweet young thing, signs with an agency, makes five films in her first week. Five directors, five actors, five times five: she gets phone calls. A hundred movies in four months. She's not a fresh face any more. Her price slips and she stops getting phone calls. Then it's, "Okay, will you do anal? Will you do gangbangs?" Then they're used up. They can't even get a phone call. The market forces of this industry use them up.

Philosophy professor Laurie Shrage and cultural critic Laura Kipnis have both argued that the violence of porn is stylized and situated in a context that is obviously fictional and meant to be either entertainment or political satire. But the political message of most mainstream pornography is one that dehumanizes women and fails to give voice to negotiation or women's actual subjective experience. Pornography puts words in women's mouths and is often gratuitously violent. Rather than stylized or computer-generated violence, the violence of pornography happens to real women who are abused in the name of a political message. In the words of Regan Starr, talking about filming *Rough Sex 2,*

> "I got the shit kicked out of me," she said. "I was told before the video— and they said this very proudly, mind you—that in this line [the Rough Sex series] most of the girls start crying because they're hurting so bad. . . . I couldn't breathe. I was being hit and choked. I was really upset, and they didn't stop. They kept filming. You can hear me say, "Turn the fucking camera off," and they kept going. (quoted in Amis 2001)

Thus, where the abolitionist argument has the most purchase is in pointing out the near silencing of women in most mainstream heterosexual pornography. This silencing is why it is an aspect of—or location of—sex work that is phenomenologically and ideologically more problematic in terms of facilitating women's agency than is prostitution. In prostitution, customers and prostitutes have to come to an agreement about what they will do together. Recall Ans's pronouncement, "What I didn't want to have happen, didn't happen."[30] But because pornography is a mode of sex work where the production and consumption are so far apart in time and space, there is less room for negotiation over the use and meaning of the product. The women in pornography cannot contest the ends to which their sexual expressions are used. Their images become a means to someone else's ends, and they can be used to silence the resistance of the flesh-and-blood women with whom pornography's male consumers are engaging.

Pornography matters for women's collective agency as well as for the individual women in it in a way that prostitution never will. Its influence is pervasive and expanding, and it serves an explicitly ideological function in shaping the imaginations of millions of viewers. Pornography is a booming industry that has grown in reach as the Internet has become a household utility and one no longer has to go to a public cinema or even a video store to see a pornographic movie.[31] With the glut of pornography available, porn has an ever-increasing power to shape the cultural narrative about sex and gender. Because pornography simply is not going away, and because it is blatantly ideological, it is important to think about how to intervene in, rather than trying to eradicate, the stories that are told about (and help construct) women's and men's sexual desires. Although MacKinnon's argument that "men treat women as who they see women as being. Pornography constructs who that is" (1987, 148) is too totalizing, sexual relations are certainly one central formative nexus of power relations that produce identity, a sense of possibility, and one's relations of freedom. Thus, pornography—because of its pervasiveness and its explicit function to "speak" sexual ideological messages—plays a much more central role in configuring sexual ideas and sexual knowledge than does prostitution.

The problem, as the abolitionists point out, is that the primary message of most mainstream heterosexual pornography is that women are less than fully human. That much pornography attempts to strip women of their humanity makes it such a fraught political practice. Feminist erotic dancer Vicky Funari is clear about the specific problem with most contemporary porn:

> Mainstream pornography does minimize participants in its economy. It reduces the man to nothing more than his dick and what "it" wants. It collapses the woman to nothing more than her cunt and what it's worth as a commodity. . . . Violent porn—like violent TV, violent politicians, and violent words—is part of a complex and pervasive feedback loop of violence. Most mainstream porn is part of a feedback loop of consumerism: boring, repetitive, quantifiable self-hypnosis. The porn industry has more power to deaden our imaginations and our passions than it has to hurt us physically. . . . Our only choice as women is to remake the system and pornography itself in our image, to surround our daughters and sons with images we want them to see and, more importantly, with a reality we want them to live. (Funari 1997, 30)

Rather than dehumanizing, sex needs to be seen as humanizing, as part of the practice of developing oneself in relationship with others. Women's sexual agency is deformed through much current pornographic production (the message of pornography). As with prostitution, this is not a necessary feature of pornography but rather is a function of its current hegemonic practice.

The problem with the abolitionist view of pornography is that it gives us no way to negotiate this ideological practice, no way to intervene and be part of the constructive process except to say no. If pornography is speech worth protecting, then competing ideas should be worth protecting equally. Obviously, to begin to equalize the playing field of sexual ideologies, women (and men) have to think outside of the existing pornography paradigm and generate new forms of sexual desire and fantasy. The question is, if pornography helps to sexualize and eroticize inequality, can it also eroticize equality, or eroticize difference without the erasure of women's subjectivity that makes up so much of the current pornographic content? It is an experiment worth undertaking precisely because of the inability to step outside of ideology. Resistance must be launched from within the system. Agency within pornography is a political stance, part of making meaning. If pornography cannot (perhaps should not) be eradicated, then the political, agentic response is appropriation, instigation, and revision. Pornography does more than reflect reality; it helps to create reality, to produce desire. Given that pornography does contain sexual speech—it is fundamentally a political message about sex, gender, and social relations—it cannot be refused. Because it is political, it is unlikely to be censored. But because of its political nature, alternative political messages about gender and sexual power must be vigorously promoted. Women must be engaged as agents in shaping these norms—not only as objects of desire, but also as subjects producing desire. Women must be empowered within the pornography industry to shift the discourse about the kinds of acts that bring women pleasure so that women's pleasure becomes part of the sexual horizon we are developing.

Pornography can model other ideological viewpoints aside from male dominance. Although much pornography speaks of women purely as objects, there are pornographic films and images that center women's desires and voices and work to develop a different argument about what women's sexuality is and looks like. In an interview with Jill Nagle, pornography actress and producer Candida Royalle argues that the problem is not the medium, but the message. The "societal attitudes toward sex that were revealed in pornography" and the exploitation of women's sexual performances while ignoring their needs are what is wrong with pornography. That was why she started to make her own: to change the message (Nagle 1997a, 156–57).

Although prostitution is criminalized in the United States in all but some rural counties of Nevada, pornography is treated as speech, and political speech at that, and is thus given broad First Amendment protections. That pornography speaks a political message is undeniable; but the content of that message (women's inequality) makes the criminalization of prostitution even more suspect. How does this legal distinction between pornography and prostitution matter? As many prostitutes make clear, they understand that this is about control (Niles 1998, 149; Almodovar 2006). When women try to control to whom they sell sex and how much gets charged, it is illegal. When other people write the narratives of women's desire and financially benefit, and the client/consumer never has directly to engage or to confront the women whose sex acts he (or she) purchases, then it is legal. My interest here is judging the structures of the decision-making contexts in which women live rather than the content of the decisions women make. And the legal structure separating pornography from prostitution makes little sense except as a way to control women's sexual autonomy. The same acts can take place, and an exchange of money takes place, but one has a camera to document the deed, and the other does not. In one (prostitution), women have some chance of negotiating the act, retaining control of the life of the act beyond the moment in which it is transacted, and controlling (to some degree) where the profits from her sex acts go. In the other (pornography), the woman has less control over which acts are performed, no benefit from the profits made, and no say over the use to which her sexual images are put. Thus the law only recognizes women's sexual commodification when it is least potentially empowering.

How the State Can Respond

Although state action is not the only source of regulation of sexual ideology and the shaping of prostitution, it is an important arena that needs to be engaged. There are three broad legal approaches available to dealing with prostitution: criminalization, decriminalization, and legalization. Decriminalization removes legal penalties from engaging in prostitution; legalization imposes some form of state regulation, which can be achieved through a number of, and different combinations of, means: zoning, mandatory health testing of prostitutes, brothel residency rules, required registration with state authorities, and so on. Criminalization is the tactic supported by radical feminists, and abolitionism has had the most success as a political and legal argument in the United States.

Unfortunately, making prostitution illegal has done nothing to decrease the demand for prostitution, the cultural understanding of prostitution, or the harms to women in prostitution. Instead, the abolition arguments help to continue to mark "whores" off from other women as a separate and stigmatized category; they vest in the state continued power over women's bodies and with it powers of domination and discipline; they essentialize male and female sexuality and their relationship to each other. At a practical level, criminalization contributes to some of the worst abuses of streetwalking in particular and makes it harder for women to leave prostitution for jobs in the licit economy, particularly if they have a criminal record because of prostitution work.

Where prostitution is criminalized, streetwalkers account for 85 to 90 percent of prostitute arrests, despite streetwalking comprising only 10 to 20 percent of all prostitution (Kuo 2002, 74). Additionally, "although women of color constitute approximately 40 percent of streetwalkers, they constitute 55 percent of those arrested for streetwalking and 85 percent of those incarcerated" (74–75). The effect of criminalization is control of already marginalized women, not the abolition of prostitution. Legalization or criminalization schemes seem to have no effect on the number of women who enter prostitution, but making women criminals does increase the dangers they face as prostitutes while doing nothing to solve the economic conditions that drive them into prostitution in the first place.[32] "Arresting prostitutes often serves only to heighten their isolation and estrangement, not only from friends, family, and the community but also from the very social services they may need in order to access alternative means of income" (Kuo 2002, 125). It also strengthens their reliance on pimps. "In prohibitionist countries like the United States, the legal harassment of street workers by the police drives prostitutes into the 'protection' of pimps and undermines the worker's ability to protect herself from dangerous clients by making speedy negotiations necessary to avoid detection and arrest" (Chapkis 2000, 183). Criminalization is a form of domination, not a means of enabling the production of new modes of relation in and beyond the sexual economy.

Critics of legalization schemes often rightly point out that legalization can be and often is at least as harmful to prostitutes' interests as criminalization. Certainly the one case of legalization in the United States—in rural counties in Nevada—has been quite poorly implemented and ought not be a model of feminist policy making. That current legalization schemes are deeply flawed does not mean all efforts at legalization have to be abandoned; it means that it needs to be done better. A brief comparison of Nevada's approach to legalization to the hybrid decriminalization/legalization model that the Netherlands has begun implementing offers some insight into how to approach the development of alternatives. The point of this brief comparison is to think about how to change the working environment for sex workers to enable them the greatest degree of control over their sexuality and income. Although these cases are not perfect comparisons—different jurisdictions (national versus state-level jurisdiction) and different political cultures (Dutch pragmatism versus U.S. moralism)—there are no other legalization or hybrid approaches within the United States with which to compare Nevada's model, and the approaches of both the Netherlands and Nevada are efforts at regulation rather than abolition, making them instructive counterpoints in some important respects.

In Nevada, prostitution is only legal in state-licensed brothels. "Because the state has given brothel owners an outright monopoly on legalized sexual commerce, all independent prostitution is a criminal offense. The effect is that no woman can work legally without agreeing to share her income with a state-licensed 'pimp'" (Chapkis 1997, 162). Further, although they have to work in brothels to avoid being criminals, the prostitutes do not count as employees but rather are categorized as independent contractors, so that they get no state-provided workers' benefits, nor can they unionize.[33] They have to live in the same place where they work, and they have to register with the police. In most brothels, if a prostitute needs to go into town during her weeks on shift, she has to be accompanied by a nonprostitute, and most are required to live outside of the town limits during their week off each month. They work a standard shift: twelve to fourteen hours per day, seven days a week, for twenty-one days straight. Fifty percent of the money earned per transaction goes back to the brothel management. In addition, prostitutes have to pay fees for room and board, purchase supplies (including condoms), and tip house employees. To be allowed to refuse a customer, the prostitute has to provide management with what it considers an "acceptable reason" (Chapkis 1997, 163; see also Kuo 2002, 82–84; Hausbeck and Brents 2000). In most brothels, women are required to participate in a lineup: "Prostitutes are required literally to line up and pose whenever a new customer enters, thus displaying 'his options'" (Kuo 2002, 83). It seems the only benefit to the prostitutes in this system is that they are not in danger of being arrested, as autonomy has been legalized out of the Nevada brothel system. Note that none of these requirements is necessary to brothel prostitution, as Kathryn Hausbeck and Barbara G. Brents (2000) explain in their social and political history of the Nevada system. Additionally, Kuo (2002) describes cooperative brothels in the Netherlands that provide a high level of physical protection for prostitutes while also giving individuals control over their working conditions, offering a very different model of brothel prostitution than that practiced in Nevada.

The Netherlands offers a different legal model premised in part on protecting the labor interests of prostitutes rather than focusing on the interests of third-party moralists or neighbors, as we see in the Nevada scheme. In the Dutch model, "acts of prostitution between consenting adults are decriminalized" (Kuo 2002, 88), but the conditions of work are matters of regulation since a change in the law in 2000. (Before the change, brothels and pimping were banned, but being a prostitute was legal.) Here, zoning of streetwalking consists primarily of safe parks *(tippelzones)* and red-light districts. In the former, police-patrolled parks are established where women are permitted to congregate for purposes of soliciting, and service centers are provided for women who need counseling. In the latter, brothels and window prostitution are located in specified zones in twelve cities (88–93). In some cities, the parks are located too far from public transportation or population centers to make them viable for most streetwalkers, so they risk arrest by working outside of the zoned areas. Brothels have to be licensed and are subject to health and safety regulations, and coercion, deceit, and abuse are ostensibly prohibited.[34] Registered, tax-paying prostitutes can get state-sponsored workers' benefits, but many prostitutes avoid registration because of the bureaucratic stigma attached and the risk of losing their anonymity. For example, being a known prostitute will get one barred from entering many countries, such as Switzerland and Austria, thus limiting prostitutes' freedom of movement and future job prospects (Chapkis 1997, 156–57; Wijers 2008).

The EU-citizen sex worker response to the changes in the law have been mixed but generally positive, noting particularly "independence (setting prices, organizing working hours and choosing what services to provide), an improvement in the image of the profession and the enforcement of rules on health and safety" as the main benefits to legalization of organized prostitution (Wijers 2008). There are still a number of problems with this system, including the variability by local jurisdiction in the licensing of establishments and enforcement of health codes. The Red Thread (the Dutch prostitutes' organization) is seeking more uniform laws, the establishment of a hotline to which prostitutes can report abuses, greater labor law enforcement, greater state support of independent operators, more licenses for small, cooperative brothels, and more support for prostitutes who want to leave the profession (Wijers 2008). One of the main problems seems to be with the licensing system, which works well for brothel owners but fails to protect prostitutes' privacy interests. But importantly and positively, "individual sex workers do not have to register [with police] and are not submitted to mandatory health checks" (Wijers 2008).

Although the Netherlands is a hybrid decriminalization/legalization model, it is also a hybrid legalization/criminalization model. The repeal of the brothel ban was motivated partly to improve women's labor interests and partly to protect EU women while further criminalizing non-EU sex workers. The political hope was that by regulating prostitution, trafficking could be eliminated, and thus the "problem" of non-EU women within the Dutch border would be ameliorated (Hubbard, Matthews, and Scoular 2008, 142; Dag Stenvoll, personal communication, September 7, 2009). Further, brothel regulation has led municipalities to decide that there is less need for safe parks for streetwalkers, and so in the last few years, cities have begun closing these spaces, further marginalizing the needs of streetwalkers. Thus, the effects of the Dutch reforms have been decidedly ambiguous. On the one hand, the health and safety of some women have been aided; on the other, the most marginalized and at-risk women are now further marginalized and at greater risk. Although the Dutch model is in many ways preferable to the Nevada model, it is hardly a panacea. (In fact, any prostitution-specific policy is going to be inadequate to address the problems of sex work.) What is clear in reviewing the Dutch model is that labor interests can be protected in a law that emphasizes cracking down on coercion (trafficking) while legalizing consensual sex work, and that state regimes are better at regulating sexuality than they are at promoting freedom. This is why I argue that decriminalization should be the default position, and women working independently should be free from state intervention in their labor.

The problem with simple decriminalization is that third parties, such as escort services or brothel owners, can still take advantage of women's labor, so although the state is no longer disciplining her sexually, her labor interests would not be improved tremendously. This is why some sex-as-work advocates argue that legalization is preferable to decriminalization because, as the current status of pornography demonstrates, if we leave it up to the goodness of the hearts of porn producers or pimps to obtain consent and insist on safer sex practices, we have not done all we can to help women (see Alexander 1998, 225). Decriminalization can aid the sex radicalism agenda, but it alone does not meet the needs pointed out by the sexed labor analysis. To shape sexual and labor relations more positively—to create different social relationships within sexual commerce—prostitutes need to be decriminalized, but any business that hires sex workers needs to be regulated in line with meeting women's interests. This will not necessarily change the violence that is faced by streetwalkers, especially in the short term. But the most significant policy change that could improve the lot of streetwalkers is a change in broader economic and social service policies, specifically drug rehabilitation and child protective services, rather than any prostitution-specific policy.

Consider the results of Ine Vanwesenbeeck's study of the experiences and psychological states of prostitutes in indoor and outdoor venues in the Dutch system, where criminalization is not a factor affecting the experience of sex workers. She found that about one-quarter of prostitute women suffer severely. About half of the women are doing far better than the stereotyped view, at or slightly less well than the average nonprostitute woman in the Netherlands. And a little more than one-quarter are faring "quite well"—even better than the average nonprostitute woman.[35] "The differences in how women fare appear to depend on five factors: childhood experiences, economic situation, working conditions, survival strategies, and interaction with clients" (Kuo 2002, 95). The first two of the five factors are nonspecific to prostitution; the final three are related to changing the structure of the job of street prostitutes. The first two factors need to be addressed by changing women's overall cultural and economic well-being so that they do not face the worst forms of prostitution as their best employment options to start with. Those who suffer under exploitative labor conditions in sex work do so for two main reasons: criminalization, and poverty and abuse outside of prostitution. Prostitution policy can only address the former. Hence, economic policy is prostitution policy. Additionally, domestic violence policy is prostitution policy: "At highest risk were those women who would never prostitute but for great economic necessity. 'Abuse by a private partner' was often the source of this extreme economic need" (96).

Economic policy is also prostitution policy for another reason. Women are not the only beings affected by exploitative labor relations and poverty. Although male violence crosses class lines, frustration and lack of a sense of control are factors leading to violence, and economically dis-empowered men are more likely to feel frustration and a lack of control. Sociologist Martin Monto's study of seven hundred men arrested for trying to hire street prostitutes indicates that most violence against prostitutes is committed by a small proportion of clients (2000, 76) and that "motives for buying sex differ according to social class. . . . Non–college graduates were more likely than college graduates to say they wanted to be in control during sex" (81). This drive for control, which can lead to more violent client–prostitute interactions, is not surprising given that these men have little control in other areas of their lives. The argument that violence correlates with men's economic frustration corresponds to the reports cited above from sex workers at the high end of the industry (call girls, escorts), who report more satisfaction with their work and much less on-the-job violence.

Legalization schemes have tended to protect community interests and brothel owners' interests, but as currently constructed, they operate almost as oppressively as criminalization for the women involved. Individual interactions may be therapeutic or resistant, but the material structure of the work environment requires serious sex-as-labor challenges in order to meet the possibilities sex workers can provide for a more open sexuality discourse while avoiding the perpetration of the harms abolitionists have documented. Thus, state policies must be a target of feminist activism. But if the only goal is abolition, not only is the policy doomed to fail, it is also doomed to punish poor women while failing to attend to the primary reason most women go into sex work: economic need. Because the state sets so much of the discursive and material framework within which women's sexuality and work are determined, the law and its enforcement are central tools for changing the framework and social meaning of prostitution and women's sex.

Ideally, feminists would move to supporting a hybrid legalization/decriminalization model that opens up space for women to operate singly or in small groups without state intervention while labor law and safety provisions were applied to any third-party business interests working with prostitutes such as escort service providers or corporate brothel owners. Certain features of current practices would not be part of an ideal state policy. For example, prostitutes must not be required to register with police, and self-employed independent operators should not be required to get a state license. Registration is a further effort to monitor and control prostitutes—to mark "whores" off from "respectable" women—and is not necessary to allowing women to engage in sex work or to receive services that might put them on the path of improving their working conditions or leaving prostitution. Registration schemes are also unlikely to work. Prostitutes across the globe generally try to avoid complying with registration imperatives, even when it would garner them public benefits. Partly this is because of the temporary nature of most prostitutes' work in the field, and partly because they wish to avoid the bureaucratic stigma of registering (Kuo 2002, 132).

Another reason to opt for a hybrid model rather than simple legalization is that the latter just shifts the site of the problem. With sex work illegal, the result is paternalism, the daddy state telling women what is good for them. The profit the state here gets is that it has a heavy hand in deciding what kind of sexuality and gender regimes are permitted and desirable, and which are not. With legalized sex work, at least as it has been practiced in Nevada, the result is the pimp state, where the state functions as an (abusive) pimp and profits from women's labor, but leaves the sex worker almost as bad off as before.

Decriminalization could begin to change the structures within which sex work—and sexuality more generally—develops and is regulated and produced. It is not meant to be a panacea for all of the harms of prostitution; nor can prostitution alone transform sexual relations between men and women (or between gays or lesbians or transgender people). But because the law helps regulate (that is, it does not determine but it shapes) not only the way we interact sexually but also the desires we have and can imagine and the relationships we build from those desires, changing the law is one important element in creating a more just sexual order. Because the state can be just as coercive as individual pimps and traffickers, it is important not to displace one source of coercion for another. The power of the state to do good—promote more equitable economic policies, for example—must be harnessed while not handing the state more paternalistic powers over women's sexual self-development.

To be clear, prostitution is a fraught, ambiguous, multivalent phenomenon (or, more accurately, phenomena). As Hynes and Raymond rightly note, "The challenge for governments today is to punish the growing numbers of sexual exploiters—traffickers, pimps, procurers, and buyers—while not penalizing the women who find themselves in conditions of sex trafficking and prostitution" (2002, 221). Hynes and Raymond then argue that prostitution needs to remain a crime, but it seems to me that turning women into criminals in order to punish their abusers does precisely what they and I agree needs to be avoided: penalizing the women involved. Women are penalized when the state marks their only lucrative career option as illegal primarily because of a rigid sexual ideology that says "good girls don't." It is important to be clear that making a job category legal does not condone harm on the job. For example, "lawyer" is a legal (noncriminal) job category, but the sexual harassment of lawyers (to use Hynes and Raymond's example) is not legal. One way to challenge the conflation of sex with violence is to insist that sex be allowed while violence is not. So long as we continue to say that to allow prostitution is to allow victimization of women, we are assuming a natural law of male sexual desire as violent. But surely men can be sexual without being violent. Although sex may be used as a tool of violence, that does not mean that sex is always violence. As with marriage, violence must be strictly not tolerated while the institution— or the sexual practice—is allowed to continue. Selling sex in some ways denaturalizes it, demystifies it, and makes it something more obviously malleable and variable.

My argument is not that prostitution is an idealized, playful free-for-all of radical sexuality; nor is it that commodification should be the model of sexuality we as a society or as feminists ought to work toward. I do contend, however, that prostitution as it currently exists has many different contexts, that most of them need to be revised, and that decriminalization is one tool to bring about necessary changes within the institution. A specific context that needs to be altered is the dire economic circumstances that drive some women into sex work. Prostitution in and of itself is neither inherently good nor bad, but prostitution engaged solely because of a lack of viable alternatives is coercive, and coercion is inherently bad in that it undermines both freedom and autonomy. Economic policies that lift wages so that the working class can make a living wage are necessary so that anyone who opts to engage in sex work only does so out of a desire for sex radicalism—to engage directly in the challenge that prostitution can provoke in the sex/gender order. When employed in sex work under conditions of autonomy, freedom, and legality, prostitution can help to dismantle the Madonna/whore dichotomy structuring women's affective, sexual, and legal lives.

CONCLUSION

Prostitution should be decriminalized not because it is an inherent good to be protected, but first because of the harms that criminalization brings with it, and second because of the role—even if limited—prostitution can play in helping to bring about a new sexual ideology where women's and men's sexual desires and imaginations are more open. Prostitution needs to be made less exploitative, and the way to do that is to shine light on it, not to cloak in under the darkness of criminality. It is not a "good enough" option for poor women, but instead, like all work available primarily to poor people, it needs to be made better through worker's protections and legal recourse for abuse. So long as women are criminals, they are seen as appropriate targets of abuse. By decriminalizing prostitutes, the state would be saying that they are worthy of respect and worthy of recognition as laborers and as agents. Decriminalizing prostitution would also make it easier to help women who are abused and who want to get out of the business. They would not have to confess to being a criminal in order to obtain help, and if they are no longer engaged in a crime, they will not be turned away from domestic violence shelters because of criminal activity. Decriminalization here functions as a form of "radical incrementalism" that collapses the distinction between reform and revolution and recognizes the power of "domination but also represents the social field as a dynamic, multi-dimensional set of relationships containing possibilities for liberation as well as domination" (Sawicki 1991, 9).

The sex-as-work analysis is an answer to the abolitionist definition of sex and gender construction that still recognizes the problems of current sexual practices. To insist on the labor value of sex work, and to insist on women's understanding of sex as work and not just as sex, is to contest the meaning of sex that says that men make women objects through sexual acts; it is to insist that the sex women have has meaning for them and not just about them. This does not require giving up any challenge to the economic system that limits women's options to sexual labor or poverty. Nor does it mean that any prostitution sex is prima facie liberating. It does mean that men do not get to define all of the terms on which sex is engaged, even under conditions of asymmetrical power relations. To change the conditions of sexual labor—to legalize it; to organize it; to bring women together to challenge male definitions and male power of ownership within prostitution (focusing on women's cooperative brothels rather than male pimps, for example)—is to wrest agency from the configurations of power within which one exists; it is to face victimization and find agency within it. To change the legal terms of prostitution is to launch a challenge to extant configurations of power, to insist the formal rules governing women's sexualized existence evolve in the face of women's sexualized challenge to the construction of sexuality as dominance/male, submission/female. Such a challenge or denunciation is a form of sexual metaphysics, a means of bringing about—or aiding the becoming of—altered sexual social relations.

From Foucault and Merleau-Ponty, we know not only that sexuality is an important component of social relations, but also that the ways in which we are inserted into the world produces the things we desire. Prostitution may well serve as a means to produce different kinds of sexual relations, but these are likely to be different in degree rather than kind. Prostitution only becomes an option for sexual and economic resistance because of the current configurations of sexual desire and economic production. Sex work cannot help but be tainted by patriarchal gender norms and sexual ideology. Although decriminalization should be implemented because it can enable the development of programs to improve prostitutes' lives directly, decriminalization will not turn a flawed system into a fully agency-enhancing one. That said, it is important to change the contours of prostitution so that fewer women are harmed through it in addition to enabling women with privilege to express sexual protest and sexual alternatives. Decriminalization is a first concrete step on the path to both ends.

Some forms of pornography and prostitution are damaging to women's sexual agency, self-determination, and bodily integrity; yet there are instantiations of pornography and prostitution that promote positive female sexuality and self-identity. The problem then is not sexual labor writ large, but certain manifestations of it. If sexuality were immaterial to agency or human flourishing, then outlawing varieties of sex work might not matter. But, as Merleau-Ponty and Foucault make clear, sexuality is central to human becoming. Further, such outlawing targets the result of the problem of sexual and economic inequality, but not the problem itself. Finally, efforts to get rid of pornography and prostitution will not work, which we know because they have not worked anywhere that they have been tried. The problem that the state should target is women's sexual victimization, exploitation, and manipulation; their lack of freedom, autonomy, and agency; and the lack of support for their efforts to build on sexually embodied knowledge. This sexual victimization is connected to women's lack of economic agency and objectification in contexts where such objectification has no positive purpose. Women need to be seen legally and culturally as fully human, and their sexuality and their life plans as fully their own. Laws that limit sexual expression while failing to redress sexual violence and economic oppression do not contribute to this view of women as fully human, a class for themselves.

CHAPTER 5

Agency and Feminist Politics

The Role of Democratic Coalitions

If agency is a temporally and structurally situated process of becoming a subject with others, what are the political possibilities for intervening overtly in the subjectification process? Although many sites and practices might potentially foster the core competencies of agency, I focus here on what has long been a central component of feminist activism: coalition politics. Acting in coalitions is a mode of political action that highlights the development and deployment of agency as ethos that I have been discussing throughout. What makes coalition politics particularly promising for my purposes is that not only can the *process* of engaging in coalition both develop and encourage the expression of agency, but the types of *outcomes* successful coalitions can produce may also be particularly suited to expanding the possibilities for agency within the different contexts of women's lives. Thus, coalition politics engages both elements of agency that I set forth at the beginning of this work: autonomy (as a deliberative, critical capacity) and freedom (the presence of enabling conditions). Although coalition politics have been discussed by numerous feminist theorists for a variety of purposes, my focus here is only on coalition politics as a site of agency, as a means of developing the conditions of agency.

Coalition politics as I discuss and develop it in this chapter is based to some degree on already conceived politicized identities, yet these bases for politics are temporary and shifting—contingent foundations, if you will. The solidarity achieved by coalitions is to a large degree political rather than ontological, taking cues from identity politics but expanding on narrow and exclusionary identity claims. Further, the coalition politics that I am advocating here brings together the trivalent dynamic of political claims that I outlined in chapter 1: redistribution, recognition, and political inclusion. It encompasses both multi-issue organizing within a group and single-issue organizing across a spectrum of differently affected groups. This approach can accommodate the need to account for shifting capacities for agency across context and time within individuals and among groups. Following Jodi Dean's lead, I argue below that because the specific remedies are worked out in participatory democratic spaces that are fluid in both membership and intended targets, they can increase the level of citizen accountability and responsiveness to specific needs for remedying group-based harms, without essentializing the group identity.

I begin this chapter by discussing the principles that guide coalitions and the activities that can render them democratic and open, making this type of political activity particularly promising for addressing the agency concerns that I have raised in this project. These principles and activities include reflective solidarity, receptive generosity, and mutual respect. Here I am borrowing from Jodi Dean, Romand Coles, and Bernice Johnson Reagon as they have considered different strategies for enacting and justifying feminist coalition politics. I then clarify how the development and deployment of political agency (both individual and collective) is linked to both political identity and the practice of coalition politics. Next, to explain and justify the type of coalition work I have in mind, I consider different bases for coalitions that can respect and foster the agency of their members, specifically identity-, issue-, and empathy-based coalitions. I conclude this chapter by thinking about the limits of coalitions in promoting the ethos necessary for agency's development, looking at the role of rights in protecting threats to agency in democratic practice.

PRINCIPLES AND PRACTICES OF COALITION:
AGONISTIC OPENNESS AND MULTIPLY FOCUSED REMEDIES

I am offering coalition politics as a way of thinking through how to do politics while being attentive to the shifting capacities and sites for agency. Opening ourselves up to the critical assessment of others, and ourselves, is not a programmatic strategy for politics so much as it is the suggestion of the reflective stance necessary for devising specific political goals and agendas. The specific policies and proposals, actions and interventions, that groups decide to engage must emerge from the actual reflective process and hard work of fighting out the meaning and necessity of different competing identities, issue stances, and political values. In all cases, part of this reflection should include considering the trivalent nature of particular problems like domestic violence or sex work. As Nancy Fraser notes, undertaking such reflection requires considering in all cases the feasibility of using measures associated with remedying one type of injustice (for example, redistributive) to address inequities associated with another type (for example, recognitive; see Fraser and Honneth 2003, 83).

A coalition politics that is geared toward significant but ultimately contingent identities as well as focused simultaneously on the multiple sites of power and types of remediation necessary to combat injustices must be based on some difficult, but ultimately quite rewarding, commitments and competencies. Ultimately, only coalitions comprising people who are committed to the hard work of agonistic, pluralistic openness and democratic debate can succeed over the long term. These groups require participants to embrace a critical perspective on power and privilege and a willingness to listen to others when the ideas espoused seem to threaten the core values and unity of the groups. Two types of activity in particular are critical for developing and sustaining such coalitions: reflective solidarity and receptive generosity. The first is developed by Jodi Dean in her 1996 work *Solidarity of Strangers*. The second is proposed by Romand Coles in his 1996 *American Political Science Review* article, "Liberty, Equality, Receptive Generosity," which brings together Bernice

Johnson Reagon's seminal coalition politics work with Nietzsche's concept of gift-giving virtue.

Both reflective solidarity and receptive generosity suppose that political unity is based on communication and an understanding that "us" and "them" do not have to be diametrically opposed or antagonistic categories.[1] Understanding both agency and identity intersubjectively requires seeing that "we" are who we are only through our engagement with, and critical reception of, "them" and who they are. In liberal theory, the achievement of both liberty and equality comes through you, the subordinated, becoming more like us, the more powerful. Reflective solidarity and an ethic of receptive generosity recast liberty and equality so that both are achieved as "we" become more like "you," and vice versa.[2] Equalizing the liberty to lead self-defined good lives conducive to the development of our capacities for agency requires, at least in part, the proliferation of radical and plural democratic spaces for generous and receptive participation. An openness to future possibilities and the freedom to achieve them are born out of the desire to know and receive the other. Coalitions built on communicative democracy do not lead necessarily to a shared identity; instead, they lead to shared commitments and a renewed reflection on who "I" am and "we" are when I do politics and engage with others (see Dean 1996, 3; Coles 1996, 387).

Such openness to others will not require us to sublimate our dignity to the will of those who are antagonistic to our claims and projects, nor work to a final position agreeable to all before moving on with the actual pressing of political claims and projects. Michaele Ferguson (2004) addresses these concerns when she discusses the potentially antagonistic relationship between individual and collective agency in democratic settings, a tension she relates to the concept of Kantian collective friendship. With this model in mind, a democratic collective agency that respects the individual's agency and projects is akin to an active, ongoing conversation. Individual subjectivity persists while individuals are in a state of collective negotiation about the content and terms of shared concerns. Furthermore, because we can never be fully transparent to each other, the conversation is ongoing, requiring repeated articulations and justifications of identity and issue boundaries as well as items on the political agenda. Thus, individuals must be committed to making normative judgments between and among citizens and their claims because the terms of connection are often in some dispute. Because we can never become precisely like other persons, we must cope with our differences by continually exercising judgment about the usefulness of particular solidarities on particular issues for our ongoing personal projects. Ergo, being open to critique and the sometimes painful confrontation with strangeness and competition in the authoring of the meaning of experience and identity does not mean *endless* openness or require us to forego making judgments about these novel claims. As with agency, democracy is not a thing; it is an ongoing drama that we enact. We are never done with coalition building, with solidarity, with achievements of increasingly amenable conditions of equality and conditions conducive to agency.[3] Nor are we ever done with considering the sources and content of our goals or the means we can and want to use to achieve them. Developing normative competence and ethical commitments is as much an ongoing process in collectives as it is within individuals.

One of the goals of an agonistic openness to others is reflective solidarity, a state that is never fully achieved but can be more or less approximated depending on the commitment of the parties in coalition. Reflective solidarity requires an openness to difference that will allow criticism and disagreement to emerge, rather than demanding unity within predetermined public identity category boundaries. It is "based on the idea that the ties we create through our discussions and questions engender shared expectations of recognition and response" (Dean 1996, 16). The multiple interconnections we share and the differences that our complex subjectivities inevitably lead to are the bases for both appeals to solidarity and the connections we can generate. These are "ties created by dissent" (29). Through truly hearing the critiques of others who want to share in our politics, we can interrogate our own privileges and construct together a more comprehensive and broadly valuable political agenda.[4] The goals and values that people devise through open democratic discussion "serve as mediations surpassing the actual interconnections among members. . . . The expectation that one will adhere to the norms of the group is the primary attribute of membership, of being validated as one of 'us'" (Dean 1996, 18). Thus it seems to me that in the same way that the conditions of our political possibility and resistance as individuals are produced through the excess and disjunctures of the imbricating subjectifying discourses producing our situation, so too coalitions generate their most radical ethical commitments and political demands through the diversity of subject positions held within and articulated through the group. Further, by pushing the group to interpolate different differences into political demands, and by doing so through reflecting on and engaging with the demands of others, one is simultaneously caring for one's own needs and ethos and the needs and ethos of the group. Agency is developed and political conditions revamped through the input of, to use Foucault's formulation, counselors and guides: friends who can be truthful with us.[5]

The need for reflective solidarity comes from the sense of hopelessness that feminists (and others on the left) sometimes encounter about the possibility for effective political activity, and paranoia surrounding efforts to do politics without engaging in acts of exclusion, which arises from the endless fragmentation and attention to the microdetails of difference and ever narrower scope of identity. Reflective solidarity, like an ethic of receptive generosity, can serve as a way of reconnecting the insights gained from antiessentialism and poststructuralist critiques of earlier feminist work to the daily practices and political needs of women. As Dean rightly reminds us, "If we forget or disregard the importance of solidarity and responsibility, we risk allowing investigations into localized configurations of power to replace our awareness of and complicity in larger relationships and interconnections" (1996, 67).

Thus, while it is important to leave open the category of "women" (or "battered women" or "sex worker" or "mother") as a site of contested meanings, and while such openness will facilitate a politics of coalition building that can allow for new identity concepts to emerge from engaged political action by those to whom the concepts will apply, such openness does not mean emptiness. Locating those facets of particular situations that have been marked, embodied, and made politically and socially meaningful can give direction and force to political action. Further, the focus on contingency needs to be balanced by an appreciation for the significance of our habitual ways of being in the world. Habits do not negate the freedom sought by contingency; rather, they mark the potential durability of changes wrested through creative approaches to existing problems, for both good and for ill. Once we have done the hard work of opening ourselves up to others and winning political battles to produce greater degrees of freedom of praxis in the world, we want them to become somewhat sedimented, habitual, and not easily erased (see Crossley 2001, 115).

Collective life and collective governance require us to articulate broadly applicable counternarratives to the dominant forces shaping both the background and foreground of our daily life, habits, and desires. As I hope my discussions in chapters 2 through 4 made clear, I am a strong proponent of celebrating the small victories and the daily acts of agency that contest imposed gender norms and identities. Still, these victories are not sufficient as political challenges to patriarchy, sexism, homophobia, racism, and the like. "Not only are microdisruptions and performative reiterations hardly enough to challenge the continued brutalization of women in their homes, the reinvigorated homophobia of the Right, and the continued economic exploitation of women across the globe, but such disruptions and reiterations themselves, as their theorists admit, can backfire, either manipulated by their opponents or co-opted into new practices of violence" (Dean 1996, 66). This is why inclusive, democratically conceived, and accountable coalitions are desperately necessary. Otherwise, counternarratives hold little threat to the status of sexist or racist hegemonic narratives as hegemonic, and little hope of becoming broadly viable, nonstigmatized alternatives.

One of the primary requirements of opening up identity categories and constructing a coalition-based politics that embraces reflective solidarity is the need to respect people as they present themselves to us. Bernice Johnson Reagon makes this point in her discussion of a "women only" event she attended. The event organizers attracted people they would not have included in the category "women," even though the attendees very much defined themselves as belonging to the group (1998, 252). As the basis of political and social organizing, a commitment to nonessentialism means that we, the organizers, do not get to be the final arbiters of the identity category's content. Allowing people to name themselves and dealing with them from their perspective is, on Reagon's terms, what it means to treat each other with respect, and respect is crucial for beginning to speak to and truly listen to each other. This is the starting point for the ethic of receptive generosity that Romand Coles develops and that I adopt here as the grounding principle of coalition politics.

He writes that coalition politics (which he aligns with radical democratic politics) must be "animated by a desire for the others' otherness, with all the cooperation and agonism this implies" (Coles 1996, 380). Although on Reagon's account coalitions can be positively brutal and run the risk of nearly destroying the agency of the less powerful members, Coles seems to assume that there is usually less hostility among coalition partners. Regardless, however difficult this cooperation and commitment to accountability might be, the alternative is worse. "Without a *generosity* born in our efforts to receive the other *as other*, . . . equality and liberty will likely take up strategic positions within imperialist identities that assimilate, smother, or explicitly deny otherness" (Coles 1996, 380, emphasis in original). The point of coalition politics is to give and receive. If we do not really listen to others and thus open ourselves to the possibility for change—if we do not act as and engage others as counselors and guides—then we end up with a politics that bears out the anti–identity politics theorists' fears of yet another viciously normalizing hegemony. If we do open ourselves up and really contemplate what we might learn from and have in common with others, we might discover something important and new about ourselves and the lives we do and can live. Thus receptive generosity is a process of becoming more open to others and an outcome that links our situations to that of others, as well as the satisfaction of our needs through creative uses of cultural politics and economic programs. We become not only better equipped but also more likely to think it necessary to tie, for example, the funding of high-tech assisted reproductive technologies to prenatal care for poor women because of a greater respect for different types of motherhood and an understanding of the importance of challenging the norm of the ideal mother.

Thus, the process is transfiguring, or it fails. "Reagon calls us . . . to agonistic dialogues with others, in an endless effort to grapple discerningly with what is foreign, to recognize and create the possibilities that the contingencies and indeterminacies infusing our own and others' identity afford" (Coles 1996, 384). Here we can see that coalition is also oriented toward the future. It has the potential to transform the actor and the people with whom she coalitions, offering at least a proliferation of options for performing and understanding identity, but it also, one hopes, transforms the material, political landscape for the better for future generations (Reagon 1998, 250–51). The process of working with others to see commonalities and to define our political concerns on our terms may touch us profoundly or very little, but at its best, it will leave us more open-minded and tolerant and less willing to impose constricting norms for roles and status positions (identities) on others.[6] As Nancy J. Hirschmann argues, "greater participation in the processes of social construction allows greater freedom not for *self*-imagining per se but for *group* imagining *within which* individuals can partially define and construct themselves. Without the discursive categories defining the larger context, the individual has no vocabulary with which to imagine the self." Further, the logic of social construction means that community must be the instrument of change; while freedom must be expressed by individuals, "its conditions are made possible by community" (2003, 237; see also Nussbaum 1999, 54).

Despite the potential of receptive generosity, caring for oneself and others, and the productive opening of the boundaries of stigmatized identities to reconfigure the possibilities for women's agency, there are also dangers. Reagon describes coalition politics as containing overwhelming pressures that threaten the core of one's identity and commitments. "Under these pressures generous receptive agonism can easily dissolve into strategies of assimilation, withdrawal, or outright subjugation" (Coles 1996, 385). These are the dangers that we must fight against, and the reasons that such work is draining and often unpleasant. At times it may be only our principles that compel us to do the hard work rather than a strong affinity for those with whom we do it. The reason we often cycle in and out of political commitments is not just because our capacity to be efficacious political agents varies across time and context, but also because we tire of being open and accountable, generous and kind to people we often quite simply do not like. As Coles writes, "Generosity . . . is not sufficient to sustain one's life in this work in an uninterrupted manner. . . . You cannot stay there, in the midst of the most agonistic difference. But generosity is one of the key virtues that keeps one coming back for more" (1996, 380). It is true that coalition politics is combative and fraught with anger, ego, and perhaps desperation, as well as some sense of danger to one's beliefs about oneself. But it is one way to stay principled and work to infuse principles into politics. In coming together to see our differences more clearly in addition to seeing our similarities, we might well further separate ourselves from others. But we can, at least at times, open ourselves up to a range of possibilities for how to be and act in the world.

Coalition Politics: Interrogating Identity and Cultivating Political Agency

Coalitions can serve as sites for deliberately bringing together people who are presumed to belong to one identity group or set of related identity categories in order to expand the meaning of identity. Within a coalition, individuals can work to articulate explicitly which interests they do and do not share, taking a first critical step in repositioning (redefining) an identity based on internal dialogue rather than solely on externally imposed meanings. This reconfiguration of the boundaries of identity also serves to advance the recognition of members of groups who may need to gain visibility and legitimacy within a marginalized group before they have the means to seek recognition outside of it. Andrea Densham describes one example of how this process worked in the groups that came together for AIDS activism, specifically under the auspices of ACT UP, in the 1980s and 1990s. In her study, she describes the process in which groups with different although sometimes overlapping identities (e.g., gay men, lesbians, feminist health workers) united under the umbrella of AIDS activism to form a larger sexual/reproductive health activist group. Internal debates about the proper goals of the group stemmed from the different subject positions of the group members. The internal debate occurred simultaneously with the presentation to the larger public of a more or less unified front. Ideological positions that were staked out during internal debates tended to correlate to the subject positions of different coalition members, so that white men tended to focus on questions of treatment and cure, while lesbians and gay men of color argued that more attention needed to be paid to day-to-day issues of housing, food, and access to health care (see Densham 1997, 287–91). Anannya Bhattacharjee provides an example of the coalition of Sakhi, the South Asian domestic violence group with a significant middle-class membership, and the Domestic Workers Committee, many of whose members are survivors of domestic violence. The groups worked together for a time on the structural economic problems affecting both domestic workers and domestic violence victims within the South Asian community, uniting under the identity of South Asian women, although ultimately class issues drove the groups apart.[7] Similarly, a number of South Asian women's domestic violence organizations worked with immigrants' rights groups to successfully lobby for the Violence Against Women Act of 1994, specifically for the self-petitioning clause for immigrant women who are abused and reliant on their husbands for their legal status in the United States (Abraham 2000, 164).

These examples demonstrate that as groups come together because of a similarity in marginalization (e.g., different reproductive and sexual health needs that are not being met because of marginalized sex and gender status), the external recognition that is lacking (thereby impeding a fuller development of agency) can be offset by gaining allies who inhabit more privileged positions or have access to greater external resources. Gaining recognition within the coalition group is the first step toward articulating political needs and developing a political voice that can begin to be heard outside the coalition group. Both a recognition within groups we say are somehow meaningfully "like us" and recognition from people who are "not like us" is important for the role that counselors and guides can play in our agentic development as well as the necessary provision of resources to make newly imagined life projects possible. Coalitions as sites of participatory democracy encourage us to listen to the self-defined needs of others rather than determining in advance what individuals or groups of people need in terms of social and political redress for their problems. Through this process, we can begin to rethink our own political demands. If we are to be successful in sustaining coalitions, we cannot assume in advance that those with whom we are agitating for change need precisely the same outcomes that we do, even if we have articulated a similar problem with the current structures of power.

So, for example, within the battered women's movement, women of color and lesbians (of all races) have had to fight for recognition from white and heterosexual activists and push for an expansion of the standard models for understanding intimate partner violence. These struggles have led to heated, and productive, debates about whether particular policies, such as mandatory arrest, should be promoted or abandoned. Many feminists within the modern battered women's movement pushed hard for mandatory arrest when police respond to domestic violence calls. But although these policies have helped in some women's cases, they have worked to increase the dual arrest rate of battered lesbians, and they have worked against the interests of many poor women and women of color who are abused, because in those situations, where the abuser is poor and has few social ties, arrest has been shown to increase the level of violence in the home once the abuser is released from jail (see Coker 2000, 1035–37). As feminists within the movement are hearing more clearly the different needs of battered women, they are beginning to articulate together with those who have been previously excluded new approaches to police and criminal justice interventions.

Throughout this project, I have given examples of how individuals are never reducible to one identity but always inhabit multiple subject positions. Taking together the multiple identities and situations of the subject, one can draw on the agency resources provided by more privileged subject positions to augment those lacking in others. Although individuals can develop some sense of agency and political efficacy on their own, group politics works to expand the types of resources available to people and begins to equalize an unequal playing field.[8] As I noted in chapter 1, the need for collective action in addition to individual resistance "arises from the context of inequality in which these efforts [to effect change in the world] occur" (Abrams 1999, 831). To redistribute resources and destigmatize and redefine various identities, collective efforts can create conditions more favorable to such changes by pooling individual resources. Such efforts aggregate the power of individual agency and cultivate the intersubjective development of agency. Marking the similarities in political inequities and locating their structural sources serves to develop critical consciousness about the sometimes insidious ways power works: to benefit particular interests (e.g., religious or economic interests relative to motherhood norms), to alienate people and groups from each other (e.g., feminists and sex workers), to create people who are particular sorts of desiring subjects (e.g., the hegemonic desire for the heteronuclear family in the context of abuse). The development of a critical consciousness promotes normative competence and weakly substantive autonomy and a potentially broader reflection on one's life plans.

I have also discussed in previous chapters the role of habit and disposition in shaping our responses to situations and the likelihood for new, more agentic engagements with our encountered world. As cognitive and emotional understandings of situations become more sedimented, actors are less likely to take novel approaches to improving their future prospects unless something jolts them out of complacency. At their best, coalitions can bring together people who have had similar experiences, but who have responded to their experiences in ways that challenge (in a good way) their own sense of the rightness of their response or reading of the event. Faced with others who have chosen differently, their own evaluation of the source and importance of different goals can be altered or more coherently articulated, leading them to respond in new ways, to change, however slightly, their standard mode of being or acting in a situation. Coalitions offer new possibilities for challenging the contexts in which we are embedded. Such subtle (or not so subtle) shifts in behavior and interaction are the ways in which the daily structures of life are resisted and give rise to new habits for being in the world. Shifts in dispositions and competencies alter the cognitive structures of action by reconfiguring our understanding of appropriate behavior or responses to given situations and types of people (see Crossley 2001, 94–96). Although creative acts are still rooted in our larger, long-term understanding of ourselves in the lives we have always known, "periodically actions and interactions give rise to new cultural forms and repertoires" (96). When these contexts are reconfigured to some degree, there is a greater possibility that the discursively constituted subject produced therein will experience more open horizons for imagining future projects. As intersections of discursive and material power are altered, some avenues may be closed off, but it is hoped that new ones will be opened.

This willingness to see others as both importantly like us and yet provocatively different from us, and to be open to what this combination of similarity and difference can teach us about our own self-understand-ings and self-defined needs, marks an important feature of coalitions as I discuss them here. Coalition politics comprises an orientation to polit-ical praxis that requires an openness to others. This openness is criti-cally important for the role that others play in the development of our agency. Caring for ourselves in order to be active agents in creating greater possibilities for freedom requires both a willingness to stand firm when we believe we must and a willingness to listen to and reflect on the (respectful) questioning of others. One way in which we saw this kind of agentic work earlier was with the discussion of battered women who adamantly want to stay with their abusers but get the violence to stop. They challenge most of us to rethink what kinds of normative and emotional commitments could make this a good choice and not just a resignation to a lack of exit options. Through this challenge, we can learn how to think about agency differently, and to think about the dif-ferent types of political responses to intimate partner violence we need to initiate. But just as we need to be open to these women in their com-mitted affront to our well-intentioned ideas about violence and leaving, they need to be open to rethinking why they are staying and what kinds of interventions they are launching into the abusive dynamic.

It is my contention that coalitions serve two simultaneous functions: they are both a *means* of resistance through the pooling of resources, and they are one of the desired *outcomes* of political action, in that they provide a space for self-definition and the articulation of political needs from the voice of the disenfranchised. As I argued in chapter 1 when drawing on the work of Merleau-Ponty, agency is shaped not only by who we are and where we are situated but also by what we do in the world. (In particular, political agency is shaped by what we do with others in the world.) Thus, who we are shapes what we bring to coali-tion politics, and what we do in coalition with others creates the hori-zon, the future conditions, for our agency and the agency of others.

Beyond this, coalitions can bring together those who are working to change economic structures, cultural representations, and the grounds for political inclusion, thereby addressing the trivalent aspects of discrimination all at once. This multiple focus is critical because the constraints on agency faced by women are multivalent, and these valances are interconnected. Thus, for example, discussions about reproductive technologies connect to assumptions about the role of motherhood in women's lives, whose motherhood options need to be expanded, and the particular ways in which this expansion can and should be accomplished. The way in which motherhood is valued in relation to the other things women can be and do is illustrated by the increasing levels of support for (some) women's infertility treatments next to the continued political nonstarter of quality, subsidized child care. A multivalent focus on the sources of interconnected agentic constraints (pronatalism, ideal mother norms, the feminization of poverty) can lead to more comprehensive solutions for coping with the differential effects of pronatalism and gender inequities.

Connections between Collective and Individual Agency and Identity

There are two types of agency considerations at play in coalition politics: individual and collective. Depending on the political arguments pursued, coalitions can expand the capacity for both types of agency; through the process of engaging in coalition work, individuals and groups can open up space and potential for self-definition and expand the possibilities for human flourishing. As coalitions bring in members and define their goals, they exhibit collective agency to the degree such activities are engaged via participatory democratic means, through dialogue and persuasion that will probably be agonistic but is at its core respectful of the differences between members.[9] Insofar as agency is shared, coalitions offer an opening for members to serve as shrewd and sympathetic interlocutors in a manner that respects each member of the coalition as equally valuable, even if in other situations clear power imbalances would be present.

I have brought together different approaches to agency in this work in order to account more fully for its both determined and determining aspects. Agency is determined through our situatedness and our "thrown" identities—those that we inhabit without having chosen them. Agency is a determining capacity in the potential for resistance to imposed meanings of thrown identities, although this potential is more complicated than liberal autonomy theory allows. Recall that the liberal perspective locates agency in the individual as a tool to be used in and against the social world. In different ways, both poststructuralism and phenomenology locate agency in the social, intersubjective realm. Although I have drawn on a liberal capacity for agency that is psychologically based and internal, I have considered this aspect of agency as it is primed and developed in different contexts on the bases of social and political configurations of power that produce particular kinds of subjects. That is, the individual has an interiority that is a crucial part of agency and that can be wielded against forces of domination, but only if she has conditions ripe for such contestation; further, this interiority (this consciousness) follows from being (her social situation). We can see the necessity for a political strategy that holds out simultaneously the importance of individual agency and the social situation or salient social groups in which she is located and from which she can draw support.

Further, examining how we absorb the imperatives of gender and racial identities at the level of habit or personal desire can help us locate places where resistance is both possible and needed. Bringing the multiple meanings of agency together demonstrates that agency is a capacity of the individual as she is uniquely situated in the world, but agency is also a possibility of the thrown identities, the collectives to which she belongs (or those into which she is placed). Constraints on the capacity for agency are similarly structured for similarly situated people. Attending to the commonalties among women's structural positions is also important for increasing the recognition and promoting the development of women's agency because it allows us to see the accumulated gains women are making, to recognize multiple types or levels of political change, and to take seriously other women's work as models for our own actions (see Naples 1998, 344). Focusing only on the local micropractices or microeffects of power offers little insight into the ways power shapes us as individuals whose personal situations are significantly like others who share our socially relevant identity markers.

Those who are part of new social movements seeking to change the political landscape to make it more just and equitable are often those defined or who define themselves as marginalized, as marked in some way as other to the dominant ideals of race, gender, or sexuality. This marginal or outsider status "shapes the contours of their political, social, and economic interactions. Similarly important are the definitions of 'self' that are developed within marginalized communities" (Densham 1997, 291). Self-identity and group identity are distinct but imbricated. In the context of uniting on the basis of thrown identities, people can use the debates within groups to challenge the content and meaning of those very identities. The process of developing an identity internally allows the group not only to establish membership, but also to set about challenging the dominant ideas about the group. "Marginalized communities, through this process of remaking an identity, are also acting to transform the parameters of political debate by, for example, actively challenging the status quo's construction of their own identity. Such a challenge opens a public discussion of who can legitimately construct a group's identity" (291). Reconstructed identities challenge the terms on which groups are considered under the law and in the economic sphere so that challenges to the imposed meanings of identity can be not just recognitive claims but redistributive ones as well. These identities are not just oppositional, of course; they are in dialogue with dominant ideals and competing internal group ideals of identity. Through negotiation and resistance, "communities produce internally constructed identities, ideologies, and, ultimately, agendas and tactics for political participation" (286).

I do not mean to suggest that the basis of coalition politics is only political rather than ontological, only rational and nonexperiential. Coalitions are based on both adopted and thrown identities, in part because both of these types of identities matter significantly to the meanings individuals give to their lives and to the ways individuals and groups are seen and treated by outsiders. "Woman" and "mother" are examples of experiential or situated, embodied knowledge identities, but even these can be evoked as political rather than ontological. As I discussed in chapter 1, the instability of identity categories, whether thrown or chosen, does not negate their usefulness for political and social purposes. Identity categories like "whore," "woman," "mother," or "battered woman" are ways of marking and claiming a space that is useful and temporarily circumscribed in some way but is not possessed of fixed borders.

Resistance is not in the service of freeing true identities from some repressed state; rather, resistance is in the service of exerting agency in the construction of future possibilities, the future discourses and institutions within which we will construct our ongoing projects (of identity and whatever else). To mark that open future, agents need a point of entry. We need a point onto which to latch our projects now and from which we can work with others to collectively challenge those discourses and institutions that are thwarting our attempts to direct the creation of our own present and future. For some, at least, the critical entry point into political dialogue with others is identity—not essentialized identity, but institutionally meaningful identities, ones that we might not like, that we want to challenge, but that we have available to us and offer us some way of making claims (see Ziarek 2001, 26).

Identities thus function as tools enabling us to make sense of the world, "to render coherent, meaningful, and viable for oneself ones' shifting commitments as well as changing attachments" (Benhabib 1999, 347). On Seyla Benhabib's account, identity serves as a marker of space and time, not a marker that is closed and fixed, but one that is woven in with the stories that others tell of their lives so that we can make sense of particular experiences and consider particular ways of rendering our situations more just. A fluid sense of the boundaries of identity is necessary if one takes seriously the intersubjective development of self-understanding. Understanding ourselves comes through understanding others and our connections to them. Moving from individual to collective identities, Benhabib argues that the multiply situated subjects who make up political groups allow a collective's identity "the capacity to generate meaning over time so as to hold past, present, and future together" (1999, 352). Although each member of the group will not have identities that map perfectly onto each other, there is some degree of synthesis in the individual's identity over time and across identity groups as well as some degree of synthesis among the group members.

Benhabib and I share a common concern in our projects: to think about how people learn from others and from seeing experiences in new ways that might provoke changes to significant attributes of the self, while still possessing some coherence to one's life. She focuses on a developing "narrative" of identity and coherence that comes through "character," which she defines as capacity to make and adopt an attitude toward politics (Benhabib 1999, 346). I borrow this particular part of her work because of my argument that working in coalition can be transformative while being based on important central understandings of oneself and the commitments that follow from particular identities. Giving coherence to one's life through the capacity to adopt a general attitude toward social and evaluative goods is akin to the receptive generosity required for sustainable coalitions. Both involve the development of a political stance that allows for a reconfiguration of aspects of identity (like the role of motherhood) through reflection with others on the reasons why these specific elements of identity carry the weight that they do. Thus, the agency enacted and developed through self-definition (both individually and collectively) is an integral part of a successful politics that extends the contexts and conditions for human flourishing.

Trivalent Injustices and Complex Coalitions: Fostering Agency and Pooling Resources

As identities are made relevant and salient through political, legal, sociocultural, and economic configurations of power, groups that work to challenge the meaning of gender and to redefine identity categories need to battle on all of these fronts; none is more primary than the other, and all are necessary targets of remedial practices. I argued in chapter 1 that gender discrimination is a trivalent phenomenon requiring a multiply focused agenda: the question of whether gender inequity is primarily a problem of misrecognition, maldistribution of resources, or political exclusion misses the way in which each of these valences of gender inequity is mutually supportive of the others. Focusing on redistributive, recognitive, or state-centered aspects of gender injustice can lead to different remedies, and each of these types of remedies is necessary for polyvalent identities that suffer stigma and discrimination.

Coalition politics can serve as an especially useful way to launch polyvalent political actions. First, because members of coalitions are differentially situated, some bring an already greater share of social capital and economic resources to the table than others. Pooling resources is one of the benefits of coalition politics. Second, bringing multiple perspectives together demonstrates a fuller range of political needs surrounding similar problems. For example, Densham discusses the way political claims became more inclusive and responsive in the case of lesbian activists in both AIDS activism and breast cancer activism. In the former case, lesbians insisted that attention be paid to the cross section of individuals affected by AIDS and the diversity of issues that were relevant to different groups living with the disease. Lesbian activists helped to develop a coalition of progressive AIDS organizations, forming the group ACT NOW to challenge ACT UP and others "to understand the medical crisis of AIDS in a larger economic, political, and social context" and to insist on inclusivity (1997, 290). The political agenda of AIDS activism was broadened by the insistence of those directly affected by the disease that the more resource-rich members of their groups listen to the many voices who had a stake in the larger political agenda. In the case of breast cancer activism, lesbians helped feminist health activist groups learn from the lessons of AIDS and additionally insisted that feminist groups attend to lesbians' specific needs for direct-care services and to the problem of sexual orientation discrimination among health care providers. The lack of research funding for and outrage about AIDS and breast cancer were linked to the broader issues of women's and poor people's access to care and the medical community's lesser regard for their sexual and reproductive health relative to white men's concerns.

As Densham observed, the tactics one uses as means of resistance come about as a result of the intersection of ideology with identity; the particular types and degree of social and political marginalization shape access to and comfort with different types of resources. "Those most disenfranchised from institutional resources will most heavily rely on internally developed institutions, such as media (alternative newspapers), philanthropic organizations (Aestra [*sic*] Foundation), or service organizations (programs like Meals on Wheels for HIV-positive people or women living with cancer), and will be less likely to look to traditional avenues for effecting change" (1997, 298). This marks another reason why coalitions among groups of people with greater and lesser economic, cultural, and political resources are so important. Without these different perspectives, the solutions that get proposed exhibit not just a failure of imagination about different ways of meeting needs (both social service and legal changes, for example), but also groups that do not have mixed voices often do not even hear what the needs of the worse off are, as we saw in the previous chapters in the case of activism around domestic violence and the kinds of legal interventions and service provisions most needed as well as the rhetoric of problem definition in the case of alternative reproduction and women's reproductive health more generally. Bringing together the sex radical critique with the sex-as-work analysis of prostitution also highlights how economic marginalization and discursive stigma are more likely to be successfully fought together than separately.

Consider the example of infertility. Marginalized women who are coping with infertility are not brought into the world of in vitro fertilization. Infertility is not seen as a problem for them in the same way that infertility among white—and especially middle-class—women is.

If these women banded together, we might end up with a social health policy that focused more on prevention by examining the social and environmental causes of infertility and ways to deal with the environmental hazards rather than after-the-fact treatment. A broader coalition on this issue might examine the money and time devoted to reproductive endocrinology rather than to universal access to quality basic gynecological care, or even women's specific risk factors and complications from other types of illness. That is, questions about why women's health care is focused on women's reproductive capacity might get asked, and answered, in a way that brings about a change in priorities. If pronatalism were less pronounced, greater relative resources would be devoted to these other types of health care concerns. This shift in funding priorities would lessen the grip of pronatalism by contributing to the alteration of the primary definition of woman as mother. This brings us back to the need to gain a greater understanding of the sources of power and the opportunities to change them if we engage broad coalitions of women who all feel the force of pronatalism, but who sit in different relationships to it.

COALITION POLITICS: UNITING AROUND IDENTITY, ISSUES, AND EMPATHY

The relationship between the agency of the individual and the agency of the collectives of which the individual is a part was addressed previously in my consideration of the boundaries of politically relevant groups and the ways in which they coalesce. Groups become politically relevant on the basis of imposed categories as well as of chosen or self-created ones. Although I am most interested here in politically relevant groups that exist because of imposed categories—those that are constructed through encountered configurations of power—I am also concerned with the way that people take up those imposed categories and combine their relationship with them with their relationship to chosen identities and interest groups. Both types of identities and interests can be significant sources of and constraints on the embodiment and development

of agency. Coalitions often become a mix of people united for an amal-
gam of reasons like identity, self-interest, and shared ethics or justice
concerns.

Developing an integrated strategy for putting justice and remediation into political practice requires public deliberation by a "counter-
hegemonic bloc of social movements" (Fraser and Honneth 2003, 86).
One could conceive of this bloc in a "united front" scenario where
groups join together to form an integrated strategy for redressing maldistribution and misrecognition along all majors axes of subordination.
Or one could conceive of a more decentralized scenario where coordi-
nation between different groups is an ongoing process and alliances are
loose and shifting across time and context, although the various groups
ideally would all be working at their more local concerns along axes of
redistribution and recognition and political remediation. My discussion
of coalition politics assumes this second scenario.

This type of coalition moves us beyond the demand assumed by
some earlier feminist activists that coalitions be based on similarity
of experience. Mary Eaton, in comparing lesbian battering with the
domestic battery of heterosexual women by their male partners (1994),
explicitly calls into question whether or not there can be a basis for the
construction of coalitions between these groups of battered women,
given the clear distinctions in some of the causes of domestic battery
in each case. But as she hints, and as I discussed in chapter 2 with the
greater success of mainstream battered women's groups when combined
with community-specific organizations, coalitions of affinity and reflective solidarity might well be appropriate in this case. More generally,
groups can be united by similar events even when there is great variation
in the experience of particular phenomena. Although there are some significant differences between lesbian and heterosexual domestic violence,
with the particular intersecting forms of power supporting lesbian battering (e.g., heterosexism/homophobia) somewhat distinct from those
supporting heterosexual battering (e.g., patriarchy, economic devaluation of women), there are also overlapping concerns (e.g., sexism, racism).

Further, with some understanding that battery, regardless of its causes, is wrong, then affinity and empathy, combined with identity-based motives, work together to form a strong, cross-cutting basis for lesbian and heterosexual women to work together on redressing domestic violence. Viable political unity does not necessarily require commonality of experience.[10] Shifting alliances can when necessary attend simultaneously to both the specificities and the commonalities of, for example, male-on-female and female-on-female violence, or the desire to stay and the desire to leave.

This is particularly true once we remember that identity is not something one is, it is something one is *in relation to* something (or someone) else and something one is *becoming* through those relationships with others. Paying attention to the contingency and ongoing development of identity and the affinities of experiences rather than requiring identical experiences, and paying attention to the political and social realities that mark certain aspects of our identities as relevant and related to others in new ways, helps us to build more meaningful coalitions. Then, as our relationships with things (structures) and other people shape our identities, refocusing on those relationships can (although it will not necessarily) remake those identities; thus, we can privilege different elements of those identities as we work to resignify their cultural and political meanings, engaging the process of becoming more self-consciously (that is, ethically).[11]

Consider, for example, the coalitions that were formed and I hope will continue to grow in the planning and executing of the April 25, 2004, March for Women's Lives. In reframing the issue motivating the demonstration from one specifically about abortion rights to a larger question of the intrusion into private medical and sexual decisions (beautifully articulated at the march by ACLU director Anthony Romero), the original organizers of the march were able to meet the ongoing critiques about class and race bias in political agendas that had been made by self-defined feminists for decades, as well as to broaden the coalition to include other stigmatized or discriminated-against groups via the articulation of shared values. So gay men and lesbians, many of whom at the march were using the reclaimed identity "queers," were marching for reproductive freedom in part because of the underlying values of privacy and antisexism that unite the groups. Additionally, Latinas and black women were brought into the center of the coalition shaping the agenda of reproductive choice around access to contraception (emergency or otherwise), prenatal health care, and nonracist medical care in addition to abortion access. The march and the coalitions built through its planning and execution reflect the mix of empathy, identity, reflective solidarity, and self-interest that any truly democratic, lasting coalition will need to survive and win important local, state, and national legislative and judicial battles.

The fact that these values are lived by embodied beings who are brought together by related experiences of marginalization and discrimination clarifies why identity remains one of the primary ways of organizing both collectives' and individuals' political values. Merleau-Ponty and Simone de Beauvoir both spoke to this point in considering why it is that certain groups are more politically relevant than others and how those groups coalesce. As "political transformations pass through the aggregated power of groups, and theory must allow that these groups are brought together less by rational calculations of interest than by common situations and cultural formation" (Whiteside 1988, 100), our theory must account for the generality of embodiment as related to and mediated by structures of economic and political inequality. Thus, both issue-oriented groups brought together through reflective solidarity and identity groups brought together through their relationships with "practico-inert structures" (Kruks 2001, 120; Young 1994) create more lasting bonds and an expanded sense of possibilities in the world without requiring precisely the same sets of experiences writ large for political communication and identification to be possible.

A purely issue-based coalition, such as that which Nancy Hirschmann seems to suggest as the way out of the problems with identity politics, is less convincing for respecting and encouraging agency and meeting the needs of new social movements than that of a coalition based on a reformulated identity politics. According to Hirschmann, "politics is about issues: the concrete identification of oppressive power in specific contexts" (2003, 218). She prefers issues as the foundation of political action because they meet her analysis of the three levels of social construction and limits on women's freedom (see chapter 1, note 12, this volume).

> Issues are temporal and specific, discursive and social constructions in the most literal sense: they come into existence as a result of expressly felt need and desire, but they must be identified and named in order to exist. Like identity, issues arise out of experiences that socially and historically constitute the meaning of who I am and what I want. Like interests, however, issues are not given or fixed but rather change in response to variable experience and material need. (Hirschmann 2003, 218–19)

Hirschmann notes that interests and issues change in response to various experiences and material needs, but as I have argued, so do salient aspects of our identity. Rather than discarding identity as the basis for political commitments or coalitions, I suggest that we need to retain identity and add to it an understanding of how issues expand both our commitments and coalitions.

The struggles we are fighting are multivalent and ongoing—and the political agency that I have been discussing also is constrained or enabled differently across situation and time. We cannot think of our interests (at least those engaged in any way with fundamental, socially and legally freighted identity categories) in the present apart from the past and future orientations of our agency and our projects. To the degree that our political praxis and political compatriots form the horizon in and with which we experience the world and engage our projects, thereby constituting the core of our personal and political agency, our identities and agency are formed through these ongoing commitments. So Jodi Dean is only partially correct when she writes that a coalition politics of tactical solidarity, such as that proposed by Hirschmann, is problematic because, in relying on "the contingent meeting of disparate interests, solidarity is reduced to a means, subject to the calculations of success of those seeking to benefit from it" (Dean 1996, 27). She claims that viewing solidarity instrumentally necessarily entails conceiving of interests and needs "statically as well as strategically." Thus, "solidarity becomes the currency used to purchase other ends" (27). Coalitions that engage only in means–end rationality do not generally serve the purpose of building community and long-term changes in recognition and redistribution, nor do they engage the crucial value negotiation and development of participatory democratic skills that are essential to a progressive politics in a multicultural society. Dean sees tactical solidarity as putting differences aside in order to achieve a specific end, thereby reducing solidarity to a means of entering the political debate rather than as a precondition for democratic discourse. Such solidarities reject identity politics by throwing out identity and focusing only on the politics (28). There are coalitions where this occurs; however, these do not have to be the only types of coalitions we engage, nor the only coalition goals for which we strive. We can have strategic coalitions that serve limited purposes, recognizing all of their flaws, while striving within our related groups to create ongoing networks for fundamental change in the economic, culturally representative, and legal systems. Although Dean is right to be wary, issue-based coalitions both strategic and empathetic have their place in our repertoire of political tools wielded to alter the discursive and material terrain producing subjects and the conditions of their agency.

The "we-ness" of the groups we might wish to encourage is mediated by something outside of or beyond the actual relationships of group members. There is a cognitive dimension to the relationship that extends beyond feeling and habit, although these may well be the things that initially draw us toward one another. Traditional identity politics have run into problems because as the groups come together, conflicts quickly arise over the goals of solidarity and criticism—that is, wanting to be united on the basis of experience or group similarities, but also wanting to attend to what often ends up being group leaders' failure of accountability for their own privilege. Because identities overlap and sometimes conflict, neither ascriptive appeals nor appeals to tradition or custom are enough to bring about any sort of lasting solidarity. This is why I began my discussion of coalition with the cognitive elements of solidarity that are necessary for justifying one's political commitments and choice of some groups over others and that help explain the mix of experience and reflection—identity and issues—at the core of our political commitments and coalitions. The only way to solve the problems with conventional solidarities and conventional identity politics is to open up communication within the group or among differing groups; otherwise, the groups are unaccountable to their members and they become homogenous and isolated.

A Juridical Injunction against Democratic Excess

What is being resisted through coalition politics is the configuration of subjectifying norms and discourses limiting the possible ways of becoming ourselves as sexual, embodied, gendered, raced beings. We are thus resisting not just the individual nexus of power within which we live, but the collective conditions of our possibility, of our mutual recognition, of the creation of both material possibilities and stigma within and across groups. Such an understanding of the purpose of coalition politics leads us to the need to be vigilant in respecting, defending, and bringing into being the rights of others and not just ourselves, as rights mark out our collective and intersubjective relationships, at least as much as they mark trumps we hold against others (see Ziarek 2001, 68).

In chapter 1, in my discussion of resignification as an aspect of resistant agency, I noted Butler's point that "resignification alone is not a politics" (2004a, 223). When Butler makes this point, she says that resignification is not sufficient in part because it can be put to both conservative and projective uses. Thus, we need to know which of those uses has value and which does not. Butler argues that the norms that help us answer these questions "cannot themselves be derived from resignification. They have to be derived from a radical democratic theory and practice; thus, resignification has to be contextualized in that way" (2004a, 224). I have offered here a particular vision of coalition politics as a way of developing that radical democratic practice in the service of agency and as means of judging and becoming competent in a range of norms that guide our actions. If resignification is not enough to open up the conditions of agency, neither is democracy, even radically democratic practice. Such (coalition, democratic) practices are important and useful as they build the capacities and become part of the shared processes of agency, but democracy is always fraught with danger, especially for individuals and groups whose conditions of possibility are limiting to the sense of self and desire that they are trying to achieve, which brings us to rights.

In part, rights are what are being fought for in coalition, but they are also a bulwark against encroaching nonrecognition by others. Rights are precisely on the order of a norm of recognition enabling us to enter into the imaginative domain of future possibilities. As Butler says, we require norms of recognition to be able to imagine these possibilities. "The thought of a possible life is only an indulgence for those who already know themselves to be possible. For those who are still looking to become possible, possibility is a necessity" (2004a, 31). That is, if we rely too heavily on democratic means to achieve the material and discursive ends of creating the conditions of normative possibility, we run a high risk of being lost in a sea of opposition to the very conditions that make self-understanding and a projective sense of agency possible. (It is the problem of majority tyranny, which can happen even in minority groups.) The state is not a foolproof bulwark against this danger, but as minorities mark out normative claims to recognition, political inclusion is essential to guard against the dangers of democracy (despite its merits). Hence, part of what a radical democratic politics tries to bring about and institute, to guard against its own potential failings, are rights claims, claims to a space within power relations that is more secure than the current positions of radical democratic actors. Rights claims change the nature of the relationships that we have with others, recreating (even if only slightly) the critical distance and relationship between self and others and self and norms. Such rights are also the conditions of, and a hard-fought product of, agency.

This demand for legal inclusion or recognition is not a demand for becoming part of a static status quo. As Ewa Ziarek reminds us, "although the performative declaration of rights by disenfranchised groups always refers to the existing laws, it also maintains within itself 'irruptive violence' enabling the repeatable break from the existing legality" (2001, 70). This performative aspect of rights guides us toward the future—the democratic ideal of creating a future habitus together that better meets our needs. As we rearticulate rights claims to render them meaningful for living and becoming in new forms, not simply for reiterating given imperatives, new subject positions, identities, and political signifiers are created. "By enabling the production of new political signifiers, the reiteration of rights not only stresses the historicity of the political form of democracy but also opens its 'incalculable' future" (71). Rights become part of a collective ethos, the collective practice of freedom. In Patricia J. Williams's formulation, "rights are to law what conscious commitments are to the psyche" (1991, 159). Rights articulation and arguments for rights-granting are thus forms of collective normative competence.

Rights are not ends in themselves, but they are markers of a point in power relationships; they are a form of recognition. As Williams writes, "For the historically disempowered, the conferring of rights is symbolic of all the denied aspects of their humanity: rights imply a respect that places one in the referential range of self and others, that elevates one's status from human body to social being" (1991, 153). Yes rights delimit and separate us, but a world without such boundaries has not meant "untrammeled vistas of possibility but the crushing weight of total— body and spiritual—*intrusion*" for African Americans, as Williams argues (164, emphasis in original), but also for would-be mothers, for battered partners, and for sex workers. Legal recognition for prostitutes, rights for reproductive autonomy, rights to protection against abuse despite the nature of one's relationship—all of these would open up vistas of possibility rather than close them off. The right not to be beaten; the right to live in a nontoxic environment; the right to reproductive health care; the right to engage in sexual commerce—these rights would refigure the place of women in relationship to men, and different groups of women in relationship to each other. To have a right to some status or to be free of some effect is not to guarantee full recognition of one's life goals and desires—nor is it to be free from stigma—but it is a rearticulation of relationship, a remarking of the shared social field within which agency develops. Thus rights also become essential tools in facilitating the collective development of agency. (This is especially true beyond the context of empathetic coalitions.) Although they are insufficient as ends in themselves, rights are important steps on the road to a radical revisioning of who counts and what is possible by establishing the norms on which we depend for our intelligibility in the social world (see Butler 2004a, 33).

CONCLUSION

Although identity does not determine agency, the source and malleability of the identity categories we choose and find ourselves thrown into are intimately related to the types and scope of individual and collective agency that we can develop and enact in the world. Coalition politics respects contingency and instability, both through its provisional capacity (coalitions can be short or long term, and organized around one or more issues) and its potential to reorganize or transfigure one's personal identity. Thus, I keep identity central to agency for two principal reasons. First, at a basic level, it is a salient concept; it is what motivates many people to engage in politics (see, generally, Monroe, Hankin, and Van Vechten 2000). Second, so long as some identities (e.g., black woman, lesbian) are still stigmatized, we need to account properly for the role of identity in politics; because gender is intimately tied to many of the most stigmatized identities, gender politics—that is, feminist politics—

must account for the imposition, legal definition, political deployment, and potential for disruption of identities. Economic structures, legal codes, and social norms still manifest themselves in discriminatory patterns on the basis of the perceived or professed identity of citizens. The world is still constructed as though identities matter. Mobilizing on the basis of oppression (in order to challenge that oppression) may require us to mobilize on the basis of identity, even if we disagree with that category or if we contest the full contents of that category.

While all marginally competent, adult persons have some capacity for agency and autonomy, understanding that agency in any meaningful, rich sense as both a capacity that is variously limited but can be honed and differentially deployed and a process that is nonlinear and inconsistent requires situating the individual in her social world and accounting for the many layers and sources of contextualizing relations of power that envelop her. I contended in chapter 1 that autonomy and agency are never found in some pure core self untouched by society, yet agency as the potential for self-consciousness about a life plan and the availability of choices as one works to achieve one's life goals does not have to be abandoned as a result of the pervasive, swirling presence of discursive and institutional power. It does require always attending to the ways that individual agency is imbricated with collective agency, such that the politically and socially significant groups in which one is a member, and the power of these groups to enact changes on the social horizon, always play a role in the availability of political, economic, and social options as well as the definition of self and goals that one constructs.

As coalitions become more than just particular demands and sediment into normative commitments about what we owe each other and share with each other and why, they can change our sense of self and our own life projects, goals, and reasons for them. If agency is a political prerogative—if agency is constituted by and through the discursive norms we are saturated with and the opportunity structures that are present to us, as these are taken up by individuals with all of their psychological quirkiness—then new ways of being can come into the world if we engage the political and change the particular constellation of norms and opportunities of our context.

I have worked throughout this project to attend to both the procedural and the substantive elements of agency in part because I have been balancing the need to account for the real, pervasive influence of the social world on individual and collective agency, and the need to avoid making an overly deterministic (and pessimistic) argument about the possibility for acting as an agent in the world. My argument is that structures shape agency, but agency is not reducible to structures, precisely because actors relate to structures in different ways across time and issues (e.g., a financially well-off, white, educated lesbian relates to the same political and legal system differently, depending on which issue she is working on and which identities she is articulating). Further, structures themselves are mutable, but the individual's agency is not necessarily tied to any specific shift in a given institution. Procedural accounts of agency as self-realization and as reiteration and performativity have been combined with substantive concerns for politically and economically opening up the conditions producing subjective desires, phenomenological locating of sites of and sources for socially significant practices of gendered embodiment, and calls for normative judgment, competence, and accountability. By insisting on a trivalent approach to coping with constraints on women's agency, I have tried to suggest ways that agency in some realms can be pressed into service in other areas where agency is lacking. A trivalent approach has also been used to argue that existing inequalities in one realm require diligence in all realms, given how imbricated the social, political, and economic spheres of life truly are. My suggestion of coalition politics to address existing limits on women's agency in different times and places continues this multiple focus. Coalitions cope with the substance and process of agency by providing a location for articulating one's needs, a context where norms and the outcomes of power relations are (I hope) challenged, judged, altered, and enacted, and a network of interaction where social goods (such as modeling of different ways of life and resources to achieve certain goals) are provided.

Thus, coalition politics offers one framework for rearticulating the problem of stunted agency, stigmatized identities, political devaluation, and economic discrimination. How can we talk about women's victimization without negating their agency or eliding the differences among and between women? By locating the source of victimization in particular structures that might feel completely oppressive but usually leave some room to maneuver; by seeing the maneuvering for what it is: hard work at self-definition and for self-respect and regard from others; by granting that one can be a victim in some circumstances and agentic in others (or both at the same time); by recognizing that systemic problems require systemic solutions, and systemic solutions do not occur through the acts of one person but by working in concert with others—even if we do not always like them—in order to engender systemic change; by recognizing that some systems oppress some women more than others, and that we can discover how to benefit more women by looking at and learning from these differences; and through the hope that empathy and ethics will motivate us to want to help others combat problems we have worked through, while remembering that helping others is not the same as saying we know that our strategies will work for everyone, or that we have any legitimate basis to decide for someone else what her "correct" interests and choices are or should be.

NOTES

Introduction

1. Both Kathi Weeks and Susan Hekman have described the impasse in feminist work on agency and subjectivity similarly to my assessment here as they, too, search for a way out of it. We want, in Weeks's words, "to endorse the critiques of humanism, functionalism, determinism, and essentialism without denying the possibility for agency" (1998, 1). Hekman's response of emphasizing the discursive subject is similar to mine. The discursively constituted subject has an "I" that is the basis of her creative engagement in the world, but that "I" is social, not presocial. The discursive subject is thus "always both constituted and constituting" (1995, 198). Hence, identity—the "I"—is deeply connected to agency as one's creative engagement in the world, a point I develop in chapter 1. There are also affinities between my account of subject formation and agency and Weeks's theory. But Weeks relies on standpoint theory—particularly labor, standpoint, and totality—as well as Nietzsche's eternal return, Kathy Ferguson's irony as feminist practice, and Antonio Negri's concept of self-valorization to bolster modernist ideals of autonomy. I turn instead to Foucault, Merleau-Ponty, and Judith Butler, among others, taking my account of the subject and her potential in slightly different directions. Ultimately, Weeks and I have similar ends—seeing the nonessential subject who is socially constituted yet has a clearly delineated *self* from which to act—achieved through different means (see Weeks 1998, 135–37).

2. I am thus aligned with Lois McNay and many feminist Foucauldians who flesh out the later work of Foucault by coping directly with both resistance and domination.

3. I see these case studies as intersectional in the third of the three types of intersectional analyses outlined by Leslie McCall; they are examples of an intercategorical intersectional approach. When examining intercategorical complexity, one "provisionally adopt[s] existing analytical categories to document relationships of inequality among social groups and changing configurations of inequality along multiple and conflicting dimensions" (2005, 1773). Adopting this approach makes strategic use of identity categories even though one knows that accepting the socially produced contours of the group for descriptive purposes can flatten some of the complexity within them.

4. I draw this distinction and this language of understanding these distinct moments of subjectification from Lois McNay (2000). Note that moments of capitulation are different from resistance that is more individualized through its mere failure to conform to expectations or the standard definition of gendered citizenship. And in neither case does one lack or enact agency in toto. "Agent" is not a descriptive characteristic like "blue eyes." It is a process engaged in different ways and in different times throughout the course of one's life, erupting or forcibly wrought in some situations and not in others.

1. CONCEIVING AGENCY

1. See Mackenzie and Stoljar (2000, 4). This distinction mirrors the divide within types of agency described by Abrams (1999). Friedman (1997) explains the ways in which autonomy as "self-determination" has been discussed within mainstream philosophy and the major feminist critiques of autonomy theory, specifically the "substantive neutrality" requirements and the insufficient attention to the social and relational development of the capacity for autonomy.

2. See Hirschmann (2003, 36–39). We can see here one way in which agency and identity are linked, both procedurally and substantively. As Seyla Benhabib has argued, the self—identity—is not a "substrate that remains self-same over time" (1999, 353). She proposes a narrative model of identity to make sense of the continuity of self ("character") despite the changes in one's commitments. She argues that the attitude toward commitments is the identity that is "stable" though the substantive commitments and parts of the self that are accentuated are different across time and place. Likewise, the agency that is tapped and developed across time and commitment varies as the context shifts, but this agency is emboldened by and embedded in the character of the actor. "The narrative model of identity is developed precisely to counteract this difficulty by proposing that identity does not mean 'sameness in time' but rather the capacity to generate meaning over time so as to hold past, present, and future together" (353), becoming the

"ungrounded ground" of Susan Hekman's (2004) work but allowing for some necessary flux in one's identity that is missing from Hekman's account.

3. There is a distinction to be drawn between "feminist agency" and "women's agency" because not all women are feminists. When I write "women's agency," I mean it inclusively. Feminist agency would be that specific form of women's agency that has a self-conscious orientation to left (some would say "progressive") politics.

4. Mackenzie and Stoljar (2000) divide theories of autonomy into five different feminist critiques of standard uses of and meanings for *autonomy*, then consider autonomy in mainstream and feminist moral psychology as divided into procedural theories (which come in structural, historical, and competency versions) and substantive theories (which have strong and weak versions).

5. Procedural accounts of autonomy are concerned only with the way in which a decision is reached or a desire developed. The content of the decision or desire is not the thing being judged by standards of procedural autonomy. Rather, so long as the actor "has subjected her motivations and actions to the appropriate kind of critical reflection," then she can be properly considered autonomous (Mackenzie and Stoljar 2000, 13–14). One standard feminist critique of procedural accounts of autonomy has been the failure to investigate fully the role that oppressive socialization can play in stunting the ability or desire to abstract oneself from the judgments of others or the imperatives of social roles when deciding on courses of action. The basic distinction between the two primary models of procedural autonomy, structural and historical, is that structural models posit autonomy as an occurent state within the person consisting of hierarchically organized motives and value judgments. Historical models attempt to deal with the socialization problem better than structural models can by considering autonomy as a capacity rather than a state of being. This capacity "enables the agent to reflect on and critically assess the various processes (socialization, parental or peer influence, etc.) by means of which one came to acquire her desires, beliefs, values, and emotional attitudes. The agent is autonomous with respect to these processes if she endorses them" (Mackenzie and Stoljar 2000, 16).

6. See Mackenzie and Stoljar (2000, 19–21). Diana Meyers (2000) is one feminist theorist who has endorsed a historical procedural account of how we cope with the question of false consciousness, for example. Many feminists have argued that if a desire for a particular thing or way of life is a result of oppressive socialization, then that desire ought to be deemed inauthentic. Meyers argues that "falseness" here cannot be judged by the content of the desire; we should only judge the process by which the desire came to be.

7. "Normative competence" is a central component of strong substantive theories as well, but Benson has developed a "weak substantive" version that I find most useful and more amenable to the normative commitments I develop throughout this work. The strong substantive version can be found in Benson (1990). The weak substantive version is developed in Benson (1994, 2000). Trudy Govier (1993) provides another useful example of a weak substantive autonomy theory.

8. Benson (1994, 2000) develops the links between a sense of self-worth, normative competence, and autonomy.

9. Note that freedom here is meant in the sense of resistance rather than liberation of a core, prepolitical self.

10. The primary focus of chapters 2 through 4 will be on uncovering these conditions of possibility for some subjective recognition and the ways in which women are arguing for opening up the normative possibilities for "women," "mother," "wives," etc.

11. Kathryn Abrams (1999) has called this aspect of agency "self-definition," which she notes "must operate within and in relation to [one's] socialization." Someone can only be a self-defining agent once she has become aware of the way in which she is socially constituted, not to transcend social conditions, but to increase her ability to "affirm, reinterpret, resist or partially replace them" (825). These potential reactions to norms are engaged both individually and collectively as "controlling images" are contesting with alternate versions of how to live within social categories (826–29).

12. My discussion and understanding of freedom are informed by Nancy Hirschmann's work in *The Subject of Liberty* (2003). In building a feminist theory of freedom, she holds on to the standard distinction between negative and positive freedom, in part to show that they are complimentary rather than opposed, and thus both necessary for a full account of freedom. She deploys both types of freedom in order to argue that to be truly free, one must be adequately unfettered by external constraints on choices, in addition to being in possession of the personal self-knowledge and empowerment to take advantage of the options available (30). As I do, she includes Foucault's "care for the self" as a crucial element of positive freedom. Such care for self as an enactment of liberty requires subjects to participate actively in shaping the contexts in which they live and make choices. Additionally, one cannot care for one's self without listening to others; people need guides and counselors who can speak the truth to them, challenge them, help them become something (210–17). We both argue that relationships among women are important in changing the discursive and material contexts in which women are oppressed by various forms of patriarchal power.

She gives the example of battered women's shelters as a context within which someone can reconceptualize her situation. In chapter 5, I give the example of building coalitions as a highly charged politicized way of doing this. Also consistent with the work I am doing here, Hirschmann articulates three levels of constraint on women's freedom: the ideological misrepresentation of reality; the material production of reality through shaping the relations of people to each other and to institutions; and the linguistic construction of meaning and interpretive frameworks, whereby we can only be the kinds of persons that our context and language allow (86–89). The third level points to Foucault's work, while the first two levels of constraint link the "discursive understandings [of self and situation] to the physical, visceral reality of oppression" (89). I focus on the second and third levels she discusses in this chapter and the chapters that follow.

13. I borrow the language of possibility from Judith Butler (2004a, 31, 219). Thinking about freedom in this way reflects, according to Helen O'Grady, Foucault's view of freedom as "an ongoing relationship of 'agonism,' of strategic contestation and renegotiation with power's limits whereby the rules of the game can be either modified or challenged" (2004, 93).

14. Consider Maurice Merleau-Ponty's observation in *Phenomenology of Perception* that "ambiguity is of the essence of human existence and everything we live or think has always several meanings" (1962, 169). The situation in which we find ourselves always synthesizes past, present, and future, the perceiver and the perceived, the self and the social world. This ambiguity is located in and exists because of our temporality, situatedness, and meaning-making potential.

15. This argument builds on Susan Hekman's work insisting on the need in feminist theory to see the distinction between personal and political identities. This distinction is important for avoiding the pitfalls of essentialism, where talk of identity is assumed to be reductionist. Political identities cannot be neatly and completely mapped onto personal identities, but these are, of course, connected. See Hekman (2004), especially chapter 1.

16. As Butler writes, "If I have any agency, it is opened up by the fact that I am constituted by a social world I never chose. That my agency is riven with paradox does not mean it is impossible. It means only that paradox is the condition of its possibility" (2004a, 3). See her discussion on multiplicity as the condition of agency (2004a, 194).

17. "The general structures of my habitual way of being-in-the-world tend to assert themselves against radical changes in my attitudes. General structures resist change by integrating particular elements into established patterns" (Whiteside 1988, 71).

18. Susan Hekman (2004) offers another view on what makes resistance possible, drawing on theories of personal identity formed through object relations.

19. "Through deliberation with others (or sometimes, self-reflexively, with themselves) about the pragmatic and normative exigencies of lived situation, actors gain in the capacity to make considered decisions that may challenge received patterns of action" (Emirbayer and Mische 1998, 994).

20. See Emirbayer and Mische (1998, 967–69) for a rich, relevant discussion of these multiple situations as developed in the work of George Herbert Mead.

21. Judith Butler picks up on this notion of horizon as well, claiming that "discourse is the horizon of agency" because agency is found in the possibilities for resignification within discourse (1995, 135). My contention here is that a perspective drawn from Merleau-Ponty is more expansive than Butler's.

22. See Crossley (2001, 101–4) for a discussion of how agents know their situation, "and their knowledge is integral to the successful accomplishment or 'doing' of that situation, but it is an embodied know-how that we are referring to here whose operation might be unnoticed by even the agent herself and whose 'principles' . . . need not be known to reflective-discursive consciousness" (103).

23. "Bodily experience forces us to acknowledge an imposition of meaning which is not the work of a universal constituting consciousness, a meaning which clings to certain contents. My body is that meaningful core which behaves like a general function" (Merleau-Ponty 1962, 147). Or, on Simone de Beauvoir's terms, the "lived body" *is* one's situation, insofar as it defines one's possibilities (1989 [1949], 34).

24. Cataldi (2001, 89) discusses this idea of disadvantage in the context of Simone de Beauvoir's work bringing Merleau-Ponty's phenomenology to bear on women's situation.

25. "Far from being constituted solely by their oppression and exclusion, group identities may be cherished as a source of strength and purpose" (Bickford 1997, 119). Or, as Linda Alcoff reminds us, "To self-identify even by a racial or sexed designation is not merely to accept the sad fact of oppression but to understand one's relationship to a historical community, to recognize one's objective social location, and to participate in the negotiation of the meaning and implications of one's identity" (2000b, 341).

26. Extensive discussions of the identity politics debates can be found in Hekman (2004, especially chapters 2 and 3), Bickford (1997, 1999), and Moya and Hames-García (2000), among many others.

27. See Butler (2004a, 223) on the limits of resignification as political intervention.

28. The Hegelian dialectic notion of recognition where the master needs the slave's recognition in order to be the master "has its allure and its truth, but it also misses a couple of important points. The terms by which we are recognized as human are socially articulated and changeable. And sometimes the very terms that confer humanness on some individuals are those that deprive certain other individuals of the possibility of achieving that status" (Butler 2004a, 2).

29. This is precisely because, as Iris Marion Young reminds us, "the material effects of political economy are inextricably bound to culture" (1997, 148). In *Justice Interruptus,* Fraser first elaborates her argument about the need to attend to both redistribution and recognition in the case of "bivalent" collectivities such as those formed on the basis of gender or race, where injustices are both economic and cultural. She expanded her analysis in response to her critics in a series of articles in the *New Left Review* (1997a, 1998, 2000). Most recently, she has published further refinements of her theory in a philosophical exchange with Axel Honneth, *Redistribution or Recognition* (2003).

30. See discussion in Koppleman (1996, 85). This is also MacKinnon's (1993) argument about why pornography is a substantive equality issue and not a free speech one.

31. Leonard Feldman (2002) expands on Nancy Fraser's bivalent recognition/redistribution framework to include specifically political forms of injustice, marking the dynamics of inclusive and exclusive power as trivalent (maldistribution, misrecognition, and political exclusion). In her critique of both Fraser's theory specifically and the idea that the distributive paradigm is sufficient to address justice claims more generally, Young has developed a fourfold categorization for determining the failures of political institutions and the frames within which we must launch our claims (distribution, division of labor, organization of decision-making power, and the construction of cultural meanings that enhance the self-respect and self-expression of all members of society) (1997, 153; 1990, chapter 1). My insistence on a trivalent politics to facilitate the development and to promote the expression of agency is informed by both works but adopts Feldman's explicitly.

32. Dan Danielsen and Karen Engle make this point as well: "It is through interpretive struggles over the meaning of sexuality in law that we participate in the production of our selves in culture" (1995, 5).

33. In both "The Ethics of Concern for the Self as a Practice of Freedom" and "The Subject and Power" interviews Foucault makes clear the need for collective action to challenge domination and includes in that collective category "political action, social movements, and cultural revolution" (McLaren 2004, 220).

34. See Bartky (1995, 189) for a discussion of this concern in particular relation to Foucault's work.

2. SHOULD I STAY OR SHOULD I GO?

1. A note on usage: How one names the problem of domestic violence is a politically loaded issue in and of itself. In addition to the term "domestic violence," variously preferred labels include "family violence," "spouse abuse," "woman abuse," "wife abuse," and "intimate partner violence." Those who prefer the phrases "woman abuse" or "wife battering" do so because most empirical evidence demonstrates that women are much more likely to be battered by a male intimate than men are to be battered by female partners. Additionally, women suffer more severe injuries in heterosexual battering incidents. Researchers who prefer the term "family violence" do so, first, because many believe that spouse battering is related to other forms of family violence such as child abuse, and they want to understand why the family is such a violent institution as a whole. A second reason some use the term is that some sociological research suggests women batter male partners as often as men batter female partners. This "mutual violence" perspective is closely associated with the Family Violence Research Program (run by Dr. Murray A. Strauss) and its studies using the Conflict Tactics Scale. This measure has many critics, however, most of whom cite its failure to distinguish acts of self-defense from acts intended to threaten or harm. (Further methodological problems with Straus's National Family Violence Survey are discussed in Tjaden and Thoennes 2000, 19–23.) Although self-defense does not explain all of the violence women commit, nearly all studies indicate that in the majority of heterosexual cases, domestic violence is directed against women by men. Finally, "intimate partner violence" is the most recent entry into the domestic violence lexicon. This term is currently preferred by the United States government in its studies. The Centers for Disease Control and Prevention include, under "intimate partner violence," physical and sexual abuse between persons of either sex who have a current or former dating, marital, or cohabiting relationship. This is the basic definition of domestic violence that I adopt in my work. In this chapter, "domestic violence" and "intimate partner violence" will be used interchangeably.

2. I should note from the outset that most of the studies I rely on to develop my understanding of how different groups of women relate to situations of intimate partner violence are qualitative; they usually use some variation on narrative life history self-reporting, with a few relying on detailed, open-ended surveys. Although I understand that this raises some methodological issues about the

ability to generalize from these findings, one cannot build the kind of contextual, situated theory I am constructing here by relying only on large-scale survey data. Additionally, my conclusions are supplemented both by large surveys (e.g., Rennison and Welchans 2000; Tjaden and Thoennes 1998) and extensive reading of numerous qualitative studies beyond those directly referenced here.

3. I am here building on and borrowing from the work of Sharon Lamb (1999), Martha Mahoney (1994), and Elizabeth M. Schneider (2000).

4. On this point, my discussion of agency in domestic violence overlaps significantly with questions of agency and decisions about reproduction that I discuss in the next chapter. In both cases, we see that as the imaginative possibilities for how one can live a good life get choked off at an early age, the potential for resistant agency to develop is inhibited, and the likelihood that one will engage in desperate acts to uphold strict gender norms is increased.

5. Obviously, purely "objective" research makes little sense in the context of social analysis, but as a matter of degree of objectivity, using the Department of Justice numbers seems to start us from a somewhat less contestable position than numbers provided by privately funded advocacy groups of various ideological stripes. But see Hoff (2001) for critiques of the government's domestic violence numbers. In this discussion, I supplement the government statistics with numbers from academic research, but I try to avoid statistics from think tanks allied with a particularly partisan position.

6. The NVAWS and the NCVS both found asymmetry in perpetration but do generate rather disparate estimates of how much partner violence occurs in particular situations. Most researchers attribute the difference to the fact that the NCVS is administered in the context of a crime survey. "Because they reflect only violence perpetrated by intimates that victims are willing to label as criminal and report to interviewers, estimates of intimate partner violence generated from the NCVS are thought to underestimate the true amount of intimate partner violence" (Tjaden and Thoennes 2000, 19). The National Family Violence Survey does not replicate the asymmetrical findings; rather, it consistently finds "mutual violence." There are a number of reasons for this disparity, the most significant of which is that the structure of the NFVS is designed to elicit greater evidence of perpetration and is prefaced with what many have termed "leading questions" and "exculpatory statements" about the prevalence of intimate partner violence. Tjaden and Thoennes (2000, 19–23) discuss these and other methodological distinctions.

7. Tjaden and Thoennes (2000, iv). The NCVS found little difference in the rates of domestic violence between Asian Americans and European Americans,

but this may be the result of underreporting among Asian Americans keen to uphold the "model minority" stereotype. Ruksana Ayyub found that, at least among South Asian immigrants, rates of domestic violence are as high as one in four (2007, 24).

8. Tjaden and Thoennes note that many studies have found that lower-income women have higher rates of domestic violence than higher-income women, but they could not analyze income in the NVAWS because of the large number of respondents who refused to provide income information (2000, 33–34).

9. "No discernible relationship emerged between intimate partner violence against males and household income" (Rennison and Welchans 2000/2002, 4).

10. For example, they fail to account for different motives for using violence, they poorly operationalize descriptions of "minor" and "severe" violence, they ignore sexual assault and rape, and they ignore the contexts and precipitating events of violence actions. For a full discussion of the problems with the findings of "mutual violence," see Dobash et al. (1992) and Showden (1999).

11. Three canonical accounts of the battered women's movement and the structural analyses it produced are Dobash and Dobash (1992), Martin (1981 [1976]), and Schechter (1982). Note that feminists in the nineteenth century also linked domestic violence to the system of male power over women in most spheres of life, but the rising prominence of psychiatric perspectives and the advent of juvenile and family courts in the early twentieth century marked the first shift (mirrored in the 1980s) to a public discourse of family violence as better handled as a personal, private concern. See Gordon (1988) for an authoritative account of relations between feminists, social service agencies, and the state from the late nineteenth through mid-twentieth centuries.

12. *Coverture* is a term in British and American law that referred to a woman's status upon marriage until the mid-nineteenth century. After marriage, the husband and wife were treated as one entity, particularly in terms of property rights. The wife's separate legal existence disappeared, and she could not own or control her own property (unless a prenuptial provision had been arranged), nor could she file any lawsuits or execute contracts. In the United States, coverture was dismantled through state-level legislation enacted between the 1840s and the 1880s, although its legacy lived on through the 1970s, with the inability of many married women to get credit in their own name, for example.

13. Chastisement comes from English common law. Specific references to chastisement are most famously found in *Bradley v. State* (Mississippi) (1824) and *State v. Black* (North Carolina) (1864). In 1871, courts in both Alabama *(Fulgham v. State)* and Massachusetts *(Commonwealth v. McAfee)* overturned previous rulings

upholding a husband's right to chastise his wife. In 1882, Maryland became the first state to pass legislation criminalizing wife beating. But although courts and legislatures became more willing to outlaw wife battering, they still were uncomfortable intervening in any but the most severe cases, on the grounds that opening the family to public scrutiny would inhibit the natural affection that could restore tranquility to the home.

14. See Pleck (1987), Schneider (2000), and Siegel (1996). "Privacy" has shielded white and economically privileged batterers far more than any other group.

15. Das Dasgupta and Jain (2007, 160–61). Das Dasgupta and Jain surveyed both U.S. immigrant and Indian Jains, and "in contradiction to the notion of gender equality advanced in Jain philosophy, almost all the interviewees acknowledged women's secondary status in the community" (161). Overall, Indian Jains were more supportive of men's right to abuse their wives than were U.S. Jains; however, more U.S. men than Indian men supported abusive conduct (51.5 percent versus 45.5 percent). Indian men and women Jains were about equal in their support of abuse, but only 17.9 percent of U.S. Jain women supported a husband's right to use violence against his wife (159).

16. For example, Ann Goetting insists that "battering takes two: a man and patriarchy. . . . Battering is an obsessive campaign of coercion and intimidation designed by a man to dominate and control a woman, which occurs in the personal context of intimacy and thrives in the sociopolitical climate of patriarchy" (1999, 4).

17. E.g., *Scott v. Hart* (1979), *Bruno v. Codd* (1978), *Thurman v. City of Torrington, CT* (1984). See discussion in Sparks (1997, 40–42) and Dobash and Dobash (1992, 165–67).

18. See discussions in Stark (1995), Dobash and Dobash (1992, 213–50; 285–98), Eaton (1994, 208), Goodmark (2008, 80–81, 119–20), Schechter (1982, 241–55), and Schneider (2000, 22–23, 87–97). There are still some expressly feminist battered women's advocates, but they are a minority of providers.

19. Individualistic explanations can include psychiatric theories of poor impulse control and poorly developed egos, social learning theories of an intergenerational cycle of violence and operant conditioning (both are part of the battered woman syndrome), and sociological theories of families as the site of inevitable conflict. As Schechter rightly observes, in answering the question of why men batter women, "most theorists fail to distinguish the different levels at which the question is being posed. Many assert that they are analyzing what causes violence, yet unwittingly they focus on why a particular man beats his wife

and what makes a particular woman a victim. Instead of developing a social theory, they analyze individuals and call the sum of their insights about these cases social causation" (1982, 210).

20. Hence, the rise of "battered woman syndrome" as the best hope for battered women who resort to killing their partners. Battered woman syndrome treats women as helpless and psychologically deficient at the same time that it tries to explain why a woman has finally wrested power from her partner in the most violent way possible. But as Charles Ewing, among others, has noted, battered women who kill are not psychologically damaged—at least, not more so than other women who are battered; they get beaten up worse (cited in Pearson 1997, 51). Traditional self-defense pleas tend to be unsuccessful for battered women who kill because self-defense is premised on a reasonable man's response to a stranger attack. Traditional self-defense is not expansive enough to account for the coercion and ongoing fear involved in severe cases of intimate partner violence; thus, it does not see and account for reasonable battered women's responses. Documenting the critiques and defenses of battered woman syndrome would require a separate volume. See Schneider (2000) and the citations therein for a solid introduction to the legal debate surrounding battered woman syndrome.

21. Leigh Goodmark has noted that "since the advent of the Violence Against Women Act (VAWA), resources have been poured into the development of criminal and civil responses to the needs of battered women. And almost all of these legal interventions are premised on the notion that battered women want to end their relationships, invoke the power of the legal system to keep their batterers away, and ultimately sever all legal ties with their abusers" (2004, 8). However, historically, the goal of the battered women's movement was to end the violence and coercion, not necessarily the relationship. This needs to become the goal again because "the reality is that a substantial number of battered women have no intention of leaving their partners," she says, citing a study in Maryland that found that the number of women who said they intended to stay with their partners fluctuated between one-quarter and one-third of the interviewees over the course of a year (20).

22. VAWA grants are dispersed through the Office on Violence Against Women in sixteen program areas. Some grants are targeted to states, tribal governments, or police departments, and others at community organizations. Half included faith-based organizations in their priority target categories. See http://www.ovw.usdoj.gov/ovwgrantprograms.htm (accessed May 7, 2009).

23. Ayyub also reports that most of the cases she has worked with involved "issues of power sharing and control. The men tend to demand total power and

control over their families. They expect their wives to submit not only to their control but also to the control of their mothers and other family members. Even in situations where the wife works outside the home, the husband holds on to the power of deciding how and where she should spend her money" (2007, 34). See also Abraham (2000, 77–80).

24. "Much of the assaultive behavior in battering relationships involves slapping, shoving, hair-pulling, and other acts which are unlikely to prompt serious medical or police concern" (Stark 1995, 985–86).

25. Kimberlé Williams Crenshaw defines structural intersectionality as "the ways in which the location of women of color at the intersection of race and gender makes our actual experience of domestic violence, rape, and remedial reform qualitatively different from that of white women" (1994, 95). See also Russo (2001). As a methodological matter, this entire project is one that combines intracategorical and intercategorical complexity in my analysis of women's agency and choices. As described by Leslie McCall, intracategorical analyses examine "particular social groups at neglected points of intersection . . . in order to reveal the complexity of lived experience within such groups" (2005, 1774); on the other hand, intercategorical analyses "provisionally adopt existing analytical categories to document relationships of inequality among social groups and changing configurations of inequality along multiple and conflicting dimensions" (1773). Although this second type of intersectionality analysis flattens some of the complexity within categories, combining these approaches allows me to account for the particularly feminized aspects of political agency while still attending to the significant and relevant differences among women.

26. Two women in the sample identified as lesbians; both were nonbattered African American women (Richie 1996, 57).

27. Richie explores the relationship between four variables in the battered African American women's lives: "culturally determined gender roles; prevailing social conditions in African-American communities; hierarchical institutional arrangements in contemporary society based on race/ethnicity; and biased practices within the criminal justice system" (1996, 19). She then compares their experiences of these four variables to the other two groups of women in her study.

28. The nonbattered women in this study had experienced violence in previous relationships, but they left soon after the onset of violence. The point is not to explain men's battering behavior through women's subjectivity, but to explain women's desires to try to mend rather than abort an abusive relationship.

29. "While sophisticated in their political and economic analysis of racism, [the battered Black women] were the least insightful about their positions as

women in the context of a racially and gender-stratified social order" (Richie 1996, 129). Richie discusses this point in relation to growing up experiences on 54–55. Goetting (1999) and Weis (2001, 156) both reached similar conclusions about the relationship between investment in the heteronuclear family and levels of abuse.

30. See also White (1998) for a similar discussion of the role of racism and adolescent dating violence.

31. South Asian immigrants include those from the countries of India, Pakistan, Bangladesh, Bhutan, Nepal, and Sri Lanka.

32. This is not just a phenomenon of South Asian immigrants. As Erez, Adelman, and Gregory found in their study of domestic violence across immigrant groups, "In the United States, most of the women (87%) reported that the gendered division of labor was clear-cut; women focused on being a wife and mother and were solely responsible for housework and child care. In a minority of cases (17%), women were responsible for grocery or child-related shopping. Most often, they did not have access to a car or did not have a driver's license (60%). Men were responsible for gainful employment and money transactions related to the family, and only in a minority of cases (13%), the women stated that their men helped with work around the house" (2009, 44).

33. This also supports Martha Mahoney's work on "separation assault," showing that the most lethal time for women is when they try to escape from their partner's control.

34. As Beverly Horsburgh explains, for Orthodox Jews, "exposing Jewish misconduct to the Christian majority is a *shanda,* a shame that brings disgrace upon all Jews in that each shoulders the burden of representing an entire people. To some Jews, she is nothing short of a traitor who undermines efforts to combat the more pressing issue of anti-Semitism" (2005, 211). Divorce may not be the optimal solution for Orthodox women anyway, because they are so thoroughly ensconced in their communities that to divorce is to shed a primary identity. "A life of abuse among her own people could seem preferable to risking the loss of all that has shaped her existence. These women are often embedded in unusually close-knit communities tied together by a value system in which their roles as wives and mothers give coherence and sanctity to daily living" (Horsburgh 2005, 221). This helps to explain why Jewish women wait, on average, longer than other women to leave their abusive situations (eight to ten years for Jewish women versus three to five years after an initial battering episode for non-Jewish women) (Horsburgh 2005, 223n17). See also Fine, Roberts, and Weis (2005) and West (2005).

35. "U.S. immigration law endangers battered immigrant women by giving near total control over the women's legal status to the sponsoring spouses, replicating the doctrine of coverture" (Erez, Adelman, and Gregory 2009, 36).

36. "Overall, women reported being raised in households where fathers and husbands were considered authoritarian decision makers with the right to wield violence as needed to secure women's compliance and that their communities expected them to reproduce such marital arrangements" (Erez, Adelman, and Gregory 2009, 47–48).

37. Economic considerations loom large too, because the women in Weis's (2001) study who were able to leave abusive situations remarked that leaving was only possible because they were able to receive welfare benefits or tuition assistance. As the social safety net is shredded, leaving will become even harder for similarly situated women. A willingness to go public with the abuse may do women less good if there are fewer resources to help them once they have reached out. Websdale's study supports this conclusion; lack of access even to safe public transportation limited poor women's ability to get to service providers (2005, 150).

38. That investment in gender norms explains the difference in ways women try to negotiate abuse, or why they might try longer to reform a relationship rather than end it, is an explanatory model that works for heterosexual relationships but does not necessarily help explain violence in lesbian and gay relationships. A different model of the structural and subjective forces producing the lesbian battering relationship is urgently needed but is beyond the scope of the discussion here.

39. This language is Gregory Merrill's, and it refers to the minority of cases where batterers have clear limits to the level which they are willing to let abuse escalate (1996, 18).

40. That culturally differentiated services are necessary is illustrated by an example Cheng Imm Tan gives of an "Asian woman and her family [who] were unable to eat the Western food served at a local shelter. When the woman cooked her own food, a child at the shelter spat at her food because it looked 'weird.' Another child made fun of the way she spoke, imitating her, and making funny noises. Others teased her by switching her bedroom lights off and on while she was inside" (1997, 109).

41. Of the nineteen battered women that Angela Moe interviewed, ten had engaged in criminal activity as a direct result of and attempt to deal with their battering: "The women described committing crimes for three primary reasons: (1) to cope with abuse by an intimate partner; (2) to keep an abusive relationship

intact and/ or appease a batterer; and (3) to survive financially upon leaving the relationship. Thus, criminality seemed to serve as both a survival strategy and as a means of resistance" (2004, 124). On resistance strategies that buy time and build resources, see Abraham (2000), Goetting (1999), and Horsburgh (2005).

42. Because moments of attempted separation are the most lethal in battering relationships, Martha Mahoney (1991, 1994) has pushed for the development of a distinct crime of "separation assault" detached from other forms of domestic battery.

43. See Gordon (1993, 130–31) for an illuminating discussion of how social-structural shifts clearly and radically changed the strategies the women in her study used for dealing with their abusive husbands. After about 1930, a new discourse of an entitlement to absolute freedom from abuse began to emerge. In the context of dealing with social work agencies, "this new discourse meant that clients felt entitled to ask for help in leaving their abusive marriages. This was a claim women began making only when they had some reasonable expectation that they could win; until then, strategies other than head-on confrontation with a husband's prerogatives were more effective" (131).

44. Richie observed that the white women in her study sought out services and assistance from outsiders more often in part because they were more apt to identify with the "battered woman" label (1996, 97). See Goetting (1999, 14) and Jones (2000).

45. In Gordon's work on women and domestic violence in the late 1800s and early 1900s, she found that even more important that the material help offered by others was the "influence on how victims defined the standards of treatment they would tolerate" once they had respectful input from others (1993, 141).

46. As Leigh Goodmark makes clear, "economic assistance, job training, and decent affordable housing may not be concerns for white, middle-class women, but often cause lower income women of color to remain in abusive relationships" (2008, 89), an observation supported by Donna Coker's work: "Economic dependency on the partner was a significant predictor of severe violence and a primary reason women gave for reuniting with their abusive partner" (2000, 1024). Additionally, in Fine, Roberts, and Weis's study of abused Puerto Rican women, they found one of the most successful resistance strategies to be the use of welfare to get the educational and employment opportunities they needed to improve their lives within the context of staying in their relationships (2005, 288). See also Neil Websdale and Byron Johnson's (2005) study of the Kentucky Job Readiness Program, which has had tremendous success in helping rural women end the violence in their relationships or leave the relationships when necessary through a

focus on affordable housing, education, transportation, day care, and job training efforts.

47. As Goldfarb makes clear, "Aside from the danger of additional abuse, a stay-away order can impose other types of harm on the victim. These include loss of access to the abuser's income and resulting impoverishment, loss of his child care assistance leading to the victim's inability to keep a job, and loss of support from extended family and community. Separation also inflects the emotional loss attendant on ending an intimate relationship and breaking up a family" (2008, 1521). Coker (2000, 1017–18) makes this point as well.

48. "The prevalence of stay-away provisions deters many women from applying for civil protection orders and prevents many women who have gotten temporary orders from completing the process of receiving a final order" (Goldfarb 2008, 1522).

49. Grewal found that "from the experiences of the twenty-five participants, it appears that South Asian women's organizations are most effective in meeting the emotional needs of survivors, while mainstream service providers, who take the time to listen and understand the needs of the survivors were most effective in providing services such as obtaining or implementing legal orders and safety planning" (2007, 177).

50. Mandatory arrest is a deeply problematic public policy response to the very real problem of police departments not taking domestic violence calls seriously. The problems with mandatory arrest are beyond the scope of what I can adequately cover here, so I direct interested readers to Goodmark (2004) and Pavlidakis (2009), who offer thorough discussions of the problem of dual arrest in mandatory arrest jurisdictions. Because arrest does not necessarily decrease violence, and in some cases it increases the severity of violence, mandatory arrest policies ought to be abandoned. But mandatory *action* policies should be maintained. That is, although specific actions should not be mandated for domestic violence victims or police, police departments must be mandated to respond in some affirmative way to women's calls for help so that we do not revert to the days where police departments failed to show up at all, or when they did show up, asked the man to take a walk around the block. As Coker reports, "In jurisdictions that have adopted mandatory or pro-arrest policies, police are frequently mandated or encouraged to provide women with information regarding community resources and legal remedies, and sometimes with direct assistance in securing resources. Interviews with victims demonstrate that battered women value this aspect of policing and further evidence suggests that the information results in enhancing women's access to resources" (2000, 1040). Giving women options

recognizes them as agents, not victims; mandating responses to them recognizes them as full citizens and as crime victims who are entitled to respectful aid—not "saving," but aid.

3. Mum's the Word

1. To be certain, Firestone did not argue that reproductive technology would necessarily be liberating, only that technologies would be liberating "*unless* they are improperly used" (1970, 187).

2. Assisted reproduction technologies manipulate eggs and sperm outside of the body before implanting them into the intended mother's body or, in the case of gestational surrogacy, the surrogate's womb. Examples of these technologies include in vitro fertilization (IVF), gamete intrafallopian transfer (GIFT), zygote intrafallopian transfer (ZIFT), and intracytoplasmic sperm injection (ICSI). Less invasive or "low-tech" forms of assisting reproduction include the use of fertility-enhancing drugs (such as clomiphene or follicle-stimulating hormone) and artificial insemination (AI).

3. I want to be clear that I am not castigating women who opt to use ART to try to become pregnant, nor do I think they are simply dupes of pronatalism. What I am trying to do is understand the role ARTs play in the larger dialogue about women's gender identity and women's potential for motherhood.

4. See Park (2002, 22) discussing negative evaluations of intentional childlessness and summarizing Heitlinger's theoretical work on pronatalism and women's equality.

5. See, for example, Stack and Burton (1994), and the "activist Web sites" discussed in Douglas and Michaels (2004, 328–30) that seek to contest the hegemonic construction of motherhood.

6. Safer (1996, 155) discusses the influence of role models on her child-free study subjects. See also Thompson (2005, 94).

7. That the dominant subjectifying discourse presumes the naturalness of maternity and the centrality of motherhood to women's identity is evidenced by the growing cottage industry of studies looking to understand the causes of voluntary childlessness among women, though not among men. Erin Taylor approaches the topic from a different angle but makes much the same argument: "Social and cultural forces, recognized by the childfree as prescriptions to procreate and stigma for those who do not, are most often geared towards women. The result is that the choices that women make, especially about having children, may not have the same bases—or elements of freedom—as those made by men" (2003, 57).

8. *Society at a Glance: OECD Social Indicators* (2006 ed.). Rates are tied with Iceland. For a comparison and discussion of reconciliation policies in OECD countries, see Henderson and Jeydel (2007, 147–79).

9. The most recent (2002) cycle of the CDC's National Survey of Family Growth began collecting infertility (although not childlessness) information on men. This was the seventh cycle of the survey; the first six surveyed only women. See Chandra et al. (2005).

10. Carolyn M. Morell's research supports this assertion. She found that because "children are often construed as necessary to complete a woman's life, women who intentionally say no to motherhood are commonly represented as unfulfilled. Whatever experience a not-mother reports is filtered by others through the lens of deficiency" (2000, 313). See also Park (2002, 22), and the studies cited in Safer (1996, 121–22).

11. It is important to note that many voluntarily childless women are quite happy with their choice and believe it was right for them. But the fact that they are called to account and are marked as deviant demonstrates that motherhood is the assumed, default, and normative identity for women.

12. If these ideas sound retrograde, that is because there is, according to Melody Rose and Mark O. Hatfield, currently a revival of "republican mother-hood" ideology (2007).

13. In Thompson's study of fertility clinics, she "found both de jure and de facto restrictions on access to the clinics focused around normative heterosexual-ity and civic comportment" (2005, 85).

14. "At the very same time that we witnessed the explosion of white celebrity moms, and the outpouring of advice to and surveillance of middle-class mothers, the welfare mother, trapped in a 'cycle of dependency,' became ubiquitous in our media landscape, and she came to represent everything wrong with America" (Douglas and Michaels 2004, 20).

15. "Of the four magazines geared especially to wives and mothers—*Redbook, Ladies' Home Journal, McCall's*, and *Good Housekeeping*—only one of their covers in 1976 featured a celebrity mom. . . . By the late 1980s and early 1990s, between one fifth and one fourth of the covers of these magazines featured celebrity moms, often featured with their gleaming, cherubic children" (Douglas and Michaels 2004, 115).

16. See Goodwin (2005) for an excellent critique of ART as a means of eliding political responsibility for the glass ceiling. Rather than changing the structure of the workplace away from the male breadwinner/wife at home model or offering substantial reconciliation policies so that women can combine career success and

economic self-sufficiency with reproduction during their prime reproductive years, ART keeps the problem private and offers a technological solution to failed family work policies.

17. Norplant was removed from the U.S. market in 2002 as a result of serious health complications associated with it. Depo-Provera is still available.

18. "The decline in 12-month infertility in the United States from 8.5% in 1982 to 7.4% in 2002 was significant" (Stephen and Chandra 2006, 516). The same study found that college graduates had significantly lower odds of infertility than non–college graduates and "non-Hispanic black women and Hispanic women were significantly more likely to be infertile than non-Hispanic white/other women" (518).

19. For women under the age of thirty-five, "the live-birth success rate for each IVF cycle" remains at about 35 percent; the rate decreases as maternal age increases (Goodwin 2005, 34).

20. Voluntary childlessness was measured at 4.9 percent of women aged fifteen to forty-four in 1982, 6.2 percent in 1988, and 6.6 percent in 1995 (Park 2002, 26–27). In 2002, the rate was 6.2 percent (National Survey of Family Growth, reported in Chandra et al. 2005).

21. Because of the way infertility is studied, precise numbers of infertile women are difficult to ascertain, as are the racial differences in the rates. Government studies query married women. Thus, from the CDC's 2002 National Survey of Family Growth (the only general study of infertility in the U.S. population), we know that infertility rates for married non-Hispanic white women, non-Hispanic black women, and Hispanic women were 7.1 percent, 11.6 percent, and 7.7 percent, respectively (Chandra et al. 2005). Most non-CDC studies examining racial differences in infertility look at women who are seeking treatment. This is a highly problematic way of studying rates of infertility because low-income women have little to no access to high-tech ARTs. To begin to address the measurement problems with these studies, Wellons et al. conducted a population-based study in four major U.S. metropolitan areas and found that black women have a twofold increase risk of infertility than white women, and "even after adjustment for socioeconomic position, marital status, and other risk factors for infertility, this disparity persisted" (2008, 4). For more on disparate usage rates of and access to ART between African American and white women, see Feinberg et al. (2006) and Seifer, Frazier, and Grainger (2008).

22. According to the EPA, the Mohawk nation's "soil and sediment . . . has been contaminated by runoff from the Site. Groundwater beneath the Site has been contaminated with PCBs and volatile organic compounds." http://www

.epa.gov/ro2earth/superfund/npl/0201644c.htm (accessed March 6, 2008; site last updated February 13, 2008).

23. Bitler and Schmidt found that state-level poverty rates significantly correspond to infertility rates (2006, 861).

24. I recognize that there are medical causes of infertility such as endometriosis and uterine fibroids that can affect women of any social and racial group, conditions for which doctors either do not know or cannot agree on the causes. If ART can help women with these conditions in the context of a society that does not insist on motherhood, then they can aid women's agency. It is unclear how much ART can currently help in these situations, however. For example, the "presence of fibroids, regardless of race, was a predictor of worse outcomes" (higher spontaneous abortion and lower live-birth rates) with ART treatment, even when access to care is equalized (Feinberg et al. 2006, 893).

25. Roberts (1997, 259) offers anecdotal evidence for this conclusion.

26. Indeed, according to a study conducted by Becker et al. in Latino communities in the San Francisco Bay Area, children are seen as "the basis of the marital relationship: a child was thought to create a bond between the couple and legitimize the relationship. . . . [Thus] childless marriages were considered failures, and there was a widespread expectation that the relationship would end if no children were born" (2006, 883). Further, specifically in Mexican and Central American cultures, "a child, rather than marriage, is the mark of adulthood, and couples are under social pressure to have children as soon as they marry. Parenthood is a critical component of gender identity and self-esteem among Latinos" (885).

27. Rose and Hatfield (2007) discuss the return of the "republican motherhood" ideology in terms of ever more stringent regulations on abortion access: "The 21st century American state throws an increasing number and type of barriers in front of women who seek to end their pregnancies, but does not ameliorate the condition of mothers through pensions, living wages, health care, or day care adjustments. It would seem the state wishes women to bear children *and* the full economic and social cost that comes with them, even when women themselves would choose otherwise" (6–7).

28. As Thompson notes, "one way to stabilize shifting notions of what is natural and normal around reproduction is to compensate with extremely conservative or stereotypical—parodic—understandings of sex, gender, and kinship" (2005, 142).

29. Kolata (2004) captures brilliantly the loss of control many couples experience when they enter into "the fertility vortex and [find] that despite themselves, they will go as far as needed, spend whatever they can scrape up, take out second

and third mortgages on their homes, and travel across the country and even overseas for tests and treatments, all in the hopes of becoming pregnant." Other narratives illustrating the loss of control are found in Ireland (1993).

30. A recent example of this is the 2007 book *The Fertility Diet* by Harvard doctors Jorge Chavarro and Walter C. Willett.

31. Average IVF costs run $7,000 to $15,000 per cycle, with most women requiring more than one implantation before a pregnancy is achieved (Mulrine 2004). Per-patient spending can run from $30,000 to $200,000 (Goodwin 2005, 16). Ertman provides similar cost estimates, citing "total cost per delivery of between $44,000 and $211,000" (2003, 13).

32. "In 2004, a total of 127,977 ART procedures were reported to CDC. These procedures resulted in 36,760 live-birth deliveries and 49,458 infants. . . . Overall, 42% of ART transfer procedures resulted in a pregnancy, and 34% resulted in a live-birth delivery (delivery of one or more live-born infants)" (Wright et al. 2007). Most, but not all, clinics report data to the CDC.

33. The problem with the technological model as the only means to achieve one's agentic ends is that technology here fails more often than it succeeds, potentially leaving one a dupe of technology, if not pronatalism.

34. Ellen Lewin's (1994) interviews with lesbian mothers provides some anecdotal evidence to support this belief.

35. See, e.g., Parents With Attitude (http://www.parentswithattitude.com/index.php/site/about/5/index.html), Happily Childfree (http://www.happilychildfree.com/index.htm), and Childfree by Choice (http://www.childfreebychoice.com/).

36. Although a similar measure has never made it out of the House since first being proposed and sent to committee in 1999, a bill is currently before Congress that would expand access to a number of the high-tech reproductive technologies. The Family Building Act of 2009 (H.R. 697; S. 1258) deals with group health insurance plans (private market and federal plans) and seeks "to amend the Public Health Service Act, the Employee Retirement Income Security Act of 1974 . . . to require coverage for the treatment of infertility" if a plan also covers obstetrical services. All nonexperimental services are included, such as Clomid, AI, IVF, GIFT, ZIFT, ICSI, but treatment must be "performed at a medical facility that conforms to the standards of the American Society for Reproductive Medicine; and is in compliance with any standards set by an appropriate Federal agency." So, for example, purchase and delivery costs for AI would not be covered if the inseminations were to take place at home (the so-called turkey baster method). Here again, more options may be made available, but women's control

does not necessarily follow. (It is unclear how the new health care reform law passed after this book was completed might affect state support for ART.)

37. Coupled with financial support for expanding ARTs availability should be a restructuring of the workplace so that the "mommy track" does not continue to be one of the most clearly social causes of infertility. If professional women who wanted to become mothers could more realistically combine a successful career with their motherhood goals when they are at their most fertile, the ART industry would lose many existing clients and be more likely to serve the larger group of infertile women.

4. WORKING IT

1. This discussion does not apply to women who are trafficked into prostitution, and it assumes that while some women are trafficked for purposes of prostitution, trafficking and prostitution are not the same thing. For a feminist argument for decoupling trafficking and prostitution as political issues, see Brooks-Gordon (2006), Ditmore (2005), Kempadoo (2005), and Sanghera (2005). Arguments for collapsing trafficking and prostitution are offered by Hynes and Raymond (2002). On legislation regarding trafficking and prostitution in the United States, see Stetson (2004).

2. Similarly, Heike Schotten (2005) argues that feminists need to focus on reconstructing male sexuality rather than pursuing the question of why women go into sex work.

3. Although O'Connell Davidson's 2002 book *Prostitution, Power, and Freedom* falls pretty comfortably into the abolitionist analysis, her more recent work on trafficking sets her analyses more at odds with MacKinnon and Pateman and the Coalition Against Trafficking in Women, the U.S.-based abolitionist anti-trafficking group that argues that all prostitution is a form of violent sexual slavery. For example, in "Will the Real Sex Slave Please Stand Up," O'Connell Davidson argues that the failure to make distinctions between kinds of sex work and degrees of exploitation and coercion makes sorting out who is and is not a "victim of trafficking" very difficult, mostly to the detriment of any sex worker who is coerced but does not present as the idealized—and brutalized—victim all prostitutes are assumed to be. Such a narrow conceptualization of prostitutes and prostitution, she argues, limits rather than enhances the duties of the state in protecting women's interests. Thus, once again, the labor interests of sex workers are elided in the name of moralism. Her more recent work on trafficking thus fits more comfortably in the sex-as-work category of prostitution analysis. I leave her in the abolitionist group here, however, because in this chapter, I am not able to

attend to the many specific concerns of trafficking in the context of my more general analysis of the place of prostitution in the social construction of sexuality.

4. Abolitionists talk only about women sex workers, although they acknowledge that there are male prostitutes and pornography actors. While the number of male prostitutes is hard to come by (and presumably most of them are catering to a male clientele), Thomas (2000) has found that between one-third and one-half of the pornography on the U.S. market is gay male porn. And of course in straight porn, there are usually male as well as female actors.

5. Many authors, both sympathetic and not to the sex radical position, point out the economic privilege of sex radicals, and that their privilege buys them better working conditions than streetwalkers because they rarely have to deal with police harassment, bad weather, or johns who refuse to pay. In addition to starting from a position of privilege, they make more money as masseuses, fetish specialists, call girls, escorts, and exotic dancers than do streetwalkers. They also are much less likely to experience violence on the job, either from clients or from pimps (as they are much less likely to work for a pimp). On working conditions, see Bernstein (1999, 110–14) and Lever and Dolnick (2000). On differing levels of violence in different prostitution venues, see Brooks-Gordon (2006, 189–90).

6. Lever and Dolnick's (2000) study had a sample size of 998, which is quite large for a sex work study. Bernstein's work corroborates this and similar studies, noting that street prostitutes are further divided into classes on the basis not of economics but of lightness or darkness of skin tone. Despite sharing the same education level, lighter-skinned women "command the most money and take the fewest risks" (1999, 102–3). See Weitzer (2000a, 4–5) for a discussion of several important distinctions between the working conditions and experiences of indoor workers versus street prostitutes.

7. This is particularly true of high-end workers: "Studies of masseuses and escorts have found that they took pride in their work, felt the job had a positive effect on their lives, and believed that they were providing a valuable service. Streetwalkers seldom make these claims, except to sometimes assert that they provide a needed service" (Weitzer 2000a, 4–5).

8. Contributors to Delacoste and Alexander's important collection of essays, *Sex Work* (1998)—including Phyllis Lumen Metal, Carole Leigh, Aline, and Nina Hartley—explain that they got into and stayed in the sex professions because they were personally empowered by the work and see themselves as therapists and healers.

9. See Chapkis (1997, 29–30). Similarly, Merri Lisa Johnson argues that "'stripper sexuality' could be considered as something akin to other nonnormative

sexual preferences or orientations such as homosexual, bisexual, or polyamorous" (2006, 163). Where "whore sexuality" is developed as a constructed alternative to heterosexual norms, it can be productive of greater subjective possibilities. Where whore sexuality is naturalized as in the arguments of some "sexual libertarians," its potential is limiting. I pick up and develop this point further below.

10. Lewis et al. argue that "it is external social and organizational factors that create risk and safety. Risks, especially those related to violence, are highest on the streets. Working independently [without a pimp] can enhance safety, regardless of the sector" (2005, 150). This finding was confirmed by Wendy Chapkis, whose work illuminates how, whether a sex worker says her experience is that of "happy hooker" or "sex work survivor" or somewhere in between, the source of the difference in experiences is usually less about the nature of erotic labor and more about the social location of the worker performing it and the conditions under which it is performed. One of the most significant factors is whether the sex worker controls which clients she accepts and services she performs, or whether a third party does (1997, 98).

11. As Lenore Kuo makes clear, streetwalking is dangerous, but sex work writ large is not nearly as dangerous as abolitionists argue, or as television and movies would have us believe. "In all of my interviews, prostitutes appeared more concerned with possible assaults or abuse by facilitators than by customers. When pressed, however, the women I interviewed acknowledged that they occasionally encountered customers who were overly rough but that they shared techniques to prevent such instances or to deal with them if they arose. Overall, with women in all forms and legal statuses of prostitution *except for streetwalking,* I consistently found that concern about customer assault was significantly less than I had expected" (2002 84–85, emphasis added). Chun noted a similar phenomenon with exotic dancers; her interviewees felt more exploited by the club owners than by the customers; they were exploited as laborers at least as much, if not more, than they were as sexualized beings (1999, 233).

12. There is some overlap here with other forms of sex work. For example, Sharon A. Abbott found that there are five main reasons that women and men go into pornography work, including money. But for pornography actors, fame and sociability are other significant motivators, which is good, because the work is not very lucrative. Those who stay in the industry are motivated by success and fame, not money (Abbott 2000, 20–28). Wesely (2003, 490–93) and Pasko (2002, 51–61) discuss the financial motives of exotic dancers.

13. This point is repeated by a number of contributors to Annie Oakley's *Working Sex* (2007). In addition to Galazia, see Brooks, Vasquez, and Blowdryer.

In Delacoste's and Alexander's *Sex Work* (1998), see Morgan, Everts, Edelstein, Helfand, "Debra," "Barbara," Niles, and West. See also Funari (1997); Kuo (2002, 69); Bremer (2006, 52); and Wesely (2003).

14. Rachel West of the United States Prostitutes Collective writes, "prostitution is about money, not about sex. If women's basic economic situation does not change, then women will continue to work as prostitutes" (1998, 283).

15. Alexander (1998, 185). Chapkis (1997, 102–3) discusses the way that this lack of respect becomes more profound the less class privilege women have and the lower down they work on the rung of the sex work hierarchy between off-street and on-street workers.

16. According to prostitute Morgan, a sex worker "knows that what she does for money is not an expression of her own sexuality" (1998, 26).

17. See also "Debra" and "Barbara," both interviewed by Carole in Delacoste and Alexander (1998, 93, 174).

18. Martha Nussbaum also makes this point—that context is essential to understanding exactly what is happening in any particular sexual act. A heterogeneous, paradoxical context determines whether objectification and sex are morally (and politically) problematic (1999, 218).

19. As sex worker Jo Doezma remarks, this is not going to be the end of the world either: "Look, we've already survived sex outside of marriage and sex without love so it's likely we can survive sex outside of desire, too" (quoted in Chapkis 1997, 121).

20. Many sex workers are themselves ambivalent about the meanings of sex work and the amount of agency they have as sexual subjects and as workers (see Egan, Frank, and Johnson 2006, xiv). The ambivalence of sex workers mirrors the ambiguity of contraposed social meanings about sex and the sexual. "American culture is characterized by rigid sexual boundaries and widespread sexual spectacles (found in advertising, sex manuals, popular music lyrics, music videos, talk shows, films, and a booming sex industry). Our cultural imagination is thus simultaneously hypersexual (wanting sex, selling sex, and making sex a spectacle) and sexually repressive for certain groups of people (claiming that sex is sacred, private, and something to be shared only within monogamous heterosexual relations)" (Egan, Frank, and Johnson 2006, xxvi–xxvii). Thus it is unlikely that sex work would have a singular meaning give that sex itself is so fraught with contradiction.

21. These forms of power include marriage and property laws, for example, or, in the cultural domain, nearly every mainstream television show and movie ever made.

22. Again, Nussbaum's analysis is instructive. Where objectification does not deny the autonomy of others, it is not necessarily a violation of the Kantian imperative to treat others as ends (1999, 220–23). She further argues that although prostitution is objectifying, it is no more so than many other forms of labor that require the use of one's body (276–98).

23. Laura Kipnis (2006) makes a similar argument when she defends *Hustler* magazine's vision of sexuality as a historically and economically situated social critique. Although I do not agree with most of Kipnis's analysis of *Hustler* in particular, I do find persuasive her general point that abolitionist feminism takes a particular view of women's sexuality and tries to impose it on all women, so that all women are posed as innocent and disgusted by male sexual desires, and male sexual desires are assumed to be inherently violent.

24. A history of sexual abuse "is more common among street-based workers than among brothel, parlor, escort, and independent out-call workers. This is largely a marker for age, however, as most adolescent prostitutes work on the street, and many street prostitutes began working before the age of eighteen." (Alexander 1998, 190–91). As Evelyn Abramovich (2005, 141–43) makes clear, the link between childhood sexual abuse and prostitution is strongest in the sense that the adolescents are fleeing an abusive home and need to support themselves financially. But the research is unclear whether childhood sexual abuse alone causes women to engage in sex work, or if it does, if it leads to any kind of sex work other than street-based prostitution, as "street-based prostitutes are currently the only population of sex workers being widely researched" (143).

25. Melissa Ditmore relates the events of a 2000 meeting of the UN's Human Rights Caucus where the representative from the abolitionist group Coalition Against Trafficking in Women tried to get antitrafficking statutes to define women who made the choice to engage in sex work as children so that their decisions could be unilaterally overruled (2005, 116). Ditmore also mentions a 2002 U.S. House Committee on International Relations meeting where abolitionists successfully lobbied to cease USAID funds to projects run by groups including Doctors Without Borders and the International Human Rights Law Group aimed at service provision for prostitutes without insisting they leave the job (because they "promote prostitution") (117–18).

26. In Merleau-Ponty's words, "To thought, the body as an object is not ambiguous; it becomes so only in the experience which we have of it, and preeminently in sexual experience, and through the fact of sexuality. To treat sexuality as a dialectic is not to make a process of knowledge out of it, nor to identify a man's history with the history of his consciousness. The dialectic is not a relationship

between contradictory and inseparable thoughts; it is the tending of an existence towards another existence which denies it, and yet without which it is not sustained. Metaphysics—the coming to light of something beyond nature—is not localized at the level of knowledge: it begins with the opening out upon 'another,' and is to be found everywhere, and already, in the specific development of sexuality" (1962, 167–68).

27. As erotic dancer Tawnya Dudash argues, "The body [is] a material object located in nature but subject to social forces within the specific historical development of economic, political, and cultural factors. The body is not only constructed by social relationships, but it also enters into the construction of these relationships and thereby contains the *agency* that is crucial for enacting change and resistance" (1997, 105).

28. I refer to pornography actors as *talent* because that is the term that they themselves use. See Abbott (2000, 18).

29. As gonzo porn becomes more prominent, anal sex has as well. But once anal sex became standard fare, then "double anal" and "triple anal" started to appear, which goes hand in hand with the mainstreaming of more violent (rough) fare.

30. This does not mean that clients will always respect women's wishes or that economic concerns will not push women beyond their limits, only that the phenomenological experience of commodified sex is highly different depending on the context.

31. "In 1975 the total retail value of all the hard-core porno in America was estimated at $5–10 million. [In 2000] Americans spent $8 billion on mediated sex" (Amis 2001).

32. Lenore Kuo found that "rates of prostitution are relatively unaffected by the adoption of differing policies" (2002, 125). Sibyl Schwarzenbach similarly finds that in most countries in Europe where aspects of prostitution have been decriminalized or legalized there is no evidence "that decriminalization causes an increase in the phenomenon of prostitution" (2006, 224). Wijers (2008) reports that both demand for and supply of prostitution services has declined over the last ten years in the Netherlands, while brothels have been legalized and prostitution maintains it decriminalized status.

33. Nevada is a "right-to-work" state, so even if they were classified as employees, they might not be able to unionize there. The point is that if prostitutes counted as employees in all states, they would be able to unionize in some of them.

34. Wijers (2008). Hubbard, Matthews, and Scoular (2008, 146) also note the improved working conditions in regulated brothels.

35. Cited in Kuo (2002, 95). A 2006 study of the effects of legalization of Dutch brothels found similar results. When prostitutes' well-being was assessed, their emotional health was found to be "more favourable than the average score of the general female population" (Wijers 2008).

5. AGENCY AND FEMINIST POLITICS

1. There are limits, of course, on how receptive I can be to others. Those whose preferred method of dealing with difference is firing off death threats are not likely to engage in reasonable, democratic discussion, nor should I necessarily want to bring them into a critical dialogue that challenges my sense of self, nor will I find that doing so will increase my capacity for living a flourishing, self-defined life. But those who are willing to meet my overtures at discussion with some openness of their own deserve my initial respect and attempts at bridging differences to find common ground.

2. Ann Russo speaks to these points when she considers where and how feminism needs to change if it is to continue to be a viable and broadly relevant political movement for all women. She reminds white women in particular that it is crucial not to conceptualize "difference" as an aspect of "other women." White is different from black in the same way that black is different from white. Only once we develop collaborative democratic structures that allow for multiple perspectives will multiracial feminist organizing truly succeed (2001, 213–23). This conception of difference is the crux of Catharine A. MacKinnon's (1989) theory of difference and dominance.

3. My description of Ferguson's project is based on her presentation of the work at the Western Political Science Association Annual Meeting in Portland, Oregon, March 11, 2004.

4. Consider here the difference between the narrow and demeaning battered woman syndrome as description of battered women's lives and as a legal defense for their actions that was developed by well-intentioned outside experts, premised on limited experience and one type of response to battery, versus the coercive control model, which was developed by well-meaning outsiders in tandem with a diverse group of battered women and advocates who were misdescribed and ill-served by battered woman syndrome. The coercive control model highlights and promotes agency, while battered woman syndrome both ignores and thwarts it.

5. Drawing from the ancient Greeks, Foucault argues that caring for the conditions of one's own life is in itself an ethical caring of and for others, and that this care can only happen through our relationships with others because our relationships are part of our social situation. "The care of the self is ethical in itself;

but it implies complex relationships with others insofar as this *ēthos* of freedom is also a way of caring for others. . . . *Ēthos* also implies a relationship with others, insofar as the care of the self enables one to occupy his rightful position in the city, the community, or interpersonal relationships, whether as a magistrate or a friend. And the care of the self also implies a relationship with the other insofar as a proper care of the self requires listening to the lessons of a master. One needs a guide, a counselor, a friend, someone who will be truthful with you. Thus, the problem of relationships with others is present throughout the development of the care of the self" (1994 [1984], 287).

6. Mary Pardo (1998) offers a compelling example of how working in community is transformative of self-identity and one's perspective of others through her study of new and established Mexican immigrant communities (see esp. 281–82).

7. Bhattacharjee (1997, 41–42). Abraham (2000) also discusses this example throughout chapter 9 of her book.

8. As Jeffrey Weeks (1995) argues, it is the collective nature of an attack on institutions at any moment that allows political actors to articulate the political boundaries for a particular battle, even if the membership in collectivities is in flux.

9. On questions of the fixity, flexibility, and necessity of group self-definition, see Bordo (1993), Collins (1990), and Young (1990). Nancy J. Hirschmann (2003, 220) also includes dialogue and persuasion as part of her political strategy.

10. This is a point made by many contemporary feminist thinkers. See, e.g., Eaton (1994, 220); Russo (2001, 21).

11. Studies of women's community activism illuminate the ways in which working in coalition with others shifts the standpoint or perspective from which one operates. These shifts "highlight the agency of the community activists. . . . Inquiries from their standpoints also reveal hidden dimensions of the powerful political-economic forces that are structuring the grounds upon which they must organize their community-based responses" (Naples 1998, 343).

BIBLIOGRAPHY

Abbott, Sharon A. 2000. "Motivations for Pursuing an Acting Career in Pornography." In Weitzer, *Sex for Sale.*

Abma, Joyce C., and Gladys M. Martinez. 2006. "Childlessness among Older Women in the United States: Trends and Profiles." *Journal of Marriage and Family* 68: 1045–56.

Abraham, Margaret. 2000. *Speaking the Unspeakable: Marital Violence among South Asian Immigrants in the United States.* New Brunswick, N.J.: Rutgers University Press.

Abramovich, Evelyn. 2005. "Childhood Sexual Abuse as a Risk Factor for Subsequent Involvement in Sex Work: A Review of Empirical Findings." In *Contemporary Research on Sex Work,* ed. Jeffrey T. Parsons. New York: Haworth Press.

Abrams, Kathryn. 1995. "Sex Wars Redux: Agency and Coercion in Feminist Legal Theory." *Columbia Law Review* 95: 304–76.

———. 1999. "From Autonomy to Agency: Feminist Perspectives on Self-Direction." *William and Mary Law Review* 40 (March): 805–46.

Alcoff, Linda Martín. 2000a. "Merleau-Ponty and Feminist Theory on Experience." In *Chiasms: Merleau-Ponty's Notion of Flesh,* ed. Fred Evans and Leonard Lawlor. Albany: State University of New York Press.

———. 2000b. "Who's Afraid of Identity Politics?" In *Reclaiming Identity: Realist Theory and the Predicament of Postmodernism,* ed. Paula M. L. Moya and Michael R. Hames-García. Berkeley: University of California Press.

Alexander, Priscilla. 1998. "Prostitution: *Still* a Difficult Issue." In Delacoste and Alexander, *Sex Work.*

Almodovar, Norma Jean. 2006. "Porn Stars, Radical Feminists, Cops and Out-law Whores: The Battle between Feminist Theory and Reality, Free Speech and Free Spirits." In Spector, *Prostitution and Pornography.*

Amis, Martin. 2001. "A Rough Trade." *Guardian Unlimited,* March 17. http://www.guardian.co.uk/Archive/Article/0,4273,4153718,00.html.

Ayyub, Ruksana. 2007. "The Many Faces of Domestic Violence in the South Asian American Muslim Community." In Das Dasgupta, *Body Evidence.*

Bartky, Sandra Lee. 1990. *Femininity and Domination: Studies in the Phenomenology of Oppression.* New York: Routledge.

———. 1995. "Agency: What's the Problem?" In *Provoking Agents: Gender and Agency in Theory and Practice,* ed. Judith Kegan Gardiner. Urbana: University of Illinois Press.

Beauvoir, Simone de. 1989 [1949]. *The Second Sex.* New York: Vintage Books.

Becker, Gay, Martha Castrillo, Rebecca Jackson, and Robert D. Nachtigall. 2006. "Infertility among Low-Income Latinos." *Fertility and Sterility* 85: 882–87.

Benhabib, Seyla. 1999. "Sexual Difference and Collective Identities: The New Global Constellation." *Signs: Journal of Women in Culture and Society* 24: 335–61.

Benson, Paul. 1990. "Feminist Second Thoughts about Free Agency." *Hypatia* 5, no. 3 (Fall): 47–64.

———. 1994. "Free Agency and Self-Worth." *Journal of Philosophy* 91: 650–68.

———. 2000. "Feeling Crazy: Self-Worth and the Social Character of Responsibility." In *Relational Autonomy: Feminist Perspectives on Autonomy, Agency, and the Social Self,* ed. Catriona Mackenize and Natalie Stoljar. Oxford: Oxford University Press.

Bernstein, Elizabeth. 1999. "What's Wrong with Prostitution? What's Right with Sex Work? Comparing Markets in Female Sexual Labor." *Hastings Women's Law Journal* 10: 91–117.

Bevir, Mark. 1999. "Foucault and Critique: Deploying Agency against Autonomy." *Political Theory* 27: 65–84.

Bhattacharjee, Anannya. 1997. "A Slippery Path: Organizing Resistance to Violence against Women." In *Dragon Ladies: Asian American Feminists Breathe Fire,* ed. Sonia Shah. Boston: South End Press.

Bickford, Susan. 1997. "Anti-Anti-Identity Politics: Feminism, Democracy, and the Complexities of Citizenship." *Hypatia* 12, no. 4 (Fall): 111–31.

———. 1999. "Reconfiguring Pluralism: Identity and Institutions in the Inegalitarian Polity." *American Journal of Political Science* 43: 86–108.

Bitler, Marianne, and Lucie Schmidt. 2006. "Health Disparities and Infertility: Impacts of State Level Insurance Mandates." *Fertility and Sterility* 85: 858–65.

Bordo, Susan. 1993. *Unbearable Weight: Feminism, Western Culture, and the Body.* Berkeley: University of California Press.

———. 1997. *Twilight Zones: The Hidden Life of Cultural Images from Plato to O.J.* Berkeley: University of California Press.

Bremer, Susan. 2006. "The Grind." In *Flesh for Fantasy: Producing and Consuming Exotic Dance,* ed. Danielle R. Egan, Katherine Frank, and Merri Lisa Johnson. New York: Thunder's Mouth Press.

Brison, Susan J. 2006. "Contentious Freedom: Sex Work and Social Construction." *Hypatia* vol. 21, no. 4 (Fall): 192–200.

Brooks, Siobhan. 2007. "An Interview with Gloria Lockett." In *Working Sex: Sex Workers Write about a Changing Industry,* ed. Annie Oakley. Emeryville, Calif.: Seal Press.

Brooks-Gordon, Belinda. 2006. *The Price of Sex: Prostitution, Policy, and Society.* Portland, Ore.: Willan Publishing.

Brown, Wendy. 1995. *States of Injury: Power and Freedom in Late Modernity.* Princeton: Princeton University Press.

Butler, Judith. 1989. "Sexual Ideology and Phenomenological Description: A Feminist Critique of Merleau-Ponty's *Phenomenology of Perception.*" In *The Thinking Muse: Feminism and Modern French Philosophy,* ed. Jeffner Allen and Iris Marion Young. Bloomington: Indiana University Press.

———. 1990. *Gender Trouble: Feminism and the Subversion of Identity.* New York: Routledge.

———. 1992. "Contingent Foundations: Feminism and the Question of 'Postmodernism.'" In *Feminists Theorize the Political,* ed. Judith Butler and Joan W. Scott. New York: Routledge.

———. 1995. "For a Careful Reading." In *Feminist Contentions: A Philosophical Exchange,* ed. Seyla Benhabib, Judith Butler, Drucilla Cornell, and Nancy Fraser. New York: Routledge.

———. 2004a. *Undoing Gender.* New York: Routledge.

———. 2004b. "Bodies and Power Revisited." In *Feminism and the Final Foucault,* ed. Dianna Taylor and Karen Vintges. Urbana: University of Illinois Press.

Carole. 1998. "Interview with Debra" and "Interview with Barbara." In Delacoste and Alexander, *Sex Work.*

Cataldi, Suzanne Laba. 2001. "The Body as a Basis for Being: Simone de Beauvoir and Maurice Merleau-Ponty." In *The Existential Phenomenology of Simone de Beauvoir,* ed. Wendy O'Brien and Lester Embree. Dordrecht, The Netherlands: Kluwer Academic Publishers.

Chandra, Anjani, Gladys M. Martinez, William D. Mosher, Joyce C. Abma, and Jo Jones. 2005. *Fertility, Family Planning, and Reproductive Health of U.S. Women: Data from the 2002 National Survey of Family Growth.* Vital Health Statistics series 23 (no. 25). Hyattsville, Md.: National Center for Health Statistics.

Chapkis, Wendy. 1997. *Live Sex Acts: Women Performing Erotic Labor.* New York: Routledge.

———. 2000. "Power and Control in the Commercial Sex Trade." In Weitzer, *Sex for Sale.*

Chun, Sarah. 1999. "An Uncommon Alliance: Finding Empowerment for Exotic Dancers through Labor Unions." *Hastings Women's Law Journal* 10: 231–52.

Coker, Donna. 2000. "Piercing Webs of Power: Identity, Resistance, and Hope in Lat Crit Theory and Praxis: Shifting Power for Battered Women: Law, Material Resources, and Poor Women of Color." *U.C. Davis Law Review* 33: 1009–55.

Coles, Romand. 1996. "Liberty, Equality, Receptive Generosity: Neo-Nietzschean Reflections on the Ethics and Politics of Coalition." *American Political Science Review* 90: 375–88.

Collins, Patricia Hill. 1990. *Black Feminist Thought: Knowledge, Consciousness, and the Politics of Empowerment.* New York: Routledge.

Compton, John J. 1982. "Sartre, Merleau-Ponty, and Human Freedom." *Journal of Philosophy* 79: 577–88.

Crenshaw, Kimberlé Williams. 1994. "Mapping the Margins: Intersectionality, Identity Politics, and Violence against Women of Color." In *The Public Nature of Private Violence: The Discoverty of Domestic Abuse,* ed. Martha Albertson Fineman and Roxanne Mykitiuk. New York: Routledge.

Crossley, Nick. 2001. "The Phenomenological Habitus and Its Construction." *Theory and Society* 30: 81–120.

Danielsen, Dan, and Karen Engle, ed. 1995. *After Identity: A Reader in Law and Culture.* New York: Routledge.

Das Dasgupta, Shamita. 2005. "Women's Realities: Defining Violence against Women by Immigration, Race, and Class." In Sokoloff, *Domestic Violence at the Margins: Readings on Race, Class, Gender, and Culture,* ed. Natalie J. Sokoloff. New Brunswick, N.J.: Rutgers University Press.

———, ed. 2007. *Body Evidence: Intimate Violence against South Asian Women in America.* New Brunswick, N.J.: Rutgers University Press.

Das Dasgupta, Shamita, and Shashi Jain. 2007. "*Ahimsa* and the Contextual Realities of Woman Abuse in the Jain Community." In Das Dasgupta, *Body Evidence.*

Dean, Jodi. 1996. *Solidarity of Strangers: Feminism after Identity Politics.* Berkeley: University of California Press.

Delacoste, Frédérique, and Priscilla Alexander, ed. 1998. *Sex Work: Writings by Women in the Sex Industry.* San Francisco, Calif.: Cleis Press.

Densham, Andrea. 1997. "The Marginalized Uses of Power and Identity: Lesbians' Participation in Breast Cancer and AIDS Activism." In *Women Transforming Politics: An Alternative Reader,* ed. Cathy J. Cohen, Kathleen B. Jones, and Joan C. Tronto. New York: New York University Press.

Denzin, Norman K. 1984. "Toward a Phenomenology of Family Violence." *American Journal of Sociology* 90: 483–513.

Ditmore, Melissa. 2005. "Trafficking in Lives: How Ideology Shapes Policy." In *Trafficking and Prostitution Reconsidered: New Perspectives on Migration, Sex Work, and Human Rights,* ed. Kamala Kempadoo. Boulder, Colo.: Paradigm Publishers.

Dobash, R. Emerson, and Russell P. Dobash. 1992. *Women, Violence, and Social Change.* New York: Routledge.

Dobash, Russell P., R. Emerson Dobash, Margo Wilson, and Martin Daly. 1992. "The Myth of Sexual Symmetry in Marital Violence." *Social Problems* 39: 71–91.

Douglas, Susan J., and Meredith W. Michaels. 2004. *The Mommy Myth: The Idealization of Motherhood and How It Has Undermined All Women.* New York: The Free Press.

Dudash, Tawnya. 1997. "Peepshow Feminism." In Nagle, *Whores and Other Feminists.*

Eaton, Mary. 1994. "Abuse by Any Other Name: Feminism, Difference, and Intralesbian Violence." In *The Public Nature of Private Violence: The Discovery of Domestic Abuse,* ed. Martha Albertson Fineman and Roxanne Mykitiuk. New York: Routledge.

Egan, R. Danielle, Katherine Frank, and Merri Lisa Johnson, ed. 2006. *Flesh for Fantasy: Producing and Consuming Exotic Dance.* New York: Thunder's Mouth Press.

Emirbayer, Mustafa, and Ann Mische. 1998. "What Is Agency?" *American Journal of Sociology* 103: 962–1023.

"Environment and Infertility." 1996. *Environmental Health Perspectives* 104: 136–37.

Erez, Edna, Madelaine Adelman, and Carol Gregory. 2009. "Intersections of Immigration and Domestic Violence: Voices of Battered Immigrant Women." *Feminist Criminology* 4: 32–56.

Ertman, Martha M. 2003. "What's Wrong with a Parenthood Market? A New and Improved Theory of Commodification." *North Carolina Law Review* 82: 1–59.

Evans, Fred, and Leonard Lawlor. 2000. "The Value of Flesh: Merleau-Ponty's Philosophy and the Modernism/Postmodernism Debate." In *Chiasms: Merleau-Ponty's Notion of Flesh*, ed. Fred Evans and Leonard Lawlor. Albany: State University of New York Press.

Faludi, Susan. 1991. *Backlash: The Undeclared War against American Women*. New York: Crown.

Feinberg, Eve C., Frederick W. Larsen, William H. Catherino, Jun Zhang, and Alicia Y. Armstrong. 2006. "Comparison of Assisted Reproductive Technology Utilization and Outcomes between Caucasian and African American Patients in an Equal-Access-to-Care Setting." *Fertility and Sterility* 85: 888–94.

Feldman, Leonard C. 2002. "Redistribution, Recognition, and the State: The Irreducibly Political Dimension of Injustice." *Political Theory* 20: 410–40.

Ferguson, Michaele. 2004. "Forgetting to be Friends: A Kantian Take on Collective Agency." Paper presented at the Western Political Science Association Annual Meeting, Portland, Ore., March 11–13.

Fine, Michelle, Rosemarie A. Roberts, and Lois Weis. 2005. "Puerto Rican Battered Women Redefining Gender, Sexuality, Culture, Violence, and Resistance." In Sokoloff, *Domestic Violence at the Margins*.

Firestone, Shulamith. 1970. *The Dialectic of Sex: The Case for a Feminist Revolution*. New York: William Morrow Press, Quill.

Foucault, Michel. 1994 [1984]. "The Ethics of the Concern for the Self as a Practice of Freedom." In *Michel Foucault: Ethics, Subjectivity, and Truth*, ed. Paul Rabinow. New York: The New Press.

———. 1994 [1981]. "Friendship as a Way of Life." In *Michel Foucault: Ethics, Subjectivity, and Truth*, ed. Paul Rabinow. New York: The New Press.

Frank, Katherine. 2002. *G-strings and Sympathy: Strip Club Regulars and Male Desire*. Durham, N.C.: Duke University Press.

Fraser, Nancy. 1993. "Beyond the Master/Subject Model: Reflections on Carole Pateman's Sexual Contract." *Social Text* 37: 173–81.

———. 1997a. "A Rejoinder to Iris Marion Young." *New Left Review* 223: 126–29.

———. 1997b. *Justice Interruptus: Critical Reflections on the "Postsocialist" Condition*. New York: Routledge.

———. 1998. "Heterosexism, Misrecognition and Capitalism: A Response to Judith Butler." *New Left Review* 228: 140–49.

———. 2000. "Rethinking Recognition." *New Left Review* 3: 107–20.

Fraser, Nancy, and Axel Honneth. 2003. *Redistribution or Recognition? A Political Philosophical Exchange.* New York: Verso.

Friedman, Marilyn. 1997. "Autonomy and Social Relationships: Rethinking the Feminist Critique." In *Feminists Rethink the Self,* ed. Diana T. Meyers. Boulder, Colo.: Westview Press.

Funari, Vicky. 1997. "Naked, Naughty, Nasty: Peep Show Reflections." In Nagle, *Whores and Other Feminists.*

Galazia, Janelle. 2007. "Staged." In *Working Sex: Sex Workers Write about a Changing Industry,* ed. Annie Oakley. Emeryville, Calif.: Seal Press.

Goetting, Ann. 1999. *Getting Out: Life Stories of Women Who Left Abusive Men.* New York: Columbia University Press.

Goldfarb, Phyllis. 1996. "Describing without Circumscribing: Questioning the Construction of Gender in the Discourse of Intimate Violence." *George Washington Law Review* 64: 582–631.

Goldfarb, Sally F. 2008. "Reconceiving Civil Protection Orders for Domestic Violence: Can Law Help End the Abuse without Ending the Relationship?" *Cardozo Law Review* 29: 1487–551.

Goodmark, Leigh. 2004. "The Legal Response to Domestic Violence: Problems and Possibilities: Law Is the Answer? Do We Know that For Sure? Questioning the Efficacy of Legal Interventions for Battered Women." *Saint Louis University Public Law Review* 23: 7–48.

———. 2008. "When Is a Battered Woman Not a Battered Woman? When She Fights Back." *Yale Journal of Law and Feminism* 20: 75–129.

Goodwin, Michele. 2005. "Assisted Reproductive Technology and the Double Bind: The Illusory Choice of Motherhood." *Journal of Gender, Race, and Justice* 9: 1–54.

Gordon, Linda. 1988. *Heroes of Their Own Lives: The Politics and History of Family Violence, Boston, 1880–1960.* New York: Viking.

———. 1993. "Women's Agency, Social Control, and the Construction of 'Rights' by Battered Women." In *Negotiating at the Margins: The Gendered Discourses of Power and Resistance,* ed. Kathy Davis and Sue Fisher. New Brunswick, N.J.: Rutgers University Press.

Govier, Trudy. 1993. "Self-Trust, Autonomy, and Self-Esteem." *Hypatia* 8, no. 1 (Winter): 99–120.

Grewal, Mandeep. 2007. "A Communicative Perspective on Assisting Battered Asian Indian Immigrant Women." In Das Dasgupta, *Body Evidence.*

Hamby, Sherry L. 2005. "The Importance of Community in a Feminist Analysis of Domestic Violence among Native Americans." In Sokoloff, *Domestic Violence at the Margins.*

Hartley, Nina. 1997. "In the Flesh: A Porn Star's Journey." In Nagle, *Whores and Other Feminists.*

Hausbeck, Kathryn, and Barbara G. Brents. 2000. "Inside Nevada's Brothel Industry." In Weitzer, *Sex for Sale.*

Heinämaa, Sara. 2003. *Toward a Phenomenology of Sexual Difference.* Lanham, Md.: Rowman and Littlefield.

Heitlinger, Alena. 1991. "Pronatalism and Women's Equality Policies." *European Journal of Population* 7: 343–75.

Hekman, Susan. 1995. "Subjects and Agents: The Question for Feminism." In *Provoking Agents: Gender and Agency in Theory and Practice,* ed. Judith Kegan Gardiner. Urbana: University of Illinois Press.

———. 2004. *Public Selves, Private Identities: Reconsidering Identity Politics.* University Park: Pennsylvania State University Press.

Henderson, Sarah L., and Alana S. Jeydel. 2007. *Participation and Protest: Women and Politics in a Global World.* New York: Oxford University Press.

Hirschmann, Nancy J. 2003. *The Subject of Liberty: Toward a Feminist Theory of Freedom.* Princeton: Princeton University Press.

Hoff, Bert H. 2001. "Women about as Likely to Initiate Dating Assault." http://www.menweb.org/dateviol/fiebertdate.htm.

Honneth, Axel. 1998. "Decentered Autonomy: The Subject after the Fall." In *Reinterpreting the Political: Continental Philosophy and Political Theory,* ed. Lenore Langsdorf and Stephen H. Watson with Karen A. Smith. Albany: State University of New York Press.

Horsburgh, Beverly. 2005. "Lifting the Veil of Secrecy: Domestic Violence in the Jewish Community." In Sokoloff, *Domestic Violence at the Margins.*

Hruska, Kathleen S., Priscilla A. Furth, David B. Seifer, Fady I. Sharara, and Jodi A. Flaws. 2000. "Environmental Factors in Infertility." *Clinical Obstetrics and Gynecology* 43: 821–29.

Hubbard, Phil, Roger Matthews, and Jane Scoular. 2008. "Regulating Sex Work in the EU: Prostitute Women and the New Spaces of Exclusion." *Gender, Place, and Culture* 15: 137–52.

Hynes, H. Patricia, and Janice G. Raymond. 2002. "Put in Harm's Way: The Neglected Health Consequences of Sex Trafficking in the United States." In *Policing the National Body: Sex, Race, and Criminalization,* ed. Jael Silliman and Anannya Bhattacharjee. Cambridge, Mass.: South End Press.

Ireland, Mardy S. 1993. *Reconceiving Women: Separating Motherhood from Female Identity.* New York: The Guilford Press.

Johnson, Merri Lisa. 2006. "Stripper Bashing: An Autovideography of Violence against Strippers." In *Flesh for Fantasy: Producing and Consuming Exotic Dance,* ed. Danielle R. Egan, Katherine Frank, and Merri Lisa Johnson. New York: Thunder's Mouth Press.

Jones, Kathleen B. 2000. *Living between Danger and Love: The Limits of Choice.* New Brunswick, N.J.: Rutgers University Press.

Josephson, Jyl. 2005. "The Intersectionality of Domestic Violence and Welfare in the Lives of Poor Women." In Sokoloff, *Domestic Violence at the Margins.*

Keck, Aries. 2009. "Study: Access to a Lawyer Strongly Decreases Domestic Violence." Public News Service, March 27. http://www.publicnewsservice.org/index.php?/content/article/8409-1.

Kempadoo, Kamala. 2005. "Sex Workers' Rights Organizations and Anti-trafficking Campaigns." In *Trafficking and Prostitution Reconsidered: New Perspectives on Migration, Sex Work, and Human Rights,* ed. Kamala Kempadoo. Boulder, Colo.: Paradigm Publishers.

Kendrick, Karen. 1998. "Producing the Battered Woman." In *Community Activism and Feminist Politics: Organizing across Race, Class, and Gender,* ed. Nancy A. Naples. New York: Routledge.

King, Leslie, and Madonna Harrington Meyer. 1997. "The Politics of Reproductive Benefits: U.S. Insurance Coverage of Contraceptive and Infertility Treatments." *Gender and Society* 11: 8–30.

Kipnis, Laura. 2006. "Desire and Disgust: *Hustler Magazine.*" In Spector, *Prostitution and Pornography.*

Kline, Marlee. 1995. "Complicating the Ideology of Motherhood: Child Welfare Law and First Nation Women." In *Mothers in Law: Feminist Theory and the Legal Regulation of Motherhood,* ed. Martha Albertson Fineman and Isabel Karpin. New York: Columbia University Press.

Kolata, Gina. 2004. "The Heart's Desire." *New York Times,* May 11. http://www.nytimes.com/2004/05/11/health/the-heart-s-desire.html.

Koppleman, Andrew. 1996. *Antidiscrimination Law and Social Equality.* New Haven, Conn.: Yale University Press.

Kruks, Sonia. 1981. *The Political Philosophy of Merleau-Ponty.* Atlantic Highlands, N.J.: Humanities Press.

———. 1990. *Situation and Human Existence: Freedom, Subjectivity, and Society.* London: Unwin Hyman.

————. 2001. *Retrieving Experience: Subjectivity and Recognition in Feminist Politics.* Ithaca, N.Y.: Cornell University Press.

Kuo, Lenore. 2002. *Prostitution Policy: Revolutionizing Practice through a Gendered Perspective.* New York: New York University Press.

Lamb, Sharon. 1999. "Constructing the Victim: Popular Images and Lasting Labels." In *New Versions of Victims: Feminists Struggle with the Concept,* ed. Sharon Lamb. New York: New York University Press.

Lang, Susan S. 1991. *Women without Children: The Reasons, the Rewards, the Regrets.* New York: Pharos Books.

Langer, Monika. 2003. "Beauvoir and Merleau-Ponty on Ambiguity." In *The Cambridge Companion to Simone de Beauvoir,* ed. Claudia Card. Cambridge: Cambridge University Press.

Lever, Janet, and Deanne Dolnick. 2000. "Clients and Call Girls: Seeking Sex and Intimacy." In Weitzer, *Sex for Sale.*

Lever, Janet, David E. Kanouse, and Sandra H. Berry. 2005. "Racial and Ethnic Segmentation of Female Prostitution in Los Angeles County." In *Contemporary Research on Sex Work,* ed. Jeffrey T. Parsons. New York: Haworth Press.

Lewin, Ellen. 1994. "Negotiating Lesbian Motherhood: The Dialectics of Resistance and Accommodation." In *Mothering: Ideology, Experience, Agency,* ed. Evelyn Nakano Glenn, Grace Change, and Linda Rennie Forcey. New York: Routledge.

Lewis, Jacqueline, Eleanor Maticka-Tyndale, Frances Shaver, and Heather Schramm. 2005. "Managing Risk and Safety on the Job: The Experiences of Canadian Sex Workers." In *Contemporary Research on Sex Work,* ed. Jeffrey T. Parsons. New York: Haworth Press.

MacKenzie, Catriona, and Natalie Stoljar, ed. 2000. *Relational Autonomy: Feminist Perspectives on Autonomy, Agency, and the Social Self.* Oxford: Oxford University Press.

MacKinnon, Catharine A. 1987. *Feminism Unmodified: Discourses on Life and Law.* Cambridge, Mass.: Harvard University Press.

————. 1989. *Toward a Feminist Theory of the State.* Cambridge, Mass.: Harvard University Press.

————. 1993. *Only Words.* Cambridge, Mass.: Harvard University Press.

Mahoney, Martha. 1991. "Legal Images of Battered Women: Redefining the Issue of Separation." *Michigan Law Review* 90: 1–94.

————. 1992. "Exit: Power and the Idea of Leaving in Love, Work, and the Confirmation Hearings." *Southern California Law Review* 65: 1283–319.

———. 1994. "Victimization or Oppression? Women's Lives, Violence, and Agency." In *The Public Nature of Private Violence: The Discovery of Domestic Abuse,* ed. Martha Albertson Fineman and Roxanne Mykitiuk. New York: Routledge.

Marcus, Isabel. 1994. "Reframing 'Domestic Violence': Terrorism in the Home." In *The Public Nature of Private Violence: The Discovery of Domestic Abuse,* ed. Martha Albertson Fineman and Roxanne Mykitiuk. New York: Routledge.

Martin, Del. 1981 [1976]. *Battered Wives.* San Francisco, Calif.: Volcano Press.

Martinez, Jacqueline M. 2000. *Phenomenology of Chicana Experience and Identity: Communication and Transformation in Praxis.* Lanham, Md.: Rowman and Littlefield.

May, Elaine Tyler. 1995. *Barren in the Promised Land: Childless Americans and the Pursuit of Happiness.* New York: Basic Books.

McCall, Leslie. 2005. "The Complexity of Intersectionality." *Signs: Journal of Women in Culture and Society* 30: 1771–800.

McIntosh, Mary. 1996. "Feminist Debates on Prostitution." In *Sexualizing the Social: Power and the Organization of Sexuality,* ed. Lisa Adkins and Vicki Merchant. New York: St. Martin's Press.

McLaren, Margaret A. 2004. "Foucault and Feminism: Power, Resistance, Freedom." In *Feminism and the Final Foucault,* ed. Dianna Taylor and Karen Vintges. Urbana: University of Illinois Press.

McNay, Lois. 2000. *Gender and Agency: Reconfiguring the Subject in Feminist and Social Theory.* Cambridge: Polity Press.

Menjívar, Cecilia, and Olivia Salcido. 2002. "Immigrant Women and Domestic Violence: Common Experiences in Different Countries." *Gender and Society* 16: 898–920.

Merleau-Ponty, Maurice. 1962. *Phenomenology of Perception.* Translated by Colin Smith. New York: Routledge.

Merrill, Gregory S. 1996. "Ruling the Exceptions: Same-Sex Battering and Domestic Violence Theory." In *Violence in Gay and Lesbian Domestic Partnerships,* ed. Claire M. Renzetti and Charles Harvey Miley. New York: Harrington Park Press.

Metal, Phyllis Luman. 1998. "The Madame." In Delacoste and Alexander, *Sex Work.*

Meyers, Diana T. 2000. "Intersectional Identity and the Authentic Self? Opposites Attract!" In *Relational Autonomy: Feminist Perspectives on Autonomy, Agency, and the Social Self,* ed. Catriona Mackenzie and Natalie Stoljar. Oxford: Oxford University Press.

————. 2002. *Gender in the Mirror: Cultural Imagery and Women's Agency.* New York: Oxford University Press.

Michie, Helena, and Naomi R. Cahn. 1997. *Confinements: Fertility and Infertility in Contemporary Culture.* New Brunswick, N.J.: Rutgers University Press.

Minow, Martha. 1997. *Not Only for Myself: Identity, Politics and the Law.* New York: The New Press.

Moe, Angela M. 2004. "Blurring the Boundaries: Women's Criminality in the Context of Abuse." *Women's Studies Quarterly* 32: 116–38.

Monroe, Kristen Renwick, James Hankin, and Renée Bukovchik Van Vechten. 2000. "The Psychological Foundations of Identity Politics." *Annual Review of Political Science* 3: 419–47.

Monto, Martin. 2000. "Why Men Seek Out Prostitutes." In Weitzer, *Sex for Sale.*

Morell, Carolyn M. 1994. *Unwomanly Conduct: The Challenges of Intentional Childlessness.* New York: Routledge.

————. 2000. "Saying No: Women's Experiences with Reproductive Refusal." *Feminism and Psychology* 10: 313–22.

Morgan, Peggy. 1998. "Living on the Edge." In Delacoste and Alexander, *Sex Work.*

Moussa, Mario. 1992. "Foucault and the Problem of Agency; or, Toward a Practical Philosophy." In *Ethics and Danger: Essays on Heidegger and Continental Thought,* ed. Arleen B. Dallery and Charles E. Scott with P. Holley Roberts. Albany: State University of New York Press.

Moya, Paula M. L., and Michael R. Hames-García. 2000. *Reclaiming Identity: Realist Theory and the Predicament of Postmodernism.* Berkeley: University of California Press.

Mulrine, Anna. 2004. "Making Babies." *U.S. News & World Report,* September 27. http://health.usnews.com/usnews/health/articles/040927/27babies.htm.

Nagle, Jill. 1997a. "First Ladies of Feminist Porn: A Conversation with Candida Royalle and Debi Sundahl." In Nagle, *Whores and Other Feminists.*

————. 1997b. *Whores and Other Feminists.* New York: Routledge.

Naples, Nancy A. 1998. "Women's Community Activism: Exploring the Dynamics of Politicization and Diversity." In *Community Activism and Feminist Politics: Organizing across Race, Class, and Gender,* ed. Nancy A. Naples. New York: Routledge.

National Crime Prevention Council. 2009. "Intimate Partner Violence Decline between 1993 and 2004." http://www.ncpc.org/publications/catalyst-newslet ter/archives/may-2007-catalyst/intimate-partner-violence-declined-between-1993-and-2004.

Niles, Donna Marie. 1998. "Confessions of a Priestesstute." In Delacoste and Alexander, *Sex Work.*

Nussbaum, Martha. 1999. *Sex and Social Justice.* New York: Oxford University Press.

Oakley, Annie, ed. 2007. *Working Sex: Sex Workers Write about a Changing Industry.* Emeryville, Calif.: Seal Press.

O'Connell Davidson, Julia. 2002. *Prostitution, Power, and Freedom.* Ann Arbor: University of Michigan Press.

———. 2006. "Will the Real Sex Slave Please Stand Up?" *Feminist Review* 83: 4–22.

O'Grady, Helen. 2004. "An Ethics of the Self." In *Feminism and the Final Foucault,* ed. Dianna Taylor and Karen Vintges. Urbana: University of Illinois Press.

Okin, Susan Moller. 1989. *Justice, Gender and the Family.* New York: Basic Books.

Pardo, Mary. 1998. "Creating Community: Mexican American Women in Eastside Los Angeles." In *Community Activism and Feminist Politics: Organizing across Race, Class, and Gender,* ed. Nancy A. Naples. New York: Routledge.

Park, Kristin. 2002. "Stigma Management among the Voluntarily Childless." *Sociological Perspectives* 45: 21–45.

Pasko, Lisa. 2002. "Naked Power: The Practice of Stripping as a Confidence Game." *Sexualities* 5: 49–66.

Pateman, Carole. 1988. *The Sexual Contract.* Stanford, Calif.: Stanford University Press.

Pavlidakis, Alexandra. 2009. "Mandatory Arrest: Past Its Prime." *Santa Clara Law Review* 49: 1201–35.

Pearson, Patricia. 1997. *When She Was Bad: Violent Women and the Myth of Innocence.* New York: Viking.

Pence, Ellen. 2001. "Advocacy on Behalf of Battered Women." In *Sourcebook on Violence against Women,* ed. Claire M. Renzetti, Jeff Edleson, and Racquel Kennedy Bergen. Thousand Oaks, Calif.: Sage Publications.

Pleck, Elizabeth. 1987. *Domestic Tyranny: The Making of Social Policy against Family Violence from Colonial Times to the Present.* New York: Oxford University Press.

Purkayastha, Bandana, Shyamala Raman, and Kshiteeja Bhide. 1997. "Empowering Women: Sneha's Multifaceted Activism." In *Dragon Ladies: Asian American Feminists Breathe Fire,* ed. Sonia Shah. Boston: South End Press.

Queen, Carole. 1997. "Sex Radical Politics, Sex-Positive Feminist Thought, and Whore Stigma." In Nagle, *Whores and Other Feminists.*

Reagon, Bernice Johnson. 1998. "Coalition Politics: Turning the Century." In *Feminism and Politics,* ed. Anne Phillips. Oxford: Oxford University Press. Originally published in Barbara Smith, ed. *Home Girls: A Black Feminist Anthology.* New York: Kitchen Table Press, 1983.

Rennison, Callie Marie, and Sarah Welchans. 2000 (revised January 31, 2002). "Intimate Partner Violence." A special report prepared for the Bureau of Justice Statistics, made available through the U.S. Department of Justice. http://bjs.ojp.usdoj.gov/index.cfm?ty=pbdetail&iid=1002.

Rich, Grant Jewell, and Kathleen Guidroz. 2000. "Smart Girls Who Like Sex: Telephone Sex Workers." In Weitzer, *Sex for Sale.*

Richie, Beth E. 1996. *Compelled to Crime: The Gender Entrapment of Battered Black Women.* New York: Routledge.

Ristock, Janice L. 2002. *No More Secrets: Violence in Lesbian Relationships.* New York: Routledge.

Roberts, Dorothy. 1997. *Killing the Black Body: Race, Reproduction, an the Meaning of Liberty.* New York: Vintage Books.

Rose, Melody, and Mark O. Hatfield. 2007. "Republican Motherhood Redux? Women as Contingent Citizens in 21st Century America." *Journal of Women, Politics, and Policy* 29: 5–30.

Russo, Ann. 2001. *Taking Back Our Lives: A Call to Action for the Feminist Movement.* New York: Routledge.

Safer, Jeanne. 1996. *Beyond Motherhood: Choosing a Life without Children.* New York: Pocket Books.

Sanghera, Jyoti. 2005. "Unpacking the Trafficking Discourse." In *Trafficking and Prostitution Reconsidered: New Perspectives on Migration, Sex Work, and Human Rights,* ed. Kamala Kempadoo. Boulder, Colo.: Paradigm Publishers.

Sawicki, Jana. 1991. *Disciplining Foucault: Feminism, Power, and the Body.* New York: Routledge.

Schechter, Susan. 1982. *Women and Male Violence: The Visions and Struggles of the Battered Women's Movement.* Boston: South End Press.

Schneider, Elizabeth M. 2000. *Battered Women and Feminist Lawmaking.* New Haven, Conn.: Yale University Press.

Schotten, C. Heike. 2005. "Men, Masculinity, and Male Domination: Reframing Feminist Analyses of Sex Work." *Politics and Gender* 1: 211–40.

Schwarzenbach, Sibyl. 2006. "Contractarians and Feminists Debate Prostitution." In Spector, *Prostitution and Pornography.*

Scott, J. L. 2007. "Mom's the Word: Yummy Mummies, Alternadads, and Other Literary Offspring." *Bitch* 35 (Spring): 71–75.

Scoular, Jane. 2004. "The 'Subject' of Prostitution: Interpreting the Discursive, Symbolic and Material Position of Sex/Work in Feminist Theory." *Feminist Theory* 5: 343–55.

Seifer, David B., Linda M. Frazier, and David A. Grainger. 2008. "Disparity in Assisted Reproductive Technologies Outcomes in Black Women Compared with White Women." *Fertility and Sterility* 90: 1701–10.

Sengupta, Somini. 2001. "A Sick Tribe and a Dump as a Neighbor; Mohawks Press G.M. over Decade-Old Impasse." *New York Times,* April 7. http://www .nytimes.com/2001/04/07/nyregion/a-sick-tribe-and-a-dump-as-a-neighbor-mohawks-press-gm-over-decade-old-impasse.html.

Showden, Carisa R. 1999. "Rejecting Ophelia: Female Subjectivity and Mutual Violence in Adolescent Dating Relationships." Master's thesis, University of North Carolina at Chapel Hill.

Shrage, Laurie. 2005. "Exposing the Fallacies of Anti-Porn Feminism." *Feminist Theory* 6: 45–65.

Siegel, Reva B. 1996. "'The Rule of Love': Wife Beating as Prerogative and Privacy." *Yale Law Journal* 105: 2117–207.

Silliman, Jael, Marlene Gerber Fried, Loretta Ross, and Elena R. Gutiérrez. 2004. *Undivided Rights: Women of Color Organize for Reproductive Justice.* Cambridge, Mass.: South End Press.

Slaughter, M. M. 1995. "The Legal Construction of 'Mother.'" In *Mothers in Law: Feminist Theory and the Legal Regulation of Motherhood,* ed. Martha Albertson Fineman and Isabel Karpin. New York: Columbia University Press.

Smith, Andrea. 2005. *Conquest: Sexual Violence and American Indian Genocide.* Cambridge, Mass.: South End Press.

Smith, Colin. 1971. "Merleau-Ponty and Structuralism." *Journal of the British Society for Phenomenology* 2: 46–52.

Sokoloff, Natalie J., ed. 2005. *Domestic Violence at the Margins: Readings on Race, Class, Gender and Culture.* New Brunswick, N.J.: Rutgers University Press.

Solinger, Rickie. 2001. *Beggars and Choosers: How the Politics of Choice Shapes Adoption, Abortion, and Welfare in the United States.* New York: Hill and Wang.

Sparks, Anne. 1997. "Feminists Negotiate the Executive Branch: The Policing of Male Violence." In *Feminists Negotiate the State: The Politics of Domestic Violence,* ed. Cynthia R. Daniels. Lanham, Md.: University Press of America.

Spector, Jessica. 2006a. "Introduction: Money, Sex, and Philosophy." In Spector, *Prostitution and Pornography.*

———, ed. 2006b. *Prostitution and Pornography: Philosophical Debate about the Sex Industry.* Stanford, Calif.: Stanford University Press.

Spivey, Sue E. 2005. "Distancing and Solidarity as Resistance to Sexual Objectification in a Nude Dancing Bar." *Deviant Behavior* 26: 417–37.

Stack, Carol B., and Linda M. Burton. 1994. "Kinscripts: Reflections on Family,
Generation, and Culture." In *Mothering: Ideology, Experience, and Agency*, ed.
Evelyn Nakano Glenn, Grace Chang, and Linda Rennie Forcey. New York:
Routledge.

Stark, Christine. 2006. "Stripping as a System of Prostitution." In Spector, *Prostitution and Pornography.*

Stark, Evan. 1995. "Symposium on Reconceptualizing Violence against Women
by Intimate Partners: Critical Issues: Re-presenting Woman Battering: From
Battered Woman Syndrome to Coercive Control." *Albany Law Review* 58:
973–1026.

Stetson, Dorothy McBride. 2004. "The Invisible Issue: Prostitution and Trafficking of Women and Girls in the United States." In *The Politics of Prostitution:
Women's Movements, Democratic States, and the Globalisation of Sex Commerce*,
ed. Joyce Outshoorn. Cambridge: Cambridge University Press.

Stephen, Elizabeth Hervey, and Anjani Chandra. 2006. "Declining Estimates
of Infertility in the United States: 1982–2002." *Fertility and Sterility* 86:
516–23.

Story, Louise. 2005. "Many Women at Elite Colleges Set Career Path to Motherhood." *New York Times*, September 20. http://www.nytimes.com/2005/09/
20/national/20women.html.

Tan, Cheng Imm. 1997. "Building Shelter: Asian Women and Domestic Violence." In *Dragon Ladies: Asian American Feminists Breathe Fire*, ed. Sonia
Shah. Boston: South End Press.

Taylor, Erin. 2003. "Throwing the Baby Out with the Bathwater: Childfree
Advocates and the Rhetoric of Choice." *Women and Politics* 24: 49–75.

Thomas, Joe A. 2000. "Gay Male Video Pornography: Past, Present, and
Future." In Weitzer, *Sex for Sale.*

Thompson, Charis. 2005. *Making Parents: The Ontological Choreography of Reproductive Technologies*. Cambridge, Mass.: MIT Press.

Thornton, Arland, and Linda Young-DeMarco. 2001. "Four Decades of Trends
in Attitudes toward Family Issues in the United States: The 1960s through the
1990s." *Journal of Marriage and Family* 63: 1009–37.

Tjaden, Patricia, and Nancy Thoennes. 1998. "Prevalence, Incidence, and Consequences of Violence against Women: Findings from the National Violence
against Women Survey." Research in Brief report of the National Institute of
Justice and the Centers for Disease Control and Prevention, made available

through the U.S. Department of Justice. http://www.ojp.usdoj.gov/nij/pubs-sum/172837.htm.

———. 2000. "Extent, Nature, and Consequences of Intimate Partner Violence: Findings from the National Violence against Women Survey." Research report of the National Institute of Justice and the Centers for Disease Control and Prevention, made available through the U.S. Department of Justice. http://www.ojp.usdoj.gov/nij/pubs-sum/181867.htm.

Ulrich, Miriam, and Ann Weatherall. 2000. "Motherhood and Infertility: Viewing Motherhood through the Lens of Infertility." *Feminism and Psychology* 10: 323–36.

Valverde, Mariana. 2004. "Experience and Truth Telling in a Post-humanist World: A Foucauldian Contribution to Feminist Ethical Reflections." In *Feminism and the Final Foucault,* ed. Dianna Taylor and Karen Vintges. Urbana: University of Illinois Press.

Venkataramani-Kothari, Anitha. 2007. "Understanding South Asian Immigrant Women's Experiences of Violence." In Das Dasgupta, *Body Evidence.*

Websdale, Neil. 2005. "Nashville: Domestic Violence and Incarcerated Women in Poor Black Neighborhoods." In Sokoloff, *Domestic Violence at the Margins.*

Websdale, Neil, and Byron Johnson. 2005. "Reducing Woman Battering: The Role of Structural Approaches." In Sokoloff, *Domestic Violence at the Margins.*

Webster, Fiona. 2002. "Do Bodies Matter? Sex, Gender, and Politics." *Australian Feminist Studies* 17: 191–205.

Weeks, Jeffrey. 1995. *Invented Moralities: Sexual Values in an Age of Uncertainty.* New York: Columbia University Press.

Weeks, Kathi. 1998. *Constituting Feminist Subjects.* Ithaca, N.Y.: Cornell University Press.

Weis, Lois. 2001. "Race, Gender, and Critique: African-American Women, White Women, and Domestic Violence in the 1980s and 1990s." *Signs: Journal of Women in Culture and Society* 27: 139–69.

Weis, Lois, Michelle Fine, Amira Proweller, Corrine Bertram, and Julia Marusza. "'I've slept in clothes long enough': Excavating the Sounds of Domestic Violence among Women in the White Working Class." 2005. In Sokoloff, *Domestic Violence at the Margins.*

Weitzer, Ronald. 2000a. "Why We Need More Research on Sex Work." In Weitzer, *Sex for Sale.*

———, ed. 2000b. *Sex for Sale: Prostitution, Pornography, and the Sex Industry.* New York: Routledge.

Wellons, Melissa F., Cora E. Lewis, Stephen M. Schwartz, Erica P. Gunderson, Pamela J. Schreiner, Barbara Sternfeld, Josh Richman, Cynthia K. Sites, and David S. Siscovick. 2008. "Racial Differences in Self-Reported Infertility and Risk Factors for Infertility in a Cohort of Black and White Women: The CARDIA Women's Study." *Fertility and Sterility* 90: 1640–8.

Wesely, Jennifer K. 2003. "'Where am I going to stop?' Exotic Dancing, Fluid Body Boundaries, and Effects on Identity." *Deviant Behavior* 24: 483–503.

West, Carolyn M. 2005. "Domestic Violence in Ethnically and Racially Diverse Families." In Sokoloff, *Domestic Violence at the Margins.*

West, Rachel. 1998. "U.S. PROStitutes Collective." In Delacoste and Alexander, *Sex Work.*

Whisnant, Rebecca. 2004. "Confronting Pornography: Some Conceptual Basics." In *Not for Sale: Feminists Resisting Prostitution and Pornography,* ed. Christine Stark and Rebecca Whisnant. North Melbourne, Australia: Spinifex Press.

White, Evelyn C. 1998. "The Abused Black Woman: Challenging a Legacy of Pain." In *Dating Violence: Young Women in Danger,* ed. Barrie Levy. Seattle, Wash.: Seal Press.

Whiteside, Kerry. 1988. *Merleau-Ponty and the Foundation of an Existential Politics.* Princeton: Princeton University Press.

Wijers, Marjan. 2008. "Prostitution Policies in the Netherlands," http://www.sexworkeurope.org.

Williams, Patricia J. 1991. *The Alchemy of Race and Rights: Diary of a Law Professor.* Cambridge, Mass.: Harvard University Press.

Wright, Victoria Clay, Jeani Chang, Gary Jeng, Michael Chen, and Maurizio Macaluso. 2007. "Assisted Reproductive Technology Surveillance—United States, 2004." *Morbidity and Mortality Weekly Report* 56 (SS06): 1–22.

Yar, Majid. 2001. "Beyond Nancy Fraser's 'Perspectival Dualism.'" *Economy and Society* 30: 288–303.

Young, Iris Marion. 1990. *Justice and the Politics of Difference.* Princeton: Princeton University Press.

———. 1997. "Unruly Categories: A Critique of Nancy Fraser's Dual Systems Theory." *New Left Review* 222 (March–April): 147–60.

Zatz, Noah D. 1997. "Sex Work/Sex Act: Law, Labor, and Desire in Constructions of Prostitution." *Signs: Journal of Women in Culture and Society* 22: 277–308.

Ziarek, Ewa Płonowska. 2001. *An Ethics of Dissensus: Postmodernity, Feminism, and the Politics of Radical Democracy.*

INDEX

Abbott, Sharon A., 245n12
Abma, Joyce C., 112
abolitionist feminist model of prostitution, 137–41, 144, 147, 148, 151–53, 154, 155, 159, 245n11, 247n23; alternatives to, 142, 174, 179, 183, 243n3; applied to pornography, 168, 169, 170, 244n4; political activity of, 149, 158, 172–73, 247n25
abortions, 110, 111, 241n27
Abraham, Margaret, 61, 65, 70, 74, 76, 90, 195–96
Abramovich, Evelyn, 247n24
Abrams, Kathryn, 2, 6, 197, 222n1, 224n11
abuse, 48, 228n1; levels of, 41, 42, 233n29, 235n39, 236n45; psychological, 47, 50–51. See also assault; battering; sex work, abuse in; violence
actions/actors, ix, 14, 26, 31, 35, 56–57, 125, 218, 223n5, 226n19; agentic, xii, xiv–xvi, 2, 6, 8, 21–23, 218, 250n11; constraints on, xi, 16; normative, 4–5, 7, 214, 215; political, 34–35, 199,

250n8; resistant, xv, 7, 16–17, 20, 33, 34, 129. See also collective action; praxis
activism, feminist, 27, 34, 100, 131, 179, 185–219. See also coalition politics
ACT NOW (AIDS group), 205
ACT UP (AIDS group), 195, 205
Adelman, Madelaine, 60, 62, 63, 64, 234n32, 235n35, 235n36
African American men, 56, 59, 60–61, 63, 65, 73
African American women: access to ARTs, 116–17, 210; childlessness among, 112; domestic violence against, 52, 54–58, 65, 66, 68, 79, 233n27, 233n29; infertility among, 114, 240n18, 240n21; involuntary sterilization of, 110; in prostitution, 136, 142, 148; race consciousness of, 61, 249n2; stereotypes of, 56, 60–61, 106, 117; violence against, 41, 42
agency, 3, 18–19, 141, 153; ARTs and, 94, 96, 118–31; autonomy in, xiii, 1–8, 10, 11, 61, 99, 217; capacities for, ix, 17, 21–22, 23, 25, 124, 163, 188, 201, 214,

269

fertility, 95, 98, 241n29. *See also* assisted reproduction technologies (ARTs); infertility

Fine, Michelle, 236n46

Firestone, Shulamith, 93, 238n1

Foucault, Michel, 221n1; on becoming, 156, 157, 162, 183, 184; on biopower, 119; on care of the self, 7, 81, 224n12, 249n5; on domination, 9, 96–97, 221n2; on freedom, 14, 162, 225n13; on friendship, 29, 190; on norms, 5–6, 157; on power, xiii, 10, 159, 227n33

Franzini, Louis, 104

Fraser, Nancy, 30, 138, 187, 227n29, 227n31

freedom, 224n9, 224n12; agency and, ix, xiii, 1–3, 5, 8–13, 108; coalition politics and, 185, 191, 193, 215; constraints on, 17, 82, 151, 164, 211, 224n12; domestic violence's effects on, 37, 47–48, 53, 60, 62–64, 68, 75–76, 78, 236n43; ethos of, 6, 7, 24, 249n5; Foucault on, 14, 162, 225n13; identity and, 13–25, 62; increasing, xi, 31, 55, 75, 80–81, 86, 88, 90, 91, 165; in prostitution, 135, 144, 146, 158, 182; reproductive, xvi–xvii, 94, 113, 119, 124, 127–28, 133, 209–10, 216, 238n1. *See also* autonomy

Friedman, Marilyn, 222n1

friendships, 156, 157, 188, 190

Funari, Vicky, 170

Galazia, Janelle, 148

gay men, 210, 235n38, 244n4. *See also* homosexuality

gender, 59, 89, 119, 141, 145, 204–7, 241n28; hierarchy in, 150, 151; intersectionality of, 37, 53, 54–69; raced expectations of, 109, 233n25. *See also* femininity; masculinity

gender entrapment, 54–55, 57, 60, 62, 75. *See also* entrapment, in domestic violence

gender identity, female: ARTs and, xvi, 119, 124, 238n3; embodied, 23, 24–25; patriarchal notions of, 58–60, 140, 141, 143–44; politics based on, x, 25; racialized, 54, 57, 61–62. *See also* femininity; womanhood; women

gender norms, xiv–xvi, 14, 191, 229n4; domestic violence related to, 42, 43–54, 64–69, 79, 89, 91, 235n38; hegemonic, 38, 56, 57, 91, 95, 165; prostitution related to, 182, 183, 184; racialized, 58–59, 61–62, 63, 66, 82, 88, 201. *See also* ideal motherhood norms; motherhood

gender relations, 19, 82, 140, 147, 152, 163–65

General Motors Company, environmental hazards from, 114

goals, xvii–xviii, 70, 72, 190. *See also* life plans

Goetting, Ann, 52, 79, 231n16, 233n29

Goldfarb, Phyllis, 46, 237n47

Goldfarb, Sally F., 84, 85

Goodmark, Leigh, 232n21, 236n46, 237n50

Gordon, Linda, 77, 236n43, 236n45

governmentality, 9, 13, 32, 96–97, 191

Govier, Trudy, 224n7

Gregory, Carol, 62, 63, 234n32

Grewal, Mandeep, 66, 87, 237n49

groups, 1, 32, 195, 207, 212–13, 217, 222n3. *See also* communities

habits, 17, 22, 23, 212; agency related to, 20, 191, 198; development of, xiii–xiv, 18, 53; gendered, 68, 201. *See also* customs; dispositions

Hamby, Sherry L., 45, 61

Hatfield, Mark O., 239n12, 241n27

Indian immigrant women, 87–88. *See also* South Asian immigrant women, domestic violence against

individuals, 32, 47–48, 188–89; heroic, x, xv; identities of, 1, 197, 202–3; resistance by, 22, 190, 197. *See also* agency, individual; self, the

inequalities, 142, 222n3, 233n25; economic, 184, 210; gender-based, 137, 158, 200, 205; marital, 44–45, 46; political, 37, 210, 218; of power, xvi, 28; of resistance, 7, 197; social, 26, 37, 218

infertility, 206–7; advice books on, 120–21; economic causes of, 127, 131–32; environmental causes of, 114–15, 117, 132, 133, 240n22; epidemic myth, 98, 101, 112; individualization of, 116, 122–23, 131, 133; medicalized model of, 108, 115–16, 122–23, 125, 131, 133, 241n24; nonmedical solutions to, 114–15, 118, 132–33; rates of, 111–15, 126, 132, 240n18, 240n21, 241n23; social causes of, 107, 116, 127, 131, 133, 243n37; workplace causes of, 114, 133. *See also* assisted reproduction technologies (ARTs); pronatalism; public policies, U.S., regarding infertility

injustices, 187, 204–7, 227n29, 227n31

institutions, xiii–xiv, 12, 13, 14, 21–22, 31, 217; constraining, 3, 203; responses to domestic violence, 82–83, 86, 91. *See also* criminal justice system, responses to domestic violence; motherhood

intersectionality, structural, 54–69, 233n25

interventions, xi, xiii, xiv, 139, 153; into domestic violence situations, xii, 43, 53, 55, 69, 71–72, 74, 80, 82–86, 196–97, 199, 230n13, 232n21

intimate partner violence, use of term, 228n1. *See also* domestic violence

Ireland, Mardy S., 123

isolation, as domestic abuse, 49, 64, 74, 75

iteration, xiii, 70, 111; agentic, 20, 23, 29, 86

Jain, Shashi, 45, 231n15

Jains, 45, 231n15

Jamison, Pollyann, 104

Jews, Orthodox, 61, 234n34

Johnson, Byron, 236n46

Johnson, Merri Lisa, 146, 244n9

Jones, Kathleen B., 72, 73, 79

judgments, 4–5, 12–13, 35, 125, 131, 189, 218, 223n5

Kant, Immanuel, 188, 247n22

Kaplan, Robert, 104

Keck, Aries, 83

Kendrick, Karen, 47

Kentucky Job Readiness Program, 236n46

King, Leslie, 126

Kipnis, Laura, 168, 247n23

knowledge: embodied, 161, 162, 203, 226n22; of self, ix, 165, 224n12; sexual, 156, 161

Kolata, Gina, 241n29

Kruks, Sonia, 12–13, 16, 23–24

Kuo, Lenore, 144, 173, 175, 245n11, 248n32

labor, 34, 135, 234n32; women's, 44–45, 160. *See also* employment; prostitution, as labor; workplaces

Lang, Susan S., 120, 130

language issues, 20, 64, 76, 87–88

Latina women, 62–63, 136, 241n26; forced sterilization of, 110; infertility rates among, 114; lack of access to

identity and, 8, 13, 15, 188; pornography's effects on, 166, 170; production of, 25, 54; theories of, ix–x, 33. *See also* agency, subjective; self, the, subjective

submission. *See* femininity, submissiveness associated with

Sullivan, Cris, 83

survivors, 61, 63; of domestic violence, 54, 75, 76, 158, 195, 235n41, 237n49

Tan, Cheng Imm, 235n40

Taylor, Erin, 238n7

technology. *See* assisted reproduction technologies (ARTs)

temporality in agency, ix, 17–21, 34, 225n14; in coercive control model, 50, 51–54; in domestic violence, 61–62, 70, 86, 90; in gender entrapment model, 55, 58; in sex work, 156, 163; political applications of, 194, 204, 211, 218

Temporary Aid to Needy Families, 75

Thoennes, Nancy, 230n8

Thomas, Joe A., 244n4

Thompson, Charis, 119, 122, 239n13, 241n28

Thornton, Arland, 108–9, 128

time. *See* temporality in agency

Tjaden, Patricia, 230n8

trafficking, sex, 243n1, 243n3, 247n25. *See also* prostitution

trivalent politics, xiv, xvii, 32, 34, 90, 186, 187, 200, 204–7, 218–19, 227n31

Ulrich, Miriam, 116, 118

understanding, 10, 11–12, 26. *See also* self, the, understanding of

United States (U.S.), ARTs in, 93–95, 99–101, 106–7, 129. *See also* public policies, U.S.

values, xii, 4, 8, 158, 190, 210

Vanwesenbeeck, Ine, 178

Venkataramani-Kothari, Anitha, 59

victimization: in domestic violence, xvi, 37–92, 158; in sex work, xvii, 135, 155, 161, 181, 184

violence, xvi, 70, 81, 191; family, 45, 46, 70, 228n1, 230n11; intersectional approach to, 53–69; in pornography, 167–68, 170, 248n29; in prostitution, 137, 147, 179, 181, 243n3, 245n10, 245n11; against women, 40–41, 45, 143, 147. *See also* abuse; assault; battering; domestic violence; sex work, abuse in

Violence Against Women Act of 1994 (VAWA), 48, 195–96, 232n21, 232n22

weak substantive autonomy, 4, 8, 56, 99, 145, 198, 224n7

Weatherall, Ann, 116, 118

Websdale, Neil, 52, 65, 68, 235n37, 236n46

Weeks, Jeffrey, 250n8

Weeks, Kathi, 221n1

Weis, Lois, 64–65, 66, 67, 233n29, 235n37, 236n46

welfare, 75, 109–10, 235n37

welfare mothers, 105–6, 108, 239n14

Wellons, Melissa F., 114, 240n21

West, Carolyn M., 42

West, Rachel, 246n14

white women, 249n2; access to ARTs, 112, 116–17; childlessness among, 112, 113, 115; domestic violence against, 39, 42, 44–45, 56, 65, 66–67, 79, 229n7, 233n25, 236n44, 236n46; infertility among, 114, 206–7, 240n18, 240n21; motherhood ideals, 106, 239n14; pronatalist appeals to, 100, 101, 103, 107–11; in prostitution, 136, 142, 148, 249

CARISA R. SHOWDEN is assistant professor of political science at the University of North Carolina at Greensboro.